GLASGOW

Varieties of English Around the World

General Editor:

Manfred Görlach
Anglistisches Seminar der Universität
Kettengasse 12
D-6900 HEIDELBERG
Germany

TEXT SERIES
Volume 3

Caroline Macafee
Glasgow

GLASGOW

by

Caroline Macafee
University of Glasgow

JOHN BENJAMINS PUBLISHING COMPANY
AMSTERDAM/PHILADELPHIA

1983

ACKNOWLEDGEMENTS

When I first planned this volume, I had a group of students who were interested in working on the local dialect, and at first it seemed possible that they would be able to collaborate with me on the volume. In the event, the work took longer and became more extensive than I had anticipated, and this proved impossible. The students - Ann Tierney, Eric Flannigan, Rowena Murray and Jan Mathieson - did, hovever, give me much very valuable assistance in the early stages in locating and selecting texts, making tapes, and forming a picture of the social background. I am also grateful to other students with whom I have had interesting discussions, in particular Wendy MacLean and Alison Kean.

Many other friends and colleagues, too numerous to mention by name, have helped me in different ways. They may have forgotten drawing my attention to something or putting me in touch with somebody, but I am grateful just the same. I must take space to acknowledge the help of Stewart Conn and Charles Woolfson, and to thank Stephen Pratt for drawing a version of Map 1, which was not used in the end because the present map superseded it. Especial thanks must go to my husband, Paul Johnston, for his help with the phonetic transcriptions, and for sharing with me his observations on Glasgow speech. The degree of detail achieved in the narrow transcriptions is due solely to him.

Seumas Simpson, Hans Speitel, Suzanne Romaine and A. J. Aitken have given me the benefit of their comments on parts of the typescript, for which I again thank them very warmly. Any remaining mistakes and inadequacies are entirely my own.

Whenever full texts or substantial parts of texts are quoted, every attempt has been made to locate the copyright holder, and to obtain their permission. I would like to thank the following: Haig Gordon and the British Broadcasting Corporation for permission to use T8 and tape, Kenneth Brown for T9 and tape, Tim Strevens and Radio Clyde for T10-14 and tape, Radio Clyde for T21-4 and tape, Billy Connolly and Transatlantic Records for T15 and tape, EMI Records for T16 and tape, Alex Mitchell, Stanley Baxter and Scottish Television for T17 and tape, Alex Mitchell and Stanley Baxter for T18, Hector Nicol and Stanley Baxter for T19, Alex Mitchell and *The Weekly News* for T67, Rikki Fulton, R. S. Andrews and Scottish Television for T20, *The Guardian* for T24a, Tom Leonard for T26, T37, T62 and T63, James Kelman for T35 and T39, Alex Hamilton for T36, T38 and T65, Tom McGrath for T43, John McGrath for T44-6, Peter Mallan and Radio Clyde for T53, Edith Little for T54, Adam McNaughton for T55, Ian Hamilton Finlay for T56-9, Stephen Mulrine for T60 and T61, Edwin Morgan for T64, *The Evening Times* for T69 and Fig. 9, Richard Bryant and the Scottish Council of Social Service for Fig. 10, Hans Speitel for Map 1, G. Melvyn Howe for Map 2, Strathclyde Regional Council for Maps 3-5, and all those who allowed me to record their voices or to use tapes which they had recorded, whether or not these actually appear in the book.

Many of the people mentioned above have gone out of their way to help me, and I hope that the use which I have made of their work will not disappoint them.

I would like to thank Michael Rigg and the staff of the Audio-Visual Services Department of the University of Glasgow for editing the tape which accompanies the volume, and my brother, Sandy McAfee, for typing the final copy. My lasting thanks are due to Manfred Görlach for his unfailing help and encouragement at each stage of the work.

To Jack Aitken,
who taught me everything I know about Scots,
with love and heartfelt gratitude.

CONTENTS

INTRODUCTION

THE ENGLISH OF GLASGOW

TEXTS: NATURAL SPEECH

STEREOTYPES

LITERATURE

4

SYMBOLS AND CONVENTIONS

V	- any vowel
C	- any consonant
⟨ ⟩	enclose graphemes, e.g. ⟨r⟩ in *real*
/ /	enclose phonemes, e.g. /r/ in *real*
[ ]	enclose segments not analysed as phonemes, in particular allophones, e.g. [ɾ] is a tap /r/, [r] is a trilled /r/.

Consonants

	Bi-labial	Labio-dental	Dental	Alveo-lar	Palato-alv.	Palatal	Velar	Pharyn-geal	Glottal
Plosive	p b			t d			k g		ʔ
Fricative	ß	f v	θ ð	s z	ʃ ʒ		x		h
Affricate					tʃ dʒ				
Nasal	m			n		ɲ	ŋ		
Lateral				l					
Tap				ɾ					
Trill				r					
Approx-imant	ʍ w			ɹ		j		ʕ	

Diacritics:

‐	- velarised, e.g. [ɫ]
̥	- voiceless, e.g. [m̥]
'	- ejective, e.g. [p'] (glottal closure with build up of pressure in oral cavity prior to release of plosive)
^	- cacuminal, e.g. [ʂ] (front rather than blade of tongue articulates with alveolar ridge)
‿	- simultaneous articulation, e.g. [ʔ͜t]
h	- aspirated, e.g. [tʰ]
ˌ	- syllabic, e.g. [n̩]

Vowels

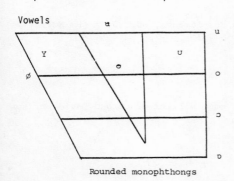

Rounded monophthongs

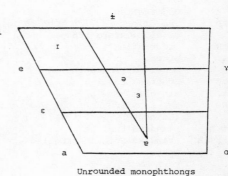

Unrounded monophthongs

6

Diacritics:

~	- nasalised, e.g. [õ]	:	- long, e.g. [eː]
.	- raised, e.g. [ẹ]	·	- half long, e.g. [e·]
ˌ	- lowered, e.g. [e̞]	◡	- rounded, e.g. [ʌ͜]
··	- centralised, e.g. [ë]	ˤ	- pharyngealised, e.g. [eˤ]
-	- retracted, e.g. [ɨ]	ᵁ ᴵ	- off-glide, e.g. [oᵁ], [æᴵ]
+	- advanced, e.g. [ɨ̟]	ᴵ	- retroflex, e.g. [ɔᴵ]

ABBREVIATIONS

adj.	adjective
Am	American
AmE	American English
aux.	auxiliary
Br	British
BrE	British English
c	century
conj.	conjunction
EDD	*The English Dialect Dictionary*, ed. Joseph Wright (London, 1898-1905).
FTA	Face-Threatening Act
HibE	Hibernian English
interj.	interjection
LAS	*Linguistic Atlas of Scotland*, eds. J. Mather and H. H. Speitel (London, 1975, vol. I).
M E	Middle English
N	Northern
n.	noun
O E	Old English
OED	*The Oxford English Dictionary* and Supplements, eds. J. A. H. Murray *et al.* (Oxford 1889-).
O Sc	Older Scots
pl.	plural
RP	Received Pronunciation
ScE	Scottish English
sg.	singular
SND	*The Scottish National Dictionary*, eds. William Grant and David Murison (Edinburgh, 1931-1975).
St E	Standard English
St ScE	Standard Scottish English
T	Text
v.	verb

INTRODUCTION

1.0 Overview

The English of Glasgow is basically the result of the mixture of two dialect systems: the local vernacular, a variety of Scots; and Standard English (St E), which became established in Scotland as a class dialect in the eighteenth century. The group of dialects known collectively as 'Scots' (sometimes 'the Scots language') are spoken in the areas of Scotland shown in Map 1, in Orkney and Shetland, and in parts of Northern Ireland. Elsewhere in Scotland, the vernacular is Highland English or Gaelic.

Although the West Mid dialect underlies the non-standard speech of Glasgow, the demographic and social conditions in the city have been quite different from those in the rural hinterland, and this is reflected in the urban dialect. Two sets of circumstances have been of particular importance: the high rate of immigration from formerly Celtic areas in the nineteenth century, and the maintenance of a fairly rigid pattern of social stratification in this century. Chapter One gives an outline of the external social forces operating on the language of Glasgow, and also provides a background for some of the topics raised in the texts. Chapter Two describes in some detail the characteristics of the urban dialect. The remainder of the volume consists of texts and transcriptions illustrating the varieties of English found in Glasgow, and their range of uses.

1.1 Scotland as a peripheral region

Glasgow is not simply a British city, although, for a time in the nineteenth century, it was the second largest city in Britain. It is specifically a Scottish city, with all that that implies. Scotland, Ireland and Wales can all be regarded historically as economically peripheral regions centred on England, as Hechter (1975) demonstrates. These three regions also contain within them the 'Celtic fringe'. The earlier Celtic population was absorbed by the Anglo-Saxons in England and Lowland Scotland, but Celtic ethnicity remains politically and culturally significant in Ireland, Wales and the Highlands of Scotland. Underdevelopment in the Celtic areas, based on an earlier stage of agricultural disadvantage, renders them particularly vulnerable to market forces, and to population loss. In the period of expansion following the Industrial Revolution, Glasgow received large numbers of migrants both from the Highlands and from Ireland, which significantly influenced the character of the city, especially in religion.

Until the recent discovery of oil in the North Sea, industrialisation in Scotland had been concentrated in a Lowland enclave stretching from Glasgow and the Clydeside conurbation in the west - see Map 2 - to Edinburgh in the east. Within this enclave there has been greater diversification than in Wales and Ireland, with coal extraction, textiles and heavy industry (iron and steel production, and shipbuilding), as well as agricultural activity. Nevertheless, the economy of Scotland has proved as vulnerable to external markets as the highly specialised economies of the other peripheral regions. Industry in these areas was particularly badly hit by the Depression of the 1930s and continued to be dependent on the traditional sectors when England was moving to petro-chemicals, synthetics, light engineering, and the new growth-leader, motor vehicle manufacture. In 1961, Scotland continued to be disadvantaged in relation to England at comparable levels of industrialisation by county, because of higher levels of unemployment (Hechter, 1975: 158).

8

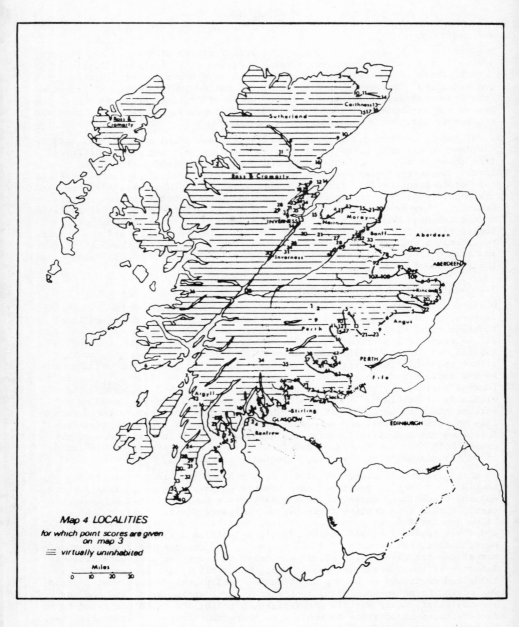

Map 1: The limit of the coherent area of Scots in mainland Scotland. The Scots speaking area is to the east and south of the line. (Speitel, 1980: 112)

9

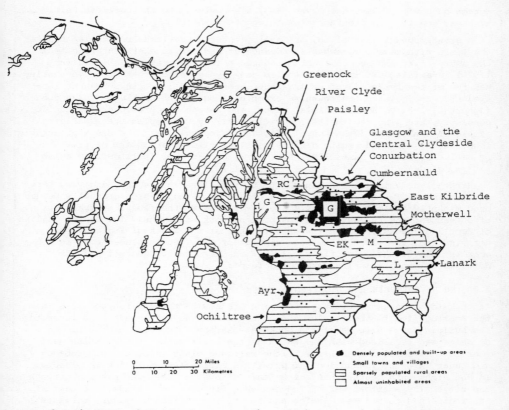

Map 2: The West of Scotland. From *Atlas of Glasgow and the West Region of Scotland* (1973: 39).

The early prosperity of the West of Scotland was serviced by local financial institutions, but by the time that its economy began to decay, London was the financial centre for Britain as a whole. At present, three quarters of the plants employing over 500 people each in the region are controlled from outside Scotland (Strathclyde Regional Council, 1976: 45). However, the peripheral regions experience unusual difficulty in attracting new industry and investment. Hechter argues that this is partly due to their bad public image, and in particular to a stereotype of Celtic backwardness. In the case of the West of Scotland, we must also recognise a stereotype of urban decay. Glasgow does indeed have serious social problems, such as alcoholism and juvenile delinquency, and its share of planning blight, but this is insufficient to explain why it has become synonymous with its own worst problems in the national press.

1.2 Early history

Glasgow was settled from a very early period. The name *Glasgow* is of p-Celtic origin (i.e. the branch of Celtic represented by Modern Welsh), and means 'green hollow'. *Clyde*, the river name, also belongs to the earliest Celtic stratum, and is formed on a root meaning 'to wash'.

Migrants speaking q-Celtic, or Gaelic, entered Scotland from the west after the Roman withdrawal, somewhat in advance of English speakers entering from the south-east, and gradually absorbed the p-Celtic speakers. Nicolaisen (1976), examining two important Gaelic name types, finds that the Clyde valley has few of the *baile* 'farm' or 'village' names which indicate permanent settlement. An isolated Renfrewshire example is *Balagiech* 'village of the goose' (Johnston, 1934). *Achadh* 'field' names, indicating the presence of a Gaelic peasantry, are also few in the lower Clyde valley. Examples are *Auchenairn* 'field of the cairn' (Johnston, 1934), and *Auchenshuggle*. The Gaels presumably found the area already quite densely settled. The supersession of p-Celtic by Gaelic is seen in names like *Barlanark*, Gaelic *barr* 'hilltop' and Welsh *lanerc* 'glade'.

Strathclyde existed as a kingdom up to the eleventh century, and was thereafter permanently incorporated into a united Scotland,[1] which gradually became predominantly English-speaking, a process linked to the feudal centralisation of government and the establishment of a network of burghs. The native English of Scotland (Scots), is continuous with that of the North of England, both deriving from the Old Northumbrian dialect of O E. Scots place-names in the area include *Nitshill* 'cattle's hill', *Kirkshaws* 'church woods', and *Baillieston* 'baillie's ('alderman's') farm'.

1.3 The seventeenth and eighteenth centuries[2]

In the mid seventeenth century, Scottish trade with the English colonies in the Americas led to the development of a port on the west coast, and later to the building of a ship canal and docks at Glasgow. Scottish access to the colonies was legalised with the Union of the Parliaments (1707), which was therefore of particular benefit to the merchant class in Scotland. Tobacco and sugar were the foundations of primitive capital accumulation in Glasgow. In the eighteenth century half of Britain's tobacco trade was passing through the city. The American War of Independence disrupted the trade, but capital was redirected to the West Indies and to the importation of sugar, molasses and rum. When trade was re-established, cotton emerged as a major import, and was integrated with an existing linen industry.

The traditional dialect of the west central area is broadly similar to other central dialects, and is well represented in the mainstream of Scottish literature. The middle classes, who were concentrated in urban centres, followed the aristocracy in adjusting their speech towards the educated speech of London in the centuries after the Union. The modern outcome of this process, known somewhat misleadingly as 'anglicisation'[3] is that the English of Lowland Scotland forms a continuum between the local dialects and St E, and that Standard Scottish English (St ScE) has stable differences from other varieties of the standard at all linguistic levels.

---

1 Excluding at this time large Norse-held areas in the North and North-West.

2 The account of the modern history of Glasgow which follows is based largely on Slaven (1975). Macaulay (1977) also includes a very useful account.

3 Misleadingly, because this term is usually applied to the advance of Anglo-Saxon over Celtic culture.

1.4 The nineteenth century

Coal and iron production began on a large scale in the West of Scotland in the second quarter of the nineteenth century. Shipbuilding on the Clyde, using local iron, was in a leading position by 1850. Glasgow was the commercial capital of an area of coal and iron to the north and east, and textiles to the south and west. A rural fringe of mixed farming supplied urban demand. This economic structure, led by external demand for ships, flourished up to the First World War.

The population of Glasgow, and of the West of Scotland generally, grew rapidly in the nineteenth century through migration from the Highlands and from rural districts into the towns. By 1870, 80 per cent of this growing population was urban. Movements of population from Ireland became important after the first of the major potato famines in 1846. Slaven (1975: 234) summarises the situation thus:

> In 1871 nearly 30 per cent of all persons in the west of Scotland were immigrants ... the Irish represented 43 per cent of all immigrants in 1871, and a third in 1901. The Highlanders added another fifth.

The effect of this influx of labour was to depress industrial wages in the region. The Irish were predominantly Catholic, in contrast to the Protestantism of the native Scots, so that religion became the main indicator of ethnic origin in the West of Scotland, and religious tensions remain to the present day, finding expression in the Orange Lodge[4] and in sectarianism in sport.

Insofar as comparisons can be made between modern Glasgow speech and Highland English, it is middle class urban speech which shows similarities, Shuken (1979) describes a high frequency of approximant /r/, and lack of conformity to the Scottish Vowel Length Rule (see below, 2.1.2) in the English of the Western Isles. Highland English has high prestige in Scotland. To a large extent, English was imposed in the Highlands and Islands through formal education, and it is therefore close to educated norms. Modern Highland English is perhaps not representative of the speech of eighteenth and nineteenth century migrants to Glasgow, many of whom must have spoken English imperfectly as a foreign language.

The languages of Ireland were, and are, Gaelic and Hibernian English (HibE), including Scots dialects based on those of the West of Scotland in parts of the North. There are numerous similarities between Northern HibE and the localised English of Glasgow, for instance the characteristic intonation pattern, the centralised realisation of /u/, and the lowered and retracted realisation of /ɪ/. It is interesting that Belfast and Glasgow share some recent developments, such as the tendency in working class speech to merge /ʍ/ as in *where* with /w/ as in *wear*, and to lenite intervocalic /ð/ (Milroy and Milroy, 1978). The tendency to merge /x/ as in *loch* with /k/ as in *lock* is also shared. Isolated items such as *wan* 'one', *wunst* 'once', *twict* 'twice' and *youse* 'you' (usually plural), are probably borrowings from HibE.

In general, conditions in nineteenth century Glasgow must have been conducive to linguistic instability and change. Part of the character of the urban dialect is negative, i.e. the erosion of traditional Scots lexis, ap-

---

4 A protestant cultural organisation, particularly active in Northern Ireland.

parently more quickly than in rural areas. The mingling of different speech
varieties no doubt exercised a levelling influence. The abrupt changes in
material and social culture must also be taken into account.

1.5 The twentieth century

The heavy industry economy of Glasgow continued to thrive up to the First
World War, by which time the coalescence of urban areas had created the
Central Clydeside Conurbation (see Map 2). During the War, there was a boom
in shipbuilding, but this did not compensate for the permanent loss of over-
seas markets cut off by the War. In the Depression which followed,

> The major industries were truncated: coal and shipbuilding barely
> operated at half the pre-war level in the late 1930s, and pig-iron
> was reduced by two-thirds: steel at best was in a stagnant con-
> dition and unemployment averaged over 20 per cent of insured labour
> throughout two decades. (Slaven, 1975: 185).

Indeed, unemployment rose to almost one third in the early 1930s. And when
the Second World War brought a recovery, it also "confirmed the region in its
traditional economic structure" (Slaven, 1975: 13).

Glasgow was not included in the 1934 Special Areas (Development and
Improvement) Act, but local attempts to attract new industry got off the
ground with the first of Glasgow's industrial estates in 1937. Fewer than
5000 jobs had been created in this way two years later. The West of Scotland
was designated a Development Area under the 1945 Distribution of Industry Act,
but the possible benefits were reduced by almost immediate government cut-
backs. By the time of the Recession, in the 1950s, Glasgow had attracted
only 29 per cent new industry, compared with a national average of 36 per
cent. Unemployment was twice the national average.

In the 1960s and 1970s, male unemployment continued to increase in the
region, especially in manufacturing and transport. Average male unemployment
in Strathclyde was 8.7 per cent at the 1971 census. But there were pockets
of very high unemployment, with figures in excess of 20 per cent in some older
urban areas, including the old coal-mining areas of Lanarkshire. The decreases
in employment were mainly in Glasgow itself. There was, however, an increase
in female employment (to 54 per cent in 1976) mainly in the New Towns of
Cumbernauld and East Kilbride, and an increase in managerial and professional
jobs. Whereas the early industrial estates were sited in Glasgow, the transfer of population from the city to the New Towns has also necessitated an
emphasis on the creation of employment there.[5]

The population of Glasgow reached its peak of 1,128,000 in 1939, and sub-
sequently declined, reaching 897,483 at the 1971 census. This was largely
the result of local authority housing and slum clearance policies, and most
of the population remained in the West of Scotland. This movement away from
Glasgow has no doubt promoted the influence of its dialect on other areas.

1.6 Language and social class

It is generally believed that there are no recognisable dialect divisions

---

5 Figures in this paragraph are from Strathclyde Regional Council (1976).
  The situation has, of course, worsened considerably in the last three
  years.

within the city at present, apart from those coinciding with social class divisions, which have been reinforced by post-war housing developments. Linguistic stratification in Glasgow was the subject of a study by R. K. S. Macaulay in the early 1970s (Macaulay and Trevelyan, 1973; Macaulay, 1977). The approach was Labovian, except that the sample was not random and speech style$_6$was held constant, the informants being formally interviewed in each case.

Macaulay's sample consisted of 48 speakers, divided equally amongst the two sexes, three age groups (10 year olds, 15 year olds, and their parents), and four social classes (defined by occupation) as follows:

    I - professional and managerial
    II - white-collar, intermediate non-manual
    III - skilled manual
    IV - semi-skilled and unskilled manual.
The sample included both Protestants and Catholics.

Five phonological variables were analysed: the phonemes /ɪ, u, a, ʌu/[7] and the glottal [ʔ] realisation of /t/. The results for the variable (i), i.e. the phoneme /ɪ/, are typical. The variants and their weightings are as follows:

    100 [ɪ]
    200 [ɛ̣, ɪ̣]
    300 [ɛ̈, ï]
    400 [ə̣]
    500 [ʌ̣]

The effect of phonetic context was consistent across age, sex and social class groups. Table 1 shows the indices for this variable by social class and sex.

	I	II	III	IV	All	III/IV
All	202	247	284	294	257	289
Males	224	279	287	300	273	294
Females	180	215	280	288	242	284

Table 1: Indices for the variable (i) by social class and sex. Based on Macaulay 1977: 32, Table 2; and 1978: 135, Table 2.

---

6 This study has been criticised by Milroy (1980) and Romaine (1980).

7 Macaulay has been criticised for treating the alternation between /ʌu/ and /u/ as a continuous variable. This is basically a difference of lexical incidence arising from divergent historical developments (see below, 2.1.4). However there is a phonetic continuum.

It will be seen that the social classes are clearly differentiated by their use of this variable. The smallest difference is between Classes III and IV, a pattern which is repeated for the other variables. Since the spread within a class was often higher than the differences between the means for these two classes, and there was overlap between Class III and Class IV speakers when rank-ordered for the four vowel indices combined, Macaulay (1978) treats Classes III and IV as one class for linguistic purposes.

As expected, females have lower indices than males in the same social class. The largest difference between the sexes is in Class II, where females are closer to the class above, and males to the class below. If we now consider male and female responses by age group, further patterns emerge - see Table 2.

	I	II	III/IV	Spread
Adults	174	238	285	111
15 yr. olds	199	249	301	102
10 yr. olds	235	261	281	46
Men	189	269	303	114
15 yr. old boys	234	279	302	68
10 yr. old boys	250	290	275	25
Women	158	206	267	109
15 yr. old girls	163	219	299	136
10 yr. old girls	220	231	286	66

Table 2: Indices for the variable (i) by age, social class and sex. Based on Macaulay 1978: 136, Table 3.

In general these results bear out Macaulay's claim (1978: 136) that "the distance between the social class groups increases with age". The unexpectedly wide spread for 15 year old girls may be traced to the fact that 15 year old Class I girls are much closer to Class I women in their use of the variable than 15 year old Class I boys are to Class I men, or than 15 year old girls are to women in other classes. Macaulay (1978: 141) points out that variability within the group of 10 year old Class I speakers, and particularly 15 year old Class l speakers, is considerably greater than variability within the group of adult Class I speakers, while in other class groups there is relatively little change in variability with age. Macaulay (1978: 139) sums up the results of this part of the study thus:

> On the whole ... the most remarkable aspect of the Glasgow survey is the great consistency of the results and the impression they give of a relatively stable, socially stratified speech community.

This study produced no evidence of differentiation between the speech of Catholics (who may be assumed to be of largely Irish descent) and Protestants. There is no religious segregation in housing or employment, but since 1918 Catholics have had their own schools within the state education system in Scotland.

1.7 Housing and the community[8]

Movements of population within Glasgow have been largely in response to official housing policy. The rapid expansion of Glasgow in the nineteenth century created classical slum conditions. Outward growth of the city was limited by the terrain, so, like Edinburgh, Glasgow expanded upwards. The most usual type of accommodation for middle and working class families was the tenement, or block of flats, usually three or four storeys high. In the most congested areas of the inner city, further tenements or factories had been built into the spaces between the original structures, leading to very high population densities, with attendant problems.

Early attempts at slum clearance, beginning with the foundation of the City Improvement Trust in 1866, resulted in a reduction of the housing stock and consequent rent increases. The Trust's chief means of creating new housing to balance demolitions was to buy land and feu it to speculative builders. After 1887, they began to build for themselves. The new housing created in this way was generally out of the price range of the lowest paid. Private construction of working class accommodation, i.e. one to three apartment houses, boomed during the 1860s and up to the collapse of the Bank of Glasgow in 1879. There was a recovery in the 1880s. However, private building for rent ceased to be profitable in the first quarter of this century, and Glasgow Corporation became the main provider of new housing stock. If we recognise that the housing problem was not simply one of densities, but also one of poverty, with the lowest paid unable to afford decent housing, it is not surprising that the Corporation succeeded mainly in producing new slums, as critics predicted as early as 1925.

The Clyde Valley Regional Development Plan of 1946 laid down the parameters of modern Glasgow. Twenty-nine redevelopment areas were designated in the inner city. The first of these to be approved was the Hutchesontown-Gorbals area in 1957. Since then, work has commenced on many others, with the aim of reducing densities by two thirds. Unfortunately, many sound buildings which could have been rehabilitated have been demolished. While the sites await rebuilding, they cast "the curse of border vacuums" (Jacobs, 1961: 271). Empty sites reduce pedestrian traffic between areas on either side, which affects shopkeepers, as does the initial loss of custom through rehousing. The presence of fewer people on the streets means less supervision of children, and less security in traversing the area after dark. Permanent obstacles to pedestrian traffic have been erected in the inner city in the form of motorways. Bryant (1972: 2) quotes a local community leader as saying, "There will soon be only two types of pedestrians left in the Gorbals: the quick and the dead." The housing estates are, of course, single function areas, with little pedestrian traffic except in and out of the estate.

Families transferred from the inner city were rehoused mainly in new estates, called 'schemes' in Scotland, on the periphery of the city. The highest densities in the city (1.5 persons per room or over) are now in the remaining privately rented inner city tenements, and in the local authority schemes. In the latter, this "is a consequence of allocating houses at the maximum occupancy standard to households which are still expanding, thereby causing overcrowding" (Strathclyde Regional Council, 1976: 182). There is also a size imbalance, with few local authority houses over four apartments. The periph-

8 Information on housing is mainly from Worsdall (1979).

eral schemes are now acknowledged to be deprived areas. The housing stock is "inadequate in many respects" (Strathclyde Regional Council, 1976: 42) - dampness is a common problem, and in tower blocks, lift breakdowns. Amenities are minimal. From an early stage, a significant proportion of tenants resisted rehousing. When The Calton was redeveloped in the 1920s, "twenty per cent of the families preferred to remain in the slum, and on top of that, ten per cent returned to their old district after being rehoused" (Worsdall, 1979: 133). The evidence in 1975 was that many households on the periphery actively sought to be rehoused nearer the city centre, where very little local authority stock remains, and that the most likely to be sold if the present (1982) government's policy of selling council houses is implemented.

Strathclyde Regional Council (1976: Figures 2.2.7 - 2.2.9) gives three maps showing the density of different types of housing in the Inner Conurbation (Glasgow plus Bearsden and part of the old county of Renfrewshire), which bring out very clearly the main areas of the city. These are reproduced as Maps 3 - 5. Map 3, showing the proportion of privately rented housing, picks out the inner city. There are large numbers of old people in the remaining tenements, some of which lack indoor toilets. Map 4, showing the proportion of owner occupied housing, picks out the suburbs of the Southside, and the dormitory districts to the north-west and south-west. Map 5, showing the proportion of local authority housing, identifies the peripheral housing schemes, the largest of which are Drumchapel in the north-west, Easterhouse in the north-east, Castlemilk in the south-east, and Pollock in the south-west. A majority of the employed in the two dormitory areas commute into Glasgow. There was also, in 1975, a significant amount of commuting back into Glasgow from the New Towns, as population transfer had got ahead of job creation there.

Milroy (1980) describes cohesive working class social structures in areas of Belfast which have, or had until recently, escaped redevelopment. Friendships tend to be within the neighbourhood, related families tend to live near each other, and those who are in waged work (especially men in traditional industries) tend to work alongside their neighbours. A similar social system flourished in Glasgow, and may still do so in some parts, but the restructuring of the city has been very extensive. There is a great deal of resentment amongst working class Glaswegians against these unpopular housing policies (cf. T8 and T35). Milroy's work suggests that they would have had a destructive effect on working class solidarity and on social reproduction, in particular the maintenance of traditional sex roles and dialectal forms of speech.

In her Belfast study, the use of several linguistic variables was shown to correlate with the speaker's degree of integration into community networks. This factor was able to explain differences in linguistic behaviour between individuals of the same age, sex and class characteristics. Particularly interesting is the contrast between the three areas studied within the city.

In Ballymacarett, where there was a long-established community and little male unemployment, sex differences in speech were large, with men favouring the more vernacular variants. Men tended to score high for membership of networks, and women, who had less opportunity for associating with neighbours at work, scored low. Thus the correlation between network membership and linguistic behaviour was strong for both sexes.

In the Clonard, there was high male unemployment, but the young women in the sample were employed and formed a cohesive group. For at least one variable, these women had more vernacular forms than young men in their neighbourhood. The Hammer was also an area of high male unemployment, and in addi-

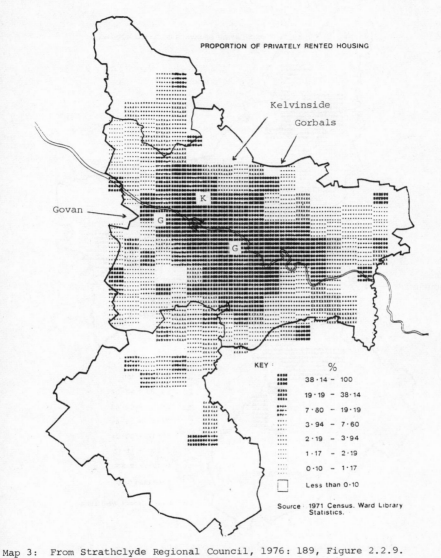

PROPORTION OF PRIVATELY RENTED HOUSING

Kelvinside

Gorbals

Govan

KEY : %
38·14 – 100
19·19 – 38·14
7·60 – 19·19
3·94 – 7·60
2·19 – 3·94
1·17 – 2·19
0·10 – 1·17
Less than 0·10

Source · 1971 Census. Ward Library Statistics.

Map 3: From Strathclyde Regional Council, 1976: 189, Figure 2.2.9.

tion most of the population had been dispersed and old houses demolished.
Here the links between linguistic variation and network scores were less
marked, and sex differences in speech smaller.

---

9 (a), the /a/ vowel except before velars, e.g. *hat, man, grass*, which has
retracted and raised back realisations in localised Belfast speech.

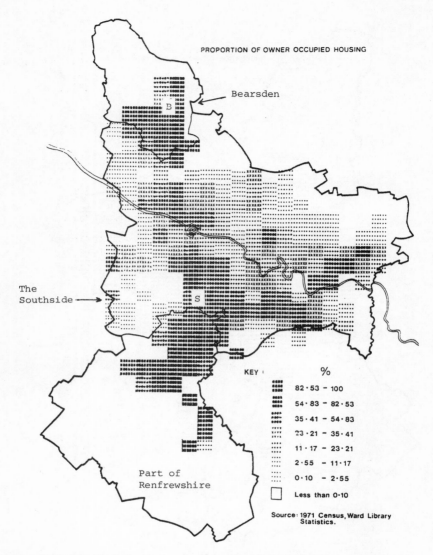

PROPORTION OF OWNER OCCUPIED HOUSING

Bearsden

The
Southside

Part of
Renfrewshire

KEY :
%
■■■■ 82·53 – 100
■■■■ 54·83 – 82·53
:::   35·41 – 54·83
:::: 23·21 – 35·41
:::: 11·17 – 23·21
:::: 2·55 – 11·17
:::: 0·10 – 2·55
☐ Less than 0·10

Source: 1971 Census, Ward Library
Statistics.

Map 4: From Strathclyde Regional Council, 1976: 188, Figure 2.2.8

This is clearly a line of investigation which needs to be pursued also in
Glasgow.

1.8 Code-switching

Code-switching is the name given to the manipulation by a single speaker of
different languages or different dialects. The definition of 'dialect' followed here is that proposed by the Linguistic Survey of Scotland and followed

19

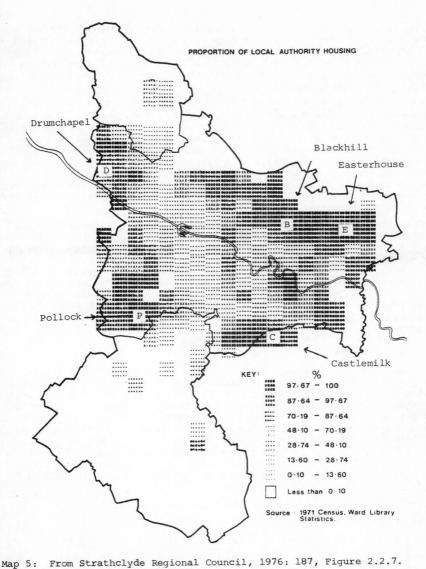

PROPORTION OF LOCAL AUTHORITY HOUSING

Drumchapel

Blackhill
Easterhouse

Pollock

Castlemilk

KEY:	%
	97·67 – 100
	87·64 – 97·67
	70·19 – 87·64
	48·10 – 70·19
	28·74 – 48·10
	13·60 – 28·74
	0·10 – 13·60
	Less than 0·10

Source : 1971 Census. Ward Library Statistics.

Map 5:   From Strathclyde Regional Council, 1976: 187, Figure 2.2.7.

by Petyt (1980: 21-3). Gross differences of lexical incidence such as those listed in 2.1.4 below are regarded as dialect differences.

Sociolinguistic studies in the tradition of Labov, such as Macaulay's in Glasgow and Milroy's in Belfast, have concentrated on phonological variables, because the phoneme systems are small, closed systems, and the full range of items can therefore be extracted from short samples of speech. Correspondingly little quantitative work has been done on lexical and syntactic variation, although Agutter's (1979) study of British slang, using Edinburgh, Glasgow and London informants, and correlating with age, sex and class, is a notable exception. Phonological variables are also assumed to be less under conscious control, so that although localised and stigmatised variants may decline in a formal situation, such as a taped interview, they are not simply suppressed, as lexical and grammatical equivalents might be.

Code-switching studies have mainly concentrated on situations where different languages, rather than dialects, are in play. The sorts of explanations put forward for this type of variation are considerably richer than those advanced for style variation in studies of phonological variants within a language. Factors of subject matter, the permanent roles of the speakers, their temporary relationship to each other in a specific situation, as well as their orientation towards that situation have all been taken into account. In phonological studies, the single factor of formality has been considered (at least until recently), and has been taken to reflect the degree of attention paid by the speaker to his language behaviour.

It is clear that the two areas are now moving towards a synthesis, though at this point no one theory has emerged to dominate the field. What I propose to do here is to apply one theory of language in society to the Glasgow situation as represented in literature. The theory is that of P. Brown and Levinson (1978), which provides a very powerful model of the speaker as a rational person using language to create and manipulate social relationships. Their actual analysis also includes useful pointers towards a model of code-switching, but this requires to be strengthened by concepts from within sociolinguistics itself. The essential features of Brown and Levinson's model are set out below.

1.8.1 The politeness model

Brown and Levinson start with the concept of the Face-Threatening Act (FTA). Almost any verbal interaction is potentially a threat to the face of one or both participants - even the conveying of information implies the ignorance, in that respect, of the hearer. Speakers have positive face, i.e. the desire and need for the attention and admiration of others, though not necessarily all others, and not necessarily the immediate interlocutor. They also have negative face, i.e. the desire and need to be private and unimpeded. All languages abound in specific verbal strategies orientated towards these facts. Brown and Levinson identify four super-strategies which are postulated as language universals. These are the choices available to a speaker wishing to perform an FTA:

1. to perform it, openly and unapologetically (baldly), e.g.

    (1) PAT Shut yer face, you! (T40/7)

    (2) Here a form - noo beat it quick! (Figure 10/2)

2. to perform it openly, but offering some gesture towards the hearer's positive face. This is more risky than the next because it involves the vulnerable assumption that the hearer desires such attention from that speaker, e.g.

    (3) ROUGER Gettin his strength up. Ah mean, a lovely girl
              like you. (T41/26)

Here the speaker is expressing lust, mitigated by complimentary remarks.

(4)   "Aye, Ah know. That road's a cryin disgrace, so it is,"
      says Andy's ma. (T38/25)

Here the speaker is doing the hearer a favour, mitigated by the reference to common ground, the difficulty of getting children to school safely.

3. to perform it openly, but offering some gesture towards the hearer's negative face, e.g.

(5)   Ah know ah'm goin on aboot this. / But ... (T64/24,5)

(6)   PAT   Aye. I go mysel' ... the odd time.

      WILLIE Sorry I spoke, then. (T40/29,30)

In the latter, the mitigation is offered retrospectively.

4. to perform it indirectly, by hints, irony, sarcasm and all kinds of indirect speech acts, e.g.

(7)   'You better get brains, son.' (T32/12)

For further discussion, see 5.2.4 below.

    The question then arises, why so speakers not simply adopt the most cautious strategy, 4., on all occasions, thus avoiding giving offence explicitly and being seen to do so? The degree of caution adopted by the speaker is a measure of the degree of risk associated with the FTA. But this risk is not simply inherent in the FTA itself (e.g. asking to borrow a car versus asking for a light). At least two other factors are also involved - the power differential between the speakers, and the social distance between them. Thus to a friend, 'Give me a light', but to a stranger, 'Do you think you could give me a light?' Or to an equal, 'No, you can't', but to someone more powerful, 'I'm afraid that under the circumstances, it wouldn't be possible just at the moment.'

    There are linguistic pointers which clarify the various factors for the hearer. For example, terms of deference like *sir*, *your honour* indicate that the hearer's power is highly rated. Terms of familiarity like ScE *hen* (to a woman) and *Jimmy* (to a man) indicate that the social distance is considered small. Modifiers like *just* can indicate that the FTA itself is not a large one e.g.

(8)   jist leeit / alane! (T62/32,3)

    Power and social distance are variables in a relationship and are manipulated and changed partly through the selection of politeness strategies and the hearer's acquiescence or otherwise in the values assigned by the speaker.

1.8.2 Politeness and dialect

Brown and Levinson associate the use of colloquial speech, non-standard dialect and vernacular language (in bilingual situations) with positive politeness (2. above), specifically as a claim to common ground with the hearer. However, there is a major complication with regard to dialects and minority languages which does not affect other realisations of 'politeness'. As well as being transient varieties in the speech of individuals, these are also permanent varieties associated with particular socially and geographically located speech communities. Consequently, the manipulation of these varieties at the micro-level must be seen as derivative from values permanently associated with them.

These rival value systems can be seen at work in T42, in the interchange between the dialect-speaking foreman and the standard-speaking manager. Each has a different kind of power. The manager's is derived from his institutional role - ultimately the power to hire and fire. The foreman's is derived from his skill and experience in the workplace, which makes him effectively indispensible. (Immediately following this scene, one of the workers goes into an epileptic fit, and the foreman explicitly states that the firm is not doing him a favour by keeping him on, as the manager suggests, because he is irreplaceable). These speakers do not converge on each other's styles. Each identifies himself through language with his respective power base.

Should we see this type of exchange, in which neither speaker employs code-switching as a conversational strategy, as an unmarked exchange? I think not, and I accept the implication that there can be no unmarked, unproblematic dialogue between standard and dialect speakers. Milroy (1980) has shown in Belfast that there is a correlation between working class speakers' use of localised variants and their degree of integration into the social networks of the community. She interprets the social role of the vernacular in terms of solidarity and that of the standard in terms of status. These are permanent ideological meanings associated with the different language varieties as manifestations of social stratification. Thus we can say that the natural everyday speech of the foreman in T42 conveys working-class values, willy-nilly. Likewise, the everyday speech of the manager conveys the dominant middle-class values, willy-nilly. There is thus a covert conflict between them which they do not attempt to mitigate. Each speaker can disassociate himself from these ideologies only by adopting the language of the other. Thus, even in a no-choice situation, where the standard speaker does not understand the dialect or minority language, and therefore the exchange can only be conducted in the standard, the use of the standard is still socially meaningful, because one speaker is forced to use a variety which is not native to him, but is native to the other.

Code-switching is not a symmetrical phenomenon, because the relationship between the varieties is not symmetrical. The standard is the norm, and in BrE is superimposed on all other varieties. For the dialect speaker to use the standard is negative politeness - he avoids imposing a local and minority norm. But, as we have seen, for the standard speaker to use the local dialect or vernacular language is positive politeness, because this is a specific compliment to the hearer. Notice that such a speaker is making the assumption that such an identification with the dialect-speaking hearer is welcomed by the latter.

Brown and Levinson's view is more general - that dialect as such is a positive politeness strategy. It would perhaps be better to see dialect exchanges between dialect speakers and standard exchanges between standard speakers as unmarked, simply confirming their permanent place in society, and all other exchanges as marked and requiring explanation in terms of the confrontation, mutual accommodation, or manipulation of rival ideologies. Within the working class community, then, dialect speech is not so much a politeness strategy at the micro-level as an expression of solidarity at the macro-level. This is consistent with Brown and Levinson's observation that working class communities tend to favour positive rather than negative politeness strategies, and Milroy's (1980) observation that social cohesion is greater in the working class than in the middle class.

1.8.3 Code-switching in practice

Code-switching between dialects is, of course, a matter of degree. There is
a common core of linguistic items, and at other points a choice between standard and non-standard alternatives. In the present state of knowledge about
Glasgow dialect - and British dialects in general - it is difficult to estimate
to what extent speakers do code-switch.

There is a widely-held belief in Scotland that speakers in rural areas
switch readily between the varieties, whereas urban speakers use either dialect
or standard habitually. However, it is probably a minority of (mostly male)
working class speakers in either rural or urban areas, who are prepared to
maintain a broad dialect style in the face of a tape-recorded interview. But
even for them, there may be other situations (in addition to reading aloud)
which would induce them to adopt the standard. (In the extreme case, there
are no choice situations, such as travelling outside Scotland, where Glasgow
dialect would be an embarrassment). They would not necessarily feel comfort-
able speaking fully standard English, or be able to keep it up for a long time
(cf. T12).

Such discomfort was described to me by an informant, a middle aged man, as
follows:

> To what extent do Ah have to think about changing from, for in-
> stance the way Ah speak in the work, and if Ah met you outside?
> Aye, it's a wee bit difficult for me with ma history and back-
> ground and the way Ah speak, you see, tae change it to speak to
> you if Ah met you just along the road. It's a wee bit of a
> struggle, Ah would say. Even Ah found it a struggle when Ah
> wis in the Labour Party, joined the local Labour Party. Most of
> the kind i people there are proper speakers. Well, for me tae
> speak, Ah would be afraid that Ah might've used the wrong grammar
> and sayed the wrong words, so this kept me quiet for a wee bit,
> ye know? It was - lots i times Ah felt lik speaking at the meet-
> ings, but Ah was afraid because of the - hearing how Ah - Ah like
> tae hear their accents, the other members - how Ah thought - an
> it was - they weren't - it was just easy for them tae speak; they
> weren't puttin anything on; they were just speaking just natu-
> rally proper. But I enjoyed listening tae them, and I used tae
> wonder how tae phrase ma questions an how tae speak.
>
> So Ah's a wee bit of a struggle there. But then Ah've discov-
> ered that that's not important; that it's not important to speak
> proper and nice, and even if Ah do sound slang, Ah felt that this
> was not important. So much so, and Ah was convinced and satisfied
> with that approach to the thing, that Ah accepted and took the job
> as chairman.

Discomfort is also an aspect of Macaulay's (1975) 'linguistic insecurity',
the lack of fluency of working class Glaswegians as perceived by school-teach-
ers and employers.

The urban/rural distinction may, however, have some validity for middle
class speakers. In rural areas of Britain class consciousness (at least between the middle and the working classes) is not so marked and a different,
historically prior, aspect of dialect is more prominent. That is, the geographical. Cutting across the solidarity-status ideological conflict, there
is the local-national one. Williams (1982) describes these two dimensions as

pertaining respectively to the state and to civil society. The local dimension is becoming more important to the middle class as they compete regionally
for state resources. This gives rise to a partial and selective identification
with non-standard dialects, precisely because they are localised.[10]

Even urban middle class speakers, whose outlook is more class oriented, are
liable to make use of occasional local dialect forms to express a sense of
place. Certain referents which are felt to be local or the ideological property of the working class tend to be named in dialect, e.g. in journalism and
reminiscences (cf. T69-71). However, an urban middle class speaker would be
unlikely to switch into broad dialect, unless he or she was upwardly mobile
from a working class background. Many such people go into teaching, and a
command of the dialect may be useful here, as a student reports:

> Teachers tended to use the dialect more when teaching the
> 'plasticine brigade' ... When dealing with them it was a way
> to try to get on equal terms. Teachers who spoke Standard
> English to them tended to set up communication barriers.

As represented, probably accurately, in Glasgow dialect writing, code-switching
is a matter of the frequency and type of dialect items selected rather than
drastic switches between fully dialectal and fully standard styles. An example
will be found in T40, where a change in the speech genre produces a drop in
the density of non-standard (written) forms.

The concept of speech genre is one which we have not so far considered. As
Brown and Levinson themselves point out, there are relevant factors in addition to those of power, social distance and the inherent threat of the FTA
incorporated into their model. But if Williams (1982) and Milroy (1980) are
correct, and there are two basic ideological positions of status versus solidarity (complicated by the local-national dimension), then it ought to be
possible to derive other factors from them. Here there is only space to point
out that certain speech genres, such as speech-making, are associated with the
public domain dominated by the middle class. So, regardless of the audience,
the model used is the standard, and the values evoked are those of status
(cf. T1). On the other hand, there are speech genres associated with the
working class. Two of these in Glasgow are *patter* and *shericking*. Patter is
the witty and creative use of language in conversation. A shericking is a
public row where a person (normally a woman) attempts to strip another of face
by inciting onlookers against him or her. In this sense, the word appears to
be localised in the Glasgow area. Either of these would be conducted only in
the vernacular.

A second example occurs in T32. Here one speaker is socially mobile and
employs a wide range of styles. The other speaks broad dialect. In the context of the former's warnings to the latter as his subordinate, mostly in the
form of veiled threats, the use of dialect plays an interesting part. Many
of the FTAs are indirect, that is, the dominant strategy is one of great cau-

---

10 Williams (1982) makes the claim that in Welsh, as a minority language,
    sociolinguistic stratification is lacking. This is the converse to the
    relative lack of regional variation in St E. The advocates of the revival
    of the Scots dialects as a language appear to be aiming at a similar sit-
    uation. But in order to extricate Scots from the solidarity-status dimen-
    sion, they have found it necessary to isolate a literary variety. Macafee
    (1981) discusses the relationship between Scottish nationalism and the
    codification of this variety.

tion. The use of dialect, because of its permanent association with working class solidarity, minimises the factor of social distance, clarifying the calculations of the speaker - power and threat are large, and even more so with social distance pegged low.

In a historical context, the question of code-switching becomes the question of language maintenance. In addition to class consciousness and language ideology, social mobility must also be taken into account.

1.9 Working class consciousness

Although Macaulay identified three class groupings on the basis of accent, for present purposes class identity in Glasgow can be thought of in terms of a dichotomy between the working classes and the middle classes. (The upper class are practically non-existent in Glasgow). The equivalent dichotomy in the dominant ideology is between 'proper' speech and 'slang'.

Amongst the working classes in the Clydeside conurbation, class consciousness is high, and there is a long history of effective mobilisation, with leadership coming largely from skilled manual workers. Before and during the First World War, Clydeside was the main centre of organised working class opposition to British participation in the War. The area was also prominent in the General Strike of 1926, and in the National Hunger Marches of the 1920s and 1930s. For Glasgow marchers, this meant five weeks on the road, usually in mid-winter. Part of the working class struggle during the Depression was the organisation of tenants against evictions, which were common at this time, because of the inability of the unemployed to pay rents. Resistance to evictions led to the setting up of a special rent fund by Glasgow City Council in 1922 (Hannington, 1936: 71). In the 1950s, many Scottish workers achieved wage parity with English workers through the trade union movement.[11] In the 1970s, the working class in Clydeside continued to struggle as workers against the loss of jobs, and as tenants against inadequate housing. Wishart (1976: 80) estimates that a quarter of all Scottish workers downed tools on 18 August 1971 in support of a work-in at Upper Clyde Shipyards, led by Jimmy Reid, against the then Conservative government's plan to liquidate the Upper Clyde Shipbuilders consortium, with the loss of seven jobs in ten. In February 1972, the government expended £25M to save three of the yards, and a fourth was sold to an American buyer. Recently, rent strikes and campaigns in the first of the redevelopment areas, Hutchesontown-Gorbals, have encouraged similar organisation in other parts of the city (Bryant, 1979). This is notwithstanding the enormous disruption of the working class community and the breaking up of its social networks in the process of rehousing.

Working class solidarity supports negative evaluations of middle class culture, including language. In response to Dowie's (1979: 59) questions, 'Where in Glasgow would you not like to stay?'[12] and 'Why would you not like to stay there?', Drumchapel schoolchildren named middle class areas amongst others, for the following reasons:

> Bearsden - "because the snobs live there and you couldn't mix in with there invirement"
> Knightswood - "it is too snobbish".

---

11 Wages in some sectors, including the shipyards, were actually higher in Scotland in the early part of the century.

12 In St ScE, to *stay* somewhere is to live there permanently.

Similar comments can be found elsewhere:

> The kids in these three closes kept together when playing and
> none of them ever played with us in the poorer closes. However,
> this didn't bother us as our parents called them "half-boiled
> toffs", and when clustered around the closes at night our moth-
> ers used to gossip about them, mimic their proper accents and
> laugh at them. (Boyle, 1977: 9).

> Whenever you are out with your friends and you accidentally say
> something politely then they laugh at you and say you are a
> snob. (12 year old girl).

Glasgow has a strong working class identity particularly as the middle
classes are numerically weak:

> It may be, indeed, that, in spite of greater mobility and mixing
> of the classes, and the reduction of the gross gap in incomes,
> the sense of class difference has heightened. Glasgow has gener-
> ated a labour force containing one of the highest proportions
> amongst British cities of workers with a low level of skills, to-
> gether with one of the lowest proportions of professional and
> managerial people, and so is increasingly a working class city.
> (Checkland, 1977: 82).

Working class Glaswegians themselves insist on friendliness and good-neigh-
bourliness as part of their character, qualities which are heavily emphasised
in nostalgic accounts of tenement life. Middle class Scots, the English, and
the rival city of Edinburgh, are perceived as correspondingly unfriendly and
reserved.

1.10 Social mobility

The chief motivation for young people to acquire the outward characteristics
of a higher class is a realistic expectation of being able to join that class,
whether through employment or marriage. All things being equal, class status
tends to be inherited:

> superficial characteristics such as styles of speech and dress
> tend to be transmitted from one generation to the next. In
> most cases these have no fundamental effect on a son's [sic]
> productivity, but they may affect his marketability or earning
> power, tending to place him in a particular occupational track.
> (Brittain, 1977: 7-8).

To some extent, the advantages and disadvantages conferred by inheritance
of status are affected by a redistribution of opportunity through formal education. But the upward social mobility of working class individuals also depends on the availability of suitable job opportunities. As we have seen,
Clydeside is an area of high unemployment and high net emigration, so that
social mobility is most readily achieved through physical mobility. Macaulay's
findings indicate that individuals who spend prolonged periods outside Glasgow
do modify their speech towards educated norms.[13]

The prevailing social immobility is reflected in a generalised lack of confidence, frequently commented on in Macaulay's study:

---

13 This opinion was held by employers and confirmed by the speech of speaker
3/9 on the attitude test tape.

> I think there is something that is lacking in Scottish people
> in general. I don't know whether it's a lack of confidence.
> They don't generally express themselves very well.... Perhaps
> it's just our dour natures.[14] (staff manageress, Macaulay, 1975:
> 37).

This perceived lack of confidence does have an objective basis. McQuaid
(1968: 45) found a high degree of anxiety and introversion amongst young people in the west of Scotland:

> the chief factors involved are, briefly, excitability, low self-
> sentiment level, high guilt proneness, tension, poor ego level,
> high threat reactivity.

1.11 The dominant ideology

The second part of Macaulay's study, already mentioned, investigated attitudes
towards localised Glasgow speech. The pattern which emerges is one of 'linguistic insecurity' amongst working class speakers, i.e. negative evaluations
of their own type of speech, and lack of confidence in interaction with middle
class speakers, as reported by teachers and employers. It is clear from the
repetitiveness and predictability of the judgements elicited from lower class
speakers that they do not reflect individual opinions in many cases, but are
individualised statements of the dominant ideology, which is, in some sense,
the 'correct' answer. Although this contradiction might indeed have reper-
cussions on individual psychology, it must surely be located in society. The
question then becomes, not 'why do some working class individuals manifest
linguistic insecurity?' but 'why are some working class individuals more willing than others to articulate the dominant ideology?'. The answer would nowadays be sought in their degree of integration with the working class community.

Middle class dislike of Glasgow dialect is sometimes expressed in peculiarly
virulent terms:

> The accent of the lowest state of Glaswegians is the ugliest
> accent one can encounter ...

for predictable reasons:

> but that is partly because it is associated with the unwashed and
> the violent. (University lecturer, Macaulay, 1975: 94).

This simply reflects the very bad reputation of Glasgow generally. This stereotype has a blighting effect on working class adolescents in Glasgow.

The slums of Britain's industrial cities consistently manifest high rates
of criminality. In Glasgow:

> The worst street in Blackhill (252 houses), produced between 1948
> and 1960 20 juvenile delinquents per 100 houses of whom 29 per
> cent became adult criminals. (Checkland, 1977: 90).

Armstrong and Wilson (1973) argue that such correlations between poor social
conditions and criminality should not be taken at face value, since "the means
whereby certain groups *become labelled* as deviant and selected for social control, is basically a *political process*" (Armstrong and Wilson, 1973: 69-70).

---

14 Notice the use of a scotticism, *dour*, and the first person *our*, as ways
of mitigating the statement.

In other words, high rates of conviction reflect not only actual law-breaking, but a concentration of official attention on those law-breakers in particular. Armstrong and Wilson describe how a group of youths in the enormous Easterhouse scheme came to be labelled delinquents. Their main leisure activities consisted of hanging around at street corners and playing or spectating at scratch football matches. Football rivalry developed into physical conflict, and at some point adult fear of 'gangs', for which Glasgow has long been notorious, especially in times of high unemployment, led to official reaction. The situation caught the attention of the media, and culminated in a much publicised campaign by a pop star to pacify the gangs. The Easterhouse youth was faced by a consensus amongst the media and official and unofficial agents of social control which identified him as a deviant member of society, and was increasingly confined to his own peer group as offering the least threat to his self-esteem. Unemployability, petty crime, prison and more serious crime follow.

This example is typical of media and official response to Glasgow's social problems in the 1960s. Since then, however, more liberal attitudes have been in evidence.[15] The media have popularised such figures as Jimmy Reid, mentioned above, and Billy Connolly, a local comedian, indicating a willingness to accept certain aspects of working class life and values. In Easterhouse itself, local initiatives have created the Easterhouse Festival, and the opportunity to present a new image of the area has been taken up by the local press:

> Last year, the Easterhouse Festival, product of citizens who wanted to tell the world they existed, went on for ages. Community drama, an unheard of concept almost anywhere else, suddenly evolved.... In this 60,000 strong part of Scotland, there are 60,000 people who refuse to accept the argument of Glasgow and the nation that they don't exist. (*The Glasgow Herald*, 9 March, 1979).

Attitudes towards Glasgow dialect have correspondingly tended to soften. Broad Glasgow speech can be heard on the local radio station, Radio Clyde, and is not necessarily treated as comic.

Perhaps because of the increasingly adult composition of the classrooms (the minimum school leaving age in Britain is now 16), ideological compromise is evident here also:

> In the past, what teachers have taught in Glasgow schools has often been an implied criticism of the way of life of a considerable proportion of parents: this is true of speech, manners and general outlook on the way life is lived. In the later 'sixties and early 'seventies this to some degree changed, with a good many teachers seeking to identify less with middle-class mores, and to find elements of intrinsic value in working-class life. (Checkland, 1977: 86).

As Macaulay's attitude survey showed, teachers and others in Glasgow do not usually (any longer) make value judgements about linguistic variation in terms of a simple good/bad (standard/non-standard) dichotomy. In the first place,

---

15 'Marginal man' in the U. K. is now the non-white, and in particular the unemployed black youth. Non-whites in Glasgow are few in number, and usually economically active.

teachers' judgements have become more sophisticated, and are expressed in terms of functional registers, i.e. the appropriateness of a given variety to a given situation. The following comment is typical:

> My class are willing to talk. When we hold a discussion, I don't correct the way they talk. I allow them to speak slang. (primary school teacher, Macaulay, 1977: 100).

Such liberal attitudes are belied not only by terms like 'correct' and 'slang', but by the fact that speech choices are made in the context of power relationships as we have seen, so that there is considerably more pressure on the working class speaker to be flexible in speech styles.

Secondly, the picture in Scotland is complicated by the considerable (and increasing) prestige of traditional forms of Scots. Glasgow dialect naturally retains various features from the underlying West Mid dialect, and these are positively valued, while innovatory features, such as the glottal stop, and those not peculiar to Scotland, such as the frequently mentioned *I done*, *I seen*, etc., are negatively valued. Thus a teacher can say with regret:

> If you read Burns nowadays, it's like reading Chaucer. When I grew up almost a third of the words were recognisable. The old Scots words which formed a fairly substantial part of the Glasgow vocabulary all now need to be explained. (secondary school teacher, Macaulay, 1977: 95).

Since working class speech, especially in casual styles, is considerably different both from St ScE and from traditional (particularly literary) Scots, the prevailing ideology is still one of 'I'm okay, you're not okay' so far as sociolinguistic variation is concerned.

1.12 Glasgow dialect literature

The development of the Glasgow novel is viewed by Burgess (1972) as a process of overcoming the dominant stereotypes - on the one hand, the violent drunken world of the mass media image, reflected in the 'gangland' novel, and on the other the nostalgic childhood world of the 'urban kailyard'.[16] The former seems to be peculiar to Glasgow within Scotland, but the latter is endemic in Scottish literature, as Campbell (1979: 411) observes:

> to this day Scottish art remains steeped in nostalgia for pre-pubescent innocence. Since the cultural bourgeoisie of the country is besotted by this ideal - hardly a week passes without some horrible new manifestation of it being lauded in the pages of the *Scotsman* - it is difficult for the artist who refuses to celebrate it to exist in Scotland.

Much of the best work of Glasgow writers has been published by small private presses. Nevertheless, and despite the prevailing climate in Scottish publishing, the 1970s have seen a great flowering of Glasgow dialect literature, and also of popular entertainment.

In the novel and short story, there are many examples of what Burgess calls 'realistic' works. Playwrights have dramatised the Glasgow working man and his doppelgänger, the Glasgow criminal, although the experience of working class women remains largely unarticulated. Glasgow poets have not only writ-

---

16 After the 'Kailyard' ('cabbage patch') school of Scottish novelists.

ten in the dialect, but have taken language as a major theme. A central feature of this newly mature literature is the distinctive orthography by which it is written down. Glasgow writers have not been concerned with setting up a local standard, but with articulating a non-standard variety as such. The appearance of illiteracy conveyed by spellings like ⟨wurd⟩ and ⟨langwij⟩ (which are purely orthographic variants, and indicate no distinctive Glasgow pronunciation) is deliberate, and in keeping with the newly, and sometimes aggressively, confident voice of Glasgow literature.

In more popular entertainment, the figure of Billy Connolly eclipses all others. Reaction to Connolly is mixed. Thomson (1976) compares his bad taste unfavourably with the intellectual bad taste of Lenny Bruce. Jimmy Reid, however, compares him to Rabelais - "big, crude, warm" - like Glasgow (1976a: 12).

THE ENGLISH OF GLASGOW

2.0 Overview

As in most English speaking areas with a historical dialect or creole, the standard variety is now thoroughly integrated with the local variety in Glasgow in such a way that the English spoken can best be described as a single linguistic system containing numerous variables grouped into standard and non-standard categories. Utterances can be placed on a continuum between fully localised and fully standardised. The continuum can be extended further in either direction in writing than in speech - not only are more formal types of St E possible in writing, but also more dense types of Scots. However, Glasgow dialect writers usually prefer a realistic mode, and avoid the latter option.[17]

The shift from a predominantly rural to a predominantly urban population, and continuing change in the means of production and in the working class way of life, have meant a decline in the quantity and currency of historical dialect forms. This is compensated by the borrowing or production of new non-standard forms, e.g. *youse*, second person plural pronoun, from HibE; *bothan* 'shebeen' from Highland English; *dowt* 'cigarette end' from England. The non-standard grammatical forms *ain't* and *them* as a deictic determiner = *those* (see below 2.4) have probably spread from England. Some items which seem to be mainly Glaswegian or in process of diffusing from Glasgow are probably local innovations: *boggin, hairy, heidbanger, hingoot, huckle, lumber, malky* and *stoatir* (in the sense of something good of its kind) (Agutter and Cowan, 1981). Others could be added, e.g. *bampot* and *bamstick*, and *staikie*. A systematic search of the SND would yield others, not necessarily still current, e.g. *snooks, smowts, snapper* and *crappy*. Partridge (1966) would add a few more, e.g. *hing-on* and *hing aff*.

St E in Scotland has certain differences from other varieties of the standard, including lexical items such as *outwith* 'outside'; *landward* 'rural'; the specialised vocabulary of Scotland's separate legal system; *glen* 'valley'; *loch* 'lake'; and others embedded in epithets and clichés, e.g. *the Wee Frees* 'the Free Church of Scotland', *furth of Scotland* 'outside Scotland', etc. There are also grammatical peculiarities, of a quantitative rather than qualitative kind, such as the Scottish (and Northern English) preference for making the operator rather than the negative particle enclitic where there is a choice, e.g. *I'll not go* rather than *I won't go*; and in negative interrogatives, a tendency to avoid inverting the negative particle over the subject, e.g. *will you not go* rather than *won't you go* (this is also the case in negative reversed polarity tags). Other points will be mentioned in connection with texts, below. Also, see Hughes and Trudgill (1979), K. Brown and Miller (1975), Millar and K. Brown (1979), K. Brown and Millar (1980).

2.1 Phonology

Only a tiny proportion of native Scots are speakers of Received Pronunciation (RP), and localised pronunciation can only usefully be related to the local standard, described by Speitel (1975) and by Abercrombie (1979). Since the

---

17 The terms *realistic* and *realism* are used here in their literary critical sense, i.e. the language so described appears to be modelled on the spoken language. There is a theoretical problem here which it is beyond the scope of the present work to discuss.

local dialect has no phonemes additional to those of St ScE,[18] it will be con-
venient here to take both together with regard to the phonemic inventory, phonetic distribution and phonetic realisation, before going on to consider the
incidence of this shared system in the lexicon.

There is a type of middle class accent known as 'Kelvinside', after an area
of the city, and popularly regarded as an affectation. It is a source of humour in the media, especially when the speaker is also portrayed as lapsing
into localised speech at other points. Some of its segmental features are
mentioned below. Other characteristics include over-careful enunciation, e.g.
separate, adjective, as three syllables, and avoidance of weak or enclitic
forms of function words. A similar phenomenon is found in Edinburgh, where it
is called 'Morningside'. Johnston (forthcoming) confirms that features associated with the stereotype do occur in Morningside, and in other parts of
Edinburgh with a similar social composition, e.g. [æ] for /a/ and the merger
of /ae/ and /ʌi/ as [æ^{I}], but are mainly confined$_{[19]}$ to upper middle class speakers over 55 and lower middle class women over 50.

2.1.1 Consonants

ScE has a phoneme /x/ in a number of words of Gaelic origin, e.g. *loch* /lɔx/;
proper names, e.g. *McCulloch* /mʌkʌlʌx/, *Auchenback* /ɔxɪnbak/; and in dialect
words, some from O E. However, /x/ appears to be losing some of its functional load in localised Glasgow speech. The forms *nicht* 'night', *fecht* 'fight',
etc., are seldom heard, and placenames such as *St. Enoch's* are heard with /k/
while this is regular for the ⟨ch⟩ of *Sauchiehall Street*.

ScE retains the phoneme /ʍ/ in contrast to /w/, e.g. *where* /ʍer/, *wear*
/wer/.$_{[20]}$ Younger speakers in Glasgow can occasionally be heard to merge with
/w/.

Post-vocalic /r/ is retained in ScE. The trilled realisation frequently
mentioned in earlier studies is in fact rare in urban speech and usually emphatic. /r/ is realised as a tap [ɾ] especially intervocalically, or as an
approximant [ɹ]. McAllister (1938: 178) links the latter with mergers involving stressed vowels before /r/ (see below, 2.1.2). The occasional loss of
post-vocalic /r/ which Romaine (1978) describes amongst working class
Edinburgh schoolchildren can also be heard in Glasgow from adult speakers.
Romaine suggests that this is a change from below in the working class in
Edinburgh, led by males, and in competition with a change, led by females,
towards the prestigious [ɹ] variant. Paul Johnston (work in progress) analyses
the 'deleted' /r/ as a pharyngeal vocalic segment, and it has been so transcribed in this volume, but he points out that as there is in any case a pharyngeal articulatory setting, the deletion interpretation is also valid.$_{[21]}$

Where RP has /tʃ/ and /dʒ/ in post-tonic position in words like *nature* and

---

18 But cf. possible near mergers involving words of the *gude* group and words
    of the *tair* group. See below, 2.1.4.

19 'Morningside' speakers also have [ʌ] for /ɔ/. Tom Leonard (personal com-
    munication) has noticed this from 'Kelvinside' speakers

20 These mergers involving /x/ and /ʍ/ also occur in Edinburgh working class
    speech (Paul Johnston, personal communication), and, as already mentioned,
    in Belfast working class speech. They appear not to be RP influenced.

21 Suzanne Romaine (personal communication) agrees that there is pharyngeal
    constriction.

and *soldier*, St ScE may have /tj/ and /dj/. Speitel (1975: 45) remarks t.
some Scottish speakers insist on the latter as the 'correct' pronunciation.

/l/ can be velarised in all positions. Middle class Scottish speakers may
correct to clear /l/ where this occurs in RP, i.e. in initial, post-consonan-
tal and intervocalic positions. Wells describes a pharyngealised /l/ in
Glasgow with an [ɒ] quality. (Wells, 1982: 411). This is a stereotype in
the football chant, "We are ra peopul".

Localised speakers may elide /ð/ initially. Both intervocalically and initially it may be merged with /r/. (McAllister, 1938: 112 gives this only
intervocalically). In words with original /r/ in a neighbouring syllable,[22]
there may be assimilation, e.g. *brother* [bɪʌɾʌ] or [bɪʌ:], *mother* [mʌɾʌ].
Localised Glasgow speakers occasionally produce /d/ for initial /ð/ (see Figure 7, and cf. HibE).

Localised speakers may have /h/ for /θ/, e.g. *think* /hɪŋk/, *something*
/sʌ(m)hm/. As elsewhere, this /h/ can be realised as the voiceless equivalent
of the following voiced segment, e.g. [sʌ(m)mm], *three* [ɪɪi:].[23] These forms
are widespread in Central Scotland. For other possible lenitions see Wells
(1982: 410).

In localised speech, post-tonic /t/ is very often realised as [ʔ] or [ʔt],
as is the initial /t/ of the word *to* [ʔʉ]. This is "the feature most frequently singled out by teachers as characteristic of a Glasgow accent" (Macaulay,
1977: 45). In fact, it is by no means confined to Glasgow: "It is thought to
be an urban phenomenon, but is in fact encountered in remote villages in
Scotland, even with old people" (Speitel, 1975: 45). Macaulay found that [ʔ]
occurs for /t/ with high frequency for all social class groups. Some environments are more stigmatised than others, especially before a pause, and word
medially before a vowel (Macaulay, 1977: 47,48), e.g. *what?* [мɪʔ], *water*
[waʔʉɪ].

To a lesser extent then /t/, post-tonic /k/ and even /p/ are realised as
[ʔ] in localised speech. When there is a following nasal, this tends to be
homorganic with the underlying plosive, e.g. *thruppence* [ɪɪʌʔms], *blacken*
[blaʔŋ].[24]

In localised Scottish speech, ejective realisations of the voiceless plosives occur in emphatic speech before a pause (Johnston, 1979: 98), e.g. *will
you please stop!* [wɪɫ jü: pɬi:z stɔpʼ].

Speitel (1975: 45) points out that in /Vnt/ and /Vrt/ combinations, the /n/
or /r/ may be deleted in localised speech before [ʔ]. The /n/ may be reduced
to nasalisation of the preceding vowel, e.g. *ninety* [nãĩʔë], and the glottal
plosive may itself be deleted, e.g. *wanting* [wã:n]. These changes are probably promoted by rapid speech rate.

22 In Edinburgh, /ð/ is sometimes deleted initially by working class speakers.
    In Belfast, speakers of the same class may lenite or delete intervocalic
    /ð/. Only in Glasgow does lenited /ð/ commonly merge with /r/.

23 *Pace* Hughes and Trudgill (1979: 72). Cf. Speitel's (1969: 52) [smmm] for
    Midlothian. A further possibility is [sʌmʔm] (A. J. Aitken, personal com-
    munication)

24 A. G. (see below, 3.6) tells how, as a child, he misunderstood the Orange
    Lodge slogan 'kick the Pope' as 'kick the poke'. Clearly there can be a
    loss of contrast between final /p/ and /k/ when both are realised as [ʔ].

r dialects, including Ulster, Berwickshire and parts of the
/t/ can be realised as a tap [ɾ] intervocalically, e.g. *let*

peech, /s/ and /z/ are occasionally realised as cacuminal
[ṣ, ẓ]. [s] does not necessarily merge with /ʃ/, and spellings with ⟨sh⟩ may
indicate this form, e.g. *minsh* 'mince'.[25]

In the clusters /rl, rm, lm, rn/, probably in that order of frequency, an
epenthetic vowel develops in localised speech, e.g. *girl* [gɪɾʌɫ], *arm* [ɛɾʌm],
film [fɪɫʌm], *torn* [toɾʌn].[26]

2.1.2 Vowels

St ScE has, minimally, the following monophthongs in stressed syllables: /i,
e, ɛ, a, ɪ, u, ɔ, o, ʌ/, which are also those of the West Mid dialect before
/t/ (Catford, 1957b: 113). Abercrombie (1979) also recognises a phoneme /ë/.
This occurs in a small number of words including *seven, heaven, never, ever,
twenty* and *shepherd*. It also occurs for /ɪ, ɛ, ʌ/ before /r/, especially in
middle class Scottish speech e.g. in *fir, earth, fur*. There is considerable
fluctuation in these mergers, and also, when /ë/ does not occur in *seven*, etc.,
speakers vary between /ɪ/ and /ɛ/. In localised speech, the realisation of
/ɪ/ is normally lowered and retracted, so that it is not possible to identify
this phoneme without eliciting minimal pairs. It is therefore transcribed as
/ɪ/ hereafter.

Middle class speakers may have additional contrasts of /æ/ with /a/, /ɒ/
with /ɔ/ and /ʊ/ with /u/ as in RP, but the incidence in the lexicon may be
different from RP. These additional contrasts are arranged in an implicational scale by Abercrombie, in the order in which they are given above, such that
the presence of the later contrasts implies the earlier ones. It is not clear
that this implicational scale holds for Glasgow (see T3 and T4 below).

As Speitel (1975: 37) points out, the realisation of /ɪ/ in ScE is generally
lower than in RP, but in localised speech it can be lowered and retracted almost to the position of /ʌ/. Berdan's (1978) analysis of Macaulay's results
for /ɪ/ show that:

> Individuals in Social Group I vary chiefly along the dimension
> of vowel height; members of the other social groups vary chief-
> ly in the use of variants differentiated by relative front-
> backness. (1978: 155).

The realisation of /u/ in ScE is often more centralised than in RP (Speitel,
1975: 39), but in Glasgow it can be fronted and lowered to [ø]. Unrounded
variants occur sporadically.[27] See T8 and T15 below.

The realisation of /a/ varies from [æ] - used only by Class I in Macaulay's
sample - through [a] to [ɑ] or [ɒ]. Macaulay conflates central and back real-

---

25 Cf. the articulatory setting with protruding lower jaw (see below, 2.1.3).

26 Two variants which are heard occasionally from young speakers are mainly
    Cockney forms: /f/ for initial /θ/ (not evidenced in this volume), and
    vocalised /l/ word finally (see T9).

27 Young working class speakers in Edinburgh also have [ø] (Paul Johnston,
    work in progress). Unrounding may explain the odd spelling ⟨dinn⟩ for
    doon 'down' in Trotter (1901: 24).

isations in his scoring system. It seems likely that most of his non-front realisation were central rather than fully back.[28] [æ] is found in the 'Kelvinside' accent.

The ranges of /e/ and /ɛ/ overlap in localised Scottish speech, with /ɛ/ tending to be raised (Speitel, 1975: 39). In the combination /er/, however, there is a merger with /ɛ/ in localised Glasgow speech, for some speakers,[29] e.g. *stair* /stɛr/. The ranges of /o/ and /ɔ/ also overlap.

Vowel length in ScE can be described as a binary system of short versus long. Aitken's (1981) Scottish Vowel Length Rule predicts that all stressed monophthongs in monosyllables and end-stressed polysyllables - except /ɪ/ and /ʌ/, which are always short - are long before /v, ð, z, ʒ, r/ or a morpheme boundary, e.g. *mood* [müd], *move* [mü:v]; *spade* [sped], *stay* [ste:], *stayed* [ste:d]. The rule operates consistently for some local dialects, but not for St ScE. Also, some speakers, including speakers of Highland English, may have contrastive length differences, e.g. *leek, made* short and *leak, maid* long (Abercrombie, 1979: 77). For localised speakers in the West of Scotland, there appears to be a second lengthening of all vowels under stress. Compare McAllister's observation (1938: 129) that Glaswegians tend to drawl.

/e/ and /o/ are usually monophthongal in ScE, but tend to become down-gliding diphthongs when lengthened under stress, especially before /r, n, l/. To a lesser extent, other vowels may develop glides under these conditions (cf. Johnston 1979: 117). Middle class Scottish speakers may have diphthongs similar to those of RP for /e/ and /o/ in any position.

The diphthongs of St ScE are /ae, ʌi, ʌu, ɔe/. Abercrombie's (1979) symbols are used here, although the first element of /ʌi/ is usually more centralised. /ae/ and /ʌi/ correspond to RP /aɪ/. The incidence in St ScE is predicted by the Scottish Vowel Length Rule, with /ae/ in long and /ʌi/ in short environments. Minimal pairs therefore usually occur only in morphologically conditioned contrasts, e.g. *sighed* /saed/, *side* /sʌid/. Genuine minimal pairs occur in dialect, where /ʌi/ can occur word finally, e.g. *aye* /ae/ 'yes', *ay* /ʌi/ 'always'. 'Kelvinside' speakers merge the two under [æⁱ] e.g. *side* [sæⁱd]. The localised realisation of /ɔe/ is [oe].

Macaulay's study included /ʌu/ as a variable. [ɑ̈u] was used more frequently by Class I, while Class II preferred [ʌu] or [əu]. Monophthongal forms with variants of /u/ were produced almost exclusively by Class III and IV speakers (1977: 42). (See below, 2.1.4).

Abercrombie (1979) identifies a three way contrast of vowels in unstressed syllables /ʌ, ɪ, e/, exemplified by *china* /tʃʌinʌ/, *pitted* /pɪtɪd/ and *pitied* /pɪted/. There is considerable fluctuation between /ɪ/ and /ʌ/ in unstressed syllables in localised speech - cf. the retracted realisation of stressed /ɪ/.

2.1.3 Suprasegmentals

Localised speakers in Glasgow tend to speak with the lower jaw protruded.[30] This is presumably what McAllister (1938) means when she refers to 'over-rounded' vowel variants.

---

28 Cf. fully back realisations in localised Edinburgh speech.

29 This is also true for some Edinburgh speakers (Speitel, 1969: 44). In addition there are a large number of words in Scots which occur with both /e/ and /ɛ/ (see below, 2.1.4).

30 This is also the case in Edinburgh (Esling, 1978: 142).

Glasgow has a very distinctive intonation, especially amongst working class speakers. This has similarities with that of Ulster (Adams, 1948), but is very different from the Edinburgh intonation patterns described by G. Brown et al. (1980). Although McClure (1980) describes intonation patterns very similar to those of Edinburgh from middle class speakers in other parts of the West of Scotland, I have the impression that the localised Glasgow pattern is rather widespread in the West, and not only from working class speakers.

Brown et al. take as their basic unit of analysis a pause bounded contour unit. Longer, or 'topic', pauses define larger units, or conversational paragraphs. Within each contour unit, stressed syllables were generally above, and unstressed syllables below, the middle of the speaker's pitch range. Most pitch movements were slight, and in a falling direction. In contour units which introduced a new topic or sub-topic, the initial peak was 'boosted' relative to following peaks. In their data, paragraph endings tended to be indecisive, but there were indications that a final non-low ending (rising pitch movement) is related to the close of a paragraph, and possibly of a conversational turn, but not of a conversation. This agrees with Cruttenden's (1981) generalisation that tunes which end with a fall are related to a group of meanings which he characterises as 'closed', while tunes which end with a rise express 'open' meanings. Cruttenden restates this at a more abstract level, with the 'closed' meanings being expressed by the unmarked tune in the system. This allows him to deal with local patterns, such as that of Glasgow.

Currie (1979) analyses a stretch of Glasgow speech in which the final peak of prominence in a contour unit is regularly reversed, occuring low in the pitch range - see Figure 1.

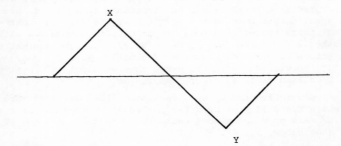

Figure 1: Idealised intonation contour of localised Glasgow English. X and Y are stressed syllables. From Currie, 1979: 390, Figure 2.

Intermediate unstressed syllables are attracted to the level of stressed ones (in Edinburgh this is only the case with unstressed syllables preceding the first stressed syllable of a contour unit), and where a tune ends with two stressed syllables the first will be attracted to the low level of the second. The movement on reversed peaks is rising.[31] Currie points out that the duration of pauses is shorter in her Glasgow than in her Edinburgh data, and suggests that the reversed peak serves to mark tone group boundaries and thus to

31 This is also the case in the transcription of a working class speaker in Macaulay and Trevelyan (1973: 240). When Macaulay (1977: 50) writes that the characteristic local contour is a rise-fall, this refers to the movement *between* syllables.

divide the discourse into smaller units.

The situation may be summarised as follows. Glasgow is intermediate between Edinburgh and Belfast (as described by Cruttenden, 1981), in that the local intonation pattern has both falls and low rises (from reversed peaks) as the unmarked terminal of contour units, with the latter perhaps predominating for many speakers in casual styles. All three cities, however, share the prevailing use in English of a high rising terminal as a marked intonation, expressing 'open' meanings. Cruttenden speculates that differences in intonation pattern might lead to misunderstandings between groups of speakers, and it would not be surprising if the frequency of rising terminals in Glasgow speech was heard by some groups as expressing hesitancy and lack of confidence.

2.1.4 Lexical incidence

There are a small number of differences in lexical incidence between St ScE and other varieties of the standard, e.g. /e/ in *there* and *where*, /ŋ/ in *sandwich* /saŋwɪdʒ/, /s/ in *raspberry* /raspɪre/, etc. The differences between St E and the local dialect in this respect are very numerous.[32] The main points are summarised below in terms of diachronic word classes.

1. O E /a:/ develops isolatively to /e/, e.g. *alane* = alone; *baith* = both; *claithes* = clothes; *ghaist* = ghost; *hail* = whole; *hame* = home; *mair* = more; *nae* = no; *naebuddy* = nobody; *nane* = none; *sae* = so; *sair* = sore; *stane* = stone; *tae* = toe.

2. O E /o:/ develops isolatively to O Sc /ø:/. This was usually spelled ⟨ui⟩ or ⟨uCe⟩, and these spellings continue in some writers, e.g. *bluidy* = bloody; *efternune* = afternoon; *gude, guid* = good; *puir* = poor; *schule* = school. Later, /ø:/ unrounded to /e/ in the long environments of the Scottish Vowel Length Rule (Aitken, 1981), e.g. *dae* = do; *flair* = floor; *shair* = sure; *tae* = to, too. In the short environments, it unrounded to /ɪ/, e.g. *blidy* = bloody; *dis* = does; *tim = tuim, toom*; *yist* = used. (The merger with /ɪ/ as in *lip*, *pin*, etc. may be only apparent.);

3. O E /u:/ remains isolatively, with loss of distinctive length, e.g. *aboot* = about; *aroon* = around; *broon* = brown; *coo* = cow, *doon* = down, *doot* = doubt; *hoor* = hour; *hoose* = house; *mooth* = mouth; *noo, nou* = now; *oor* = our; *roon* = round; *Toonheid* = Townhead; *troosers* = trousers;

4. O Sc /ɛ:/ develops isolatively to /i/, e.g. *breid* = bread; *deid, deed* = dead; *heid* = head; NO

5. O Sc /o/ or /ɔ/ develops to /a/ in labial environments in a number of words, e.g. *aff* = off; *drap* = drop; *saft* = soft. Elsewhere it appears as /o/, e.g. *boady* = body; *boather* = bother; *boatle* = bottle; *boax* = box; *coarpiration* = corporation; *Croass* = Cross; *doactur* = doctor; *Goad* = God; *goat, gote* = got; *hoaspital* = hospital; *hoat* = hot; *joab* = job; *knoatit* = knotted; *loak* = lock; *loast* = lost; *moarnin* = morning; *oaffer* = offer; *oaffice* = office; *oan* = on; *cumoan* = come on; *Scoatch* = Scotch; *shoap*, *shope* = shop; *shoart* = short; *spoat* = spot; *stoap* = stop;

6. O Sc /a/ remains after /w/, e.g. *squaad* = squad; *waant, wahnt* = want; *waash* = wash; *waater, watter* = water;

7. O E /aŋg/ gives /aŋ/, e.g. *alang* = along; *belang* = belong; *lang* = long;

---

32 For convenience, loan words and length adjustments are not taken into account, but see Aitken (1977).

thrang = throng; *wrang* = wrong;

8. /e/ and /ɛ/ are found in a number of words from earlier /a/, especially before /r/, e.g. *mairrit* = married; *pairty* = party; *yaird* = yard; and also e.g. *aipple* = apple; *faimlies* = families; *faither* = father;

9. Before /r/ and /n/ there is a back vowel often spelled ⟨au⟩ and usually described as /ɔ/, e.g. *caur* = car; *taur* = tar; *corrie (-fisted)* = carr, *ken*; *bawr* = bar 'joke'; *haun* = hand; *staun* = stand. *Bauchle* = bachle, *tottie* = *tattie* and *miroclous* = miraculous also have this vowel. More easterly dialects have this vowel also in *cat*, *lamb*, etc. (Again, the merger may only be apparent);

10. O Sc /ai/ develops to /ʌi/ finally in a number of words, e.g. *gey* = gay (but see Glossary); *pey* = pay; *stey* = stay; *wey* = way; *anywey* = anyway. This is also the development in *bailie* and *jile* = jail.

11. Unstressed final /ʌ/ occurs in a number of words where more easterly dialects have /ɘ/, e.g. *barra* = barrow; *fella, f'lla* = fellow; *morra* = morrow; *tabacca* = tobacco;

12. /l/ is vocalised following O Sc /a, o, u/. /al/ develops to /ɔ/, e.g. *aw, a', aa* = all; *aaready* = already; *baw* = ball; *faut* = fault; *faw* = fall; *haud* = hold; *hauf* = half; *sma'* = small; *wa* = wall. However, following /d/ blocks the loss of /l/, e.g. *aul(d)* = old; *cauld* = cold.[33]   /ol/ develops to /ʌu/, e.g. *gowd* = gold. /ul/ develops to /u/, e.g. *fu, fou', foo* = full; *pu'* = pull; *shoolder* = shoulder. Where this fails, the outcome is /ʌl/, e.g. *bull, full, pull*;

13. /d/ is lost after /l/, e.g. *aul* = old; *chiel* = child (but see Glossary). /d/ is likewise lost after /n/, e.g. *foon* = found; *haun* = hand; *hielan* = highland; *hunners* = hundreds; *mine* = mind; *san* = sand; *spen* = spend; *staun* = stand; *unnerstaun* = understand;

14. /d/ final in an unstressed syllable is devoiced, e.g. *bastart* = bastard; *hundret* = hundred; *-it* = -ed as in *mairrit*, above (but see 2.4);

15. /v/ is vocalised medially and finally, e.g. *de'il* = devil; *gie, gi'*, *gey, gee* = give; *hae, ha'e* = have; *lea', lee* = leave; *o', o, a* = of; *owre* = over; *twal'* = twelve;

16. /θ/ final is deleted in a small number of words, e.g. *claes, claithes* = clothes; *Sooside* = Southside; *wi', wi* = with.

2.2 Orthography

Traditionally, Scots orthography has adopted standard spellings for items where there is no contrast between Scots and St ScE, e.g. ⟨force, east, lamp boat⟩, and has provided contrastive spellings for Scots lexis and word forms, except that the resources of the shared system are not always capable of expressing the difference, e.g. ⟨finger⟩ for Scots /fɪŋʌr/, St ScE /fɪŋgʌr/; ⟨bull⟩ for Scots /bʌl/, St ScE /bul/. Spellings such as ⟨aw, a', ha'e, puir⟩ above are typical of old-fashioned Scots. Notice that ⟨ui⟩ and ⟨uCe⟩ spellings for O Sc /ø:/ are inappropriate for its modern reflexes. Notice also the use of apostrophes for vocalised or deleted consonants. Traditional orthographic practice can be observed in 18th and 19th century texts, in journalism, and

---

33 Forms with /ʌu/, e.g. *owld* 'old' also occur occasionally in Glasgow, as in Kintyre and Ulster.

in the work of some serious writers, e.g. William McIlvanney, who have not
concerned themselves with orthographic problems. There is naturally less attention to orthography in drama than in other types of writing, and here there
is often a mixture of recent innovations and traditional spellings, e.g. with
apostrophes.

In 1947, the Makars Club, which included most of the important writers of
the 'Scottish Renaissance', made a series of recommendations concerning the
spelling of Scots which are embodied in *The Scots Style Sheet* (1947). The
most widely observed of these recommendations is the dropping of apostrophes.
The continued use of $\langle uCe \rangle$ and $\langle ui \rangle$, and the use of $\langle aa \rangle$ for the /ɔ/ which
results from /al/, can be attributed to *Style Sheet* influence, as can the use
of $\langle ou \rangle$ for /u/ as in *nou* = now. In general, the *Style Sheet* is employed by
writers of 'Lallans', a revived form of Scots.

There is also a distinctive Glasgow orthography. This appears to have originated in a series of television sketches written by Alex Mitchell, called
"Parliamo Glasgow", which first appeared in 1960 (see 4.2 below). The running
joke was to make Glasgow dialect look like a foreign language by means of
spellings. The 'foreign' words were revealed as Glasgow phrases when read
aloud. One much imitated device was to run words together, thus adding to the
confusion. However, many of these respellings were, of necessity, phonemic,
and it is these which have been taken up and improved upon by serious writers.

There is nevertheless a great deal of variation amongst the writers who use
all or some of the conventions listed below. The writers chiefly involved are
Alan Spence, Stephen Mulrine, Tom Leonard, Alex Hamilton and James Kelman,
with the early precedent of Ian Hamilton Finlay's *Glasgow Beasts* (see chapter
5).

The main characteristics of the resulting local orthography include extended
use of $\langle k \rangle$ for /k/, e.g. $\langle praktiklli \rangle$, and of $\langle z \rangle$ for /z/, e.g. $\langle cawz \rangle$. $\langle u \rangle$
is restored where St E has $\langle o \rangle$ as a result of the need to avoid sequences of
minim strokes in M E, e.g. $\langle nuthin \rangle$. The lowered, retracted realisation of
/ɪ/ is spelled $\langle u \rangle$, e.g. *buld* = build; *durty* = dirty; *luvin* = living; *thurd*
= third; *wull* = will; *Yorkhull* = Yorkhill. There is a great deal of fluc-
tuation between $\langle i \rangle$ and $\langle u \rangle$ in unstressed syllables, e.g. *hiv*, *huv* = have. An
$\langle h \rangle$ is introduced after some vowels, and often before $\langle t \rangle$ e.g. $\langle thaht \rangle$. This
draws attention to the possibility of a localised realisation, but it is some-
times arguable whether it is to be associated with a back realisation of the
vowel or a glottal realisation of the /t/, or both. Syllabic consonants can
stand alone word finally, e.g. $\langle bettr, aippl, fukn \rangle$. The inflection -*ed* is
spelled $\langle t \rangle$ when pronounced /t/ after a voiceless consonant, e.g. $\langle pickt \rangle$.

When unstressed function words are phonetically enclitic to a preceding or
following item, they are shown as continuous with it, without the use of an
apostrophe as in St E, but often with doubling of consonant graphs, e.g.
whissup = what's up; *furryi* = for you; *nscraipt* = and scraped. A much wider
range of items is involved than in St E. Function words also vary in spelling
within a text according to whether they are stressed, e.g. *ya*, *ye* = you. Word
division can be adjusted to show the transfer of a closing consonant to a following word beginning with a vowel, e.g. $\langle a \; nexaggeratiun \rangle$.

Local spellings of an earlier date (at least the 1930s) include the use of
$\langle err \rangle$ to spell the /ɛr/ which develops from /er/, e.g. $\langle squerr \rangle$. One of the
commonest early uses of this is in the name *Mary*, and it seems possible that
the spelling actually arose from the coincidence that *Merry* is also a possible
name. The use of $\langle oa \rangle$ for /o/ when contrasting with St E /ɔ/, e.g. $\langle moarnin \rangle$,

× too late - cf. E. Gaitens: Dance of the Apprentices (1948)!

is traditional, as is the use of $\langle$oo$\rangle$ for /u/ when contrasting with St E /ʌu/. However, both are avoided by users of *The Scots Style Sheet*, probably because they do not occur in O Sc. Glasgow writers sometimes use $\langle$oo$\rangle$ where St ScE also has /u/, e.g. $\langle$trooth$\rangle$, thus drawing attention to the existence of a localised realisation.

The attention focussed on orthography by some writers provides in addition many *ad hoc* spellings, sometimes representing detail at the level of phonetic realisation, e.g. Leonard, in "Tea Time" (1975: unpaginated), shows the lengthening of tonic syllables:

> ahm thaht depehhhhndint
> hingoanti ma vowwwwwulz
> hingoanti ma maaaammi.[34]

Some further points appear to be confined to comic literature, imitative, at least in this respect, of "Parliamo Glasgow". The /r/ which develops from /ð/ is spelled $\langle$r$\rangle$ e.g. $\langle$ra$\rangle$ 'the', as is the [ɾ] realisation of /t/, e.g. $\langle$burra$\rangle$ 'butter'. Words are run together beyond the realistic practise described above, e.g. $\langle$yekanniwhakram$\rangle$ 'you can't whack them'.[35] Another device with limited currency is the use of an apostrophe for [ʔ]. This appears from time to time, but as most serious writers have now discontinued the use of apostrophes in dialect forms, this is also largely avoided.

The popularity of the local spelling system is shown by a recent letter in the Glasgow *Evening Times* (27 June 1980):

> Re. The letter from reader about amusing notice of "Keep Oot" erected by workmen in the city centre. When our new shopping centre was being built the workmen erected a notice which read - "PLEAZE YOUS UTHER FITPATH."

On the other hand, many of the improvements on standard spellings coincide with common spelling errors, and this allows different writers to arrive independently at the same conventions. It also helps to give the system the character of an anti-standard rather than a local standard.

A particularly interesting feature of the local spelling system as used in serious as well as comic texts, is that it potentially applies right across the lexicon (i.e. to standard as well as dialectal word forms). Such standard spellings as are retained are mainly those which are phonemically analysable, so that the system as a whole is both more consistent and more precise than that operating in most varieties of English. Characteristics of the local standard, such as the unstressed vowel /ʌ/, and the vowel of *never* $\langle$nivir$\rangle$, are specified. Indeed, in many of the texts using this orthography, dialectal lexis is almost entirely absent, and what is presented is basically St ScE, apart from the orthography itself.

The general effect of this radically non-standard orthography and in particular its comic forms, is to exaggerate the unintelligibility (to outsiders) of Glasgow speech. Far from being easier to read than St E, this system requires a high degree of literacy in the ordinary reader, precisely because it is so divergent from the standard. In the transcriptions below, a compromise is attempted. Standard spellings are retained where nothing is lost thereby,

---

34 'I'm so dependent; hang on to my vowels; hang on to my Mummy.'

35 Also in other comic dialect literature, e.g. Newcastle.

and the local orthography is used to show local forms, for the most part at the phonemic level. Conventional word divisions are retained, and ambiguity is minimised.

2.3 Lexis

2.3.1 Scots dialect lexis

The main source of information about Modern Scots dialect lexis is *The Scottish National Dictionary* (SND), published in 10 volumes between 1931 and 1975. This is based on a corpus of written texts from 1700, supplemented by the observations of a number of local authorities who provided comments on the words in each volume. Thus in the SND, a word is often given as known in a particular area at a particular date. For certain words, detailed information on their geographical distribution is also provided by the two lexical volumes (vols. I and II) of the *Linguistic Atlas of Scotland* (LAS: Mather and Speitel, 1975, 1977).

O Sc had distinctive vocabulary in all semantic fields, but with the adoption of London English as the standard in Scotland, Scots fell out of use in learned and official registers, with a consequent loss of lexis. However, the Scottish legal system continued to have its own terminology. Also, dialect forms of polysyllabic and Romance words often remain in speech. Speitel (1969: 31) cites *bigotted*, *blasphemous*, *cambric*, *precise* and others in Midlothian as differing from St E in lexical incidence, and comments:

> This is another contribution to the destruction of the myth that
> a dialect speaker has a very limited vocabulary and has difficulty
> in expressing abstract things.

Compare also reduced forms like *swedger* from *assuage* and *mickey* from *micturating pot*.

A great deal of Scots vocabulary without St E cognates also survives, although not all of this is very commonly used. Macaulay (1977: 55) found in a small lexical test, involving ten items, that his middle class informants knew more 'old Scots words' than his working class ones. Aitken (1979: 108) is no doubt correct in explaining this phenomenon in terms of the middle classes being better read in Scottish literature. Macaulay also found a marked age difference, with 15 year old speakers knowing less than half of the items known to adults. However, there seems every chance that this is a phenomenon of age stratification. Many dialect words are probably learned as part of the child's earliest vocabulary, but many others are little used or have a historical (or at least antiquarian) reference, so that it would not be surprising if they were learned later in life as part of an extended adult vocabulary.[35]

The situation has been best stated by Aitken, whose comments are worth quoting at length (1976: 48,9):

> Innovations in the grammatical system of world English, and,
> still more obviously, the profusion of new loan words, compounds,
> coinages and new uses of established words which are constantly
> enriching our vocabulary, supply further additions to the 'common
> core': expressions like *chaffeur*, *chain store*, *macaroni* ... ...
> are of course just as much at the disposal of 'dialect speakers'

---

36   Cf. also the point made by Agutter and Cowan (1981), that the concepts
     involved may be beyond children of a given age.

as of 'speakers of standard English'.

This is one way in which those elements in the system which are not distinctively Scottish have come more and more to dominate it - in which it is gradually becoming less Scottish. ... ...

In such ways as these, as is regularly claimed ... ... 'Scots' is indeed 'dying'. But these claims are commonly greatly exaggerated. So gradual is the 'decline' that all of the statements made above about current Scots could be applied with equal validity to the 18th century itself. And, despite all that has been said, the number of distinctive Scots expressions which continue in daily currency remains astonishingly large - as a glance at some of the *Scottish National Dictionary's* 30,000 or so entries, few of which are noted in the Dictionary as wholly obsolete, will remind us.

2.3.2 Glasgow as a focal area

The two volumes of the LAS report on two postal questionnaires on lexis. Vol. 1 includes returns for a single Glasgow informant, a woman in her fifties. She gives a nil response for 48 out of 90 items. This is unsurprising since many of these relate to rural life (e.g. 'gizzard (of fowl)', 'mould board', 'meal bin','couch grass'), although this does not account for all the blanks. Some might feel that a single informant is better than none for a large city; on the other hand the results might be seen as invalid for any but small rural settlements.

One would expect Glasgow to emerge as a focal area, i.e. that there would be distributions of varying sizes centred on Glasgow, and few differences between it and neighbouring locations. Some variants do seem to centre on Glasgow in this way, e.g. *stank* for 'the grating (over drain opening)', *simmit* for 'undervest (man's)', *baggie* for 'the fry of a minnow'. In a few cases, it seems clear that the form found in Glasgow is an innovating form, - *sapples* for 'soap suds' is a newer term than eastern *graith*, which, however, is found alongside *sapples* up to the borders of Glasgow. Likewise western *wallies* for 'broken pieces of china' is more recent than eastern *piggies* (though not actually recorded from the Glasgow informant).

However, there are a surprisingly large number of isoglosses cutting through the Clydeside conurbation. To some extent the Survey may have uncovered genuine differences between Glasgow and surrounding towns which still have a separate identity. However, the picture is often confused, with a number of different variants for an item being recorded in the immediate vicinity of Glasgow Also, some of the informants for neighbouring localities were born in Glasgow or have a Glasgow parent. A further problem is that for four items - *theevil* for 'porridge stick', *skalie* for 'slate pencil', *netterie* for 'spider' and *groser* for 'gooseberry' - the Glasgow informant gives an item which is otherwise mainly found in the east, north of the Tay. For these items, Glasgow emerges as a *relic* area.

One is forced to conclude that the information is insufficient, both in terms of the source items used and the data collected, to support any inferences about the status of Glasgow as a focal area or not.

2.3.3 Slang

Glasgow dialect literature differs from Scottish literature as a whole in the frequency with which slang occurs, i.e. non-standard forms which have a wide urban distribution in Britain, and/or forms which are innovations in a Scottish context. Some of these are transient (see comments on T29, T30). Others are perhaps on their way to establishing themselves in Central Scotland. Of course, when they become established outside of urban centres, such items cease to be regarded as slang, and become dialectal. The distinction is partly one of attitudes, and is related to the ideologies discussed in 1.8.2 above.

This peculiarity of Glasgow dialect literature may be the result of a greater preference for realism amongst Glasgow writers. But it would also seem reasonable to assume that Glasgow is the main point of entry into Scotland for items spreading from urban centres elsewhere, and that it is likewise the centre from which these, and native innovations, are most likely to spread initially within Scotland.

Alex Mitchell (see T17, T18, T67 below) was kind enough to draw up for me a list of some Glasgow terms known to him, of which a number fall into this category, e.g. *bramah, cadie, chavver*. His *waarmur* and *miroclous* are words which have passed into British slang from Scottish usage. Mackie's (1978) Glossary of Glasgow terms again includes British slang, e.g. *bender, bint, chancer, dick, jam, map, prig, bung. Batter* 'booze' seems to be from a misunderstanding of *on the batter* (see Glossary, below).

Mitchell and Mackie can be taken as members of the oldest age group. A younger group is represented by the subjects of Patrick's (1973) study of Glasgow gangs, although many of these boys had been in legal custody, and their language is perhaps not typical of their age group. Interestingly, they used English legal terminology such as *grievous bodily harm* (also known as GBH) rather than the Scottish *serious assault*. Their 'gangs' were known as *teams*, and the ringleader as the *leader-aff* (cf. dance hall terminology). Patrick (1973: 15) makes this comment on the difficulty of understanding their in-group slang:

> Born and bred in Glasgow, I thought myself *au fait* with the local dialect and after two years of part-time work with these boys I considered myself reasonably familiar with their slang - another serious mistake as it turned out. So confused was I on the first night that I had to 'play daft' to avoid too many questions and also to enable me to concentrate on what was being said.

Again their language was a mixture of the localised and general British slang.

The slang of a younger age group again was provided by P. MacLaren (personal correspondence) who has collected items considered slang by his pupils, non-academic classes aged 12-15. These include Scots items, e.g. *swedger, pap, plunk, dog*, and others not attested for other areas and presumably local, e.g. *heidbanger, boufing, grog* 'spit'. His pupils also knew a great deal of British slang, e.g. *barney, cally dosh, clock, yellowbelly, sky, grass. Chinex* 'chewing gum' is perhaps related to *chinny* 'sugar'. *Biff* 'the tawse' appears to be the same as the Australian *biffs* 'a caning'. *Take a powder, fuzz* and *busies* are ultimately U. S. slang. *Hog* and *dingy* as nouns and *slag* as a verb are probably from slang words which are attested as other parts of speech (see Glossary, below). *Teaboy* is probably a variant of *teaman*, and *crawbag* of *crawfish*.

An interesting aspect of MacLaren's survey was the unusual definitions of-

fered for some items, e.g. *crash the ash* 'give me a cigarette' rather than
'put out a cigarette', *rookies* 'policemen' rather than 'recruits', and *bombed
out* 'not wanted' rather than 'forced out'. This fluidity of reference and
connotation appears to be a characteristic of slang terms, presumably commenc-
ing at the point where in-group language begins to gain wider currency.
Agutter (1979) found a great deal of variability in the contexts in which different informants (mainly from Glasgow and Edinburgh) were prepared to accept
slang terms, mostly terms for women in her study. One common semantic development is the amelioration of derogatory terms, e.g. Mackie (1978: 14) asserts
that *tart* is a neutral term in Glasgow, but Agutter (1979: 117) is perhaps
nearer the mark when she points out that many informants were willing to use
this in a "gratuitously derogatory manner".[37] Other such terms were also a-
vailable, for some, in neutral contexts. In Partridge (1966) also, the earliest sense given for terms like *stumer* and *jane* is rather different from that
given for Glasgow.

2.3.4 Word creation

There are certain areas of meaning where many slang synonyms exist, in Glasgow
and in English slang generally. Where strong tabus or judgemental attitudes
are involved, rapid semantic change can take place in the form of amelioration
(e.g. *gallus* as a term of praise, *bint* or *jane* meaning 'girlfriend') or pejo-
ration (e.g. *stumer* or *warmer* as insults). It is apparently to counterbalance
this tendency that word creation is particularly active in these fields.

A few examples will illustrate the point for Glasgow:

1. names for the police. *Polis* and *bobby* are probably the oldest terms in use.
Bell's (1933) Glossary includes *nick* 'policeman', but this usually means 'the
jail'. Mackie (1978) gives *dick* 'detective'. Patrick (1973) has *screws* and
busies, while MacLaren has these and also *fuzz* and *rookies*;

2. names for girls and women. Mackie gives *bint* and *tart*. Mitchell gives
jane, pejorative *judy* and *chavver*, and ameliorative *bramah*. McCormick (1977)
has the latter as *brammer* with hyper-dialectal /r/, and also *stoatir*. Patrick
records pejorative *cow* and *hing-oot*, and *lumber* 'a date', cf. earlier *click*.
MacLaren's pupils gave only *hog* and *boot*, both pejorative;

3. terms for 'drunk'. Mitchell gives *blin' fu'*, *canned*, *fleein'*, *fu' as a
puggie*, *miroclous* (i.e. *miraculous*), *pie-eyed*, *smugged*, *stewed*, *stocious*.
Mackie has *drucken* and *smashed*, plus *bender* for a booze-up and *batter* for
booze. McCormick adds *blootered* and *steaming*. Patrick adds *puggled*, *bevied*
and *stoatin*;

4. terms for 'losing one's head'. Bell has *(to become) peery-heidit*. Mackie
has *(he went) beldyheidit*, literally 'bald-headed'. At present, phrases based
on *take a ...* are current, e.g. *take a flakey* from MacLaren's pupils, and also
take a hairy and *take a berkie* from a middle aged male informant who commented
that they are used by children. In the appropriate 'berserker' context, these
are not necessarily pejorative. Similarly with Mitchell's *heidcase* and
Patrick's *heidbanger*, both literally 'lunatic'. The amelioration of *gallus* is
paralleled by the use of *mental*, *crack-pot* and *psychie* (= *psychiatric*) as terms
of approval in Patrick.

Patrick appears to be the first to mention productive rhyming slang in

---

37 It is also possible that the original non-pejorative sense had remained
    in Glasgow since the last century.

Scottish usage, although Mackie (1978: 24 ff.) suggests that it has a long
history in Glasgow. Some slang terms are, of course, derived from rhyming
slang without this being generally recognised, e.g. *china (plate) = mate, on
one's Tod (Sloan) = on one's own,(plink) plonk = vin blanc*. The productivity
of rhyming slang in Scotland is evidenced by rhymes such as *winners and losers
= troosers* 'trousers', *Milngavie* (spelling pronunciation) = *lavvie* 'lavatory',
both from a middle aged male informant; *Askit pooders (Askit powders*, a brand
name) = *shooders* 'shoulders' (also reduced, e g. *shove in your askits*) from a
student; *Benny Lynch* (a Glasgow boxer) = *cinch* and *get off your Elky (Clark)*
(a Glasgow boxer) = *get off your mark* (Mackie, 1978: 25).

Another productive means of word formation is the addition of the suffix
-ie, -y:

1. to adjectives to form nouns, e.g. *gemmie* 'someone who is game', *riddie* 'a
red neck'. MacLaren's pupils also gave *brassie* 'a brass neck', which they
took to be a synonym of *riddie*;

2. to nouns or verbs to form adjectives, e.g. *chuckie stanes, shitey, slevvery,
squinty, swerry-words* 'swear words'.

This suffix is also freely used in shortened polysyllables, e.g. *bookie* from
bookmaker, techie from *Technical College, sanny* from *sandshoe, Clenny* from
Cleansing Department, psychie from *psychiatric, chanty* from *chamber pot, dunny*
from *dungeon, wellies* from *Wellington boots*, and *cludgie* from *(water) closet*.

Some items seem to be coined on phonesthetic principles. An example is the
nonce word *floompy* in T4. If this is meaningful, it would seem to be through
its phonological similarity to other words beginning with *fl - ? fluffy,
fluttery, flippant, floppy* - and to vocal gestures lexicalised as *oops, whoops*,
and to words ending in *mp - ? bump, clump, stump, plump*. That is, it combines
connotations abstracted from groups of existing words with phonological and
semantic similarities. The unit of meaning here, the phonestheme, is a structure smaller tham the word, but not identifiable with the morpheme. Its existence is inferred from its productivity.

A second example is the nonce word *scrimle* in T20. This appears to be a
diminutive of *scramle = scramble*, in the same way as *scritch* is a variant of
scratch implying a less forceful motion. *Minging* 'smelly' seems to be the
basis of *ginging* and *clinging* (but see Glossary), with the additional rein-
forcement of *humming, bogging* and *boufing* (all six synonyms from MacLaren).

Ram- as in *ramfeezle* was formerly productive in Scots, and has an intensive
sense, connoting forcefulness. Although it behaves like a bound morpheme, it
should perhaps be regarded as a phonestheme, since it is of obscure origin and
usually combines with other elements of obscure origin. The same holds for
-foisted in *gumple-foisted* and other similar compounds meaning 'sulky', and
probably also for *hum-* as in *humdudgeon* and *cam-* as in *camstairy*, although
etymologies have been suggested for these (see SND).

2.3.5 Swearing

Swear words, like other socially stigmatised forms, are heard with greatest
frequency from men. *Bass* in the challenge *ya bass*, often seen in graffiti,
appears to be a reduced form of *bastard*. In reported speech, the words
fucking bastard can be conveniently reduced to *f...in b...*, pronounced
/ɛfɪn bi/.[38] *Fucked* means 'ruined', as in the cliché "the fuckin fucker's
fucked". In British English, swear words can be inserted within polysyllables,
e.g. "See that bloke Avery. He's a million-fuckin-aire 'cause o me!" (Bryden,

1975: 78).

2.3.6 American influence

An education report of 1935 (Research Committee of Glasgow Local Association
of the Educational Institute of Scotland, 1935: vi) notes some Americanisms in
use amongst Glasgow schoolchildren, which it attributes to the cinema, e.g.
bump him off, *to make tracks*, *O. K.*, *yeah* and *on the level*, all now well integrated into BrE. A continuing influence of AmE can be observed, e.g. in this
notice from the polar bear enclosure at Glasgow's Calderpark Zoo (1979):

> The barrel has been deliberately put in the pool as something for
> the bears to play with. It is one of the few things which we
> have been able to think of which floats, and which they cannot
> destruct [sic].

or in this student poster (1979):
> Strut your funky stuff at the Erectors Club Disco.

2.3.7 The gravity model

The status of Glasgow as a point of reception and transmission for innovations
(if such is the case) can be explained in terms of the 'gravity model'
(Chambers and Trudgill, 1980: 196 ff.). This is a means, widely used in human
geography, of predicting the influence of one population centre on another as
a function of population size and distance. It is usual to include a weighting
factor to take account of the existing degree of similarity and the ease of
communication between centres. However, in the case of lexis, which can be
borrowed freely within a language, even raw figures may be revealing. Table 3
shows the predicted pull on and from Glasgow of a number of centres. Notice

	1971 Population	Road distance in Miles	Pull on Glasgow	Pull from Glasgow
Glasgow	897 483			
London, Outer Metropolitan Area	7 475 385	397	93.1	4.85
Edinburgh	453 584	44	70.6	139.7
Belfast	362 100	137	5	12.3
Dundee	182 204	84	3.9	19.3
Aberdeen	182 071	145	1.3	6.5

Table 3: The unweighted 'pull' of selected centres on and from Glasgow. See
Chambers and Trudgill, 1980: 196 ff.

---

38 This is the point of McGinn's (1976: unpaginated) verses, "The bee from the
old town of Effen":

> He kept bees in the old town of Effen
> An Effen beekeeper was he
> and one day this Effen beekeeper
> was stung by a big Effen bee.

the importance of London as a potential influence on Glasgow, and of Belfast
as a place likely to be influenced by it. It is interesting to note that
Agutter (1979) gives some indications of slang on the move, e.g. *boot*, mainly
Edinburgh, but also Glasgow; *lumber*, mainly Glasgow (first in Patrick, 1973),
in Edinburgh and even in London. British slang contains a small proportion of
items of ultimately Scottish origin, e.g. *click*, *melt*, *fly*, *chin*, and *miraculous* and *warmer*, already mentioned. It is likely that Glasgow played a part
in the wider dissemination of such items.

2.4 Grammar

2.4.0 Scots grammar

The grammar of Scots differs from that of St E mainly in superficial features
such as the form of inflections and function words, and rules of concord. Many
of these differences are shared with other non-standard varieties and some,
e.g. multiple negation, are almost universal in non-standard English. In the
account which follows, items are not peculiar to the West of Scotland unless
so stated.

2.4.1 Sentence processes

Negation. The forms of the enclitic negative particle in the West Mid dialect
are /nʌ/ spelled <-na> and /ne/ spelled <-nae> or <-ny>. The latter seems to
be spreading from the East of Scotland. *No* is the usual form of the isolate
negative particle. There is also a form *nut*, which occurs in sentence fragments expressing denial, e.g.

(1) "And I'm tellin ye it was the *Sixth*." ... ... "It was *nut*,"
    the stranger asserted. "But it was *sut*," cried Danny
    angrily. (Blake, 1935: 91).

Multiple negation, where the negative particle is semantically reinforced by
the negative determiner and its compounds, is common, e.g.

(2) jis shows ye, canny leave nuthin alane (T60/8)

The isolate negative particle can take as its scope the main verb (rather than
operator) of the clause, e.g.

(3) Will you not put too many on there in case they fall in the
    street, please? (Heard in Glasgow, 1979).

As Brown and Millar (1980: 106) point out, negation of the operator and the
main verb can occur in the same clause. This is not multiple negation in the
usual sense, since these negatives are not mutually reinforcing, e.g.

(4) He isnae still no working (Brown and Millar, 1980: 105).

The form *int* (= *ain't*) occurs only as a form of *be* (not *have*) plus enclitic
negative particle, and only in reversed polarity tags, in Scots, e.g.

(5) We're aw happy, int wi'? Ah mean we've aw earned a bit an'
    that's whit matters intit? (T. McGrath and Boyle, 1977: 27).[39]

The passive. The auxiliary of the passive is frequently *get*, even when an
animate agent is expressed, e.g.

(6) we just got chased by the parkies (Hamilton, 1976a: 2).[40]

---

39 But see Petyt (1978) where West Yorkshire *int* [ɪnt] is treated as a secondary contraction of *isn't*.

The preposition governing the agent is commonly *fae* 'from' or *wi* 'with', e.g.

> (7) "Heh, Ah'm gonnae get killt fae ma ma!" (Hamilton, 1976a: 13).
> (8) 'Ah'm no feart fae gypsies ur tinkers ur naebody!' (Spence, 1977: 52).
> (9) except when it's their weans that get battert wi some other weans (T5/28).

The imperative. A superficial subject pronoun *you* can occur in imperatives in Scots, even when these are positive. This is usually the second word in the sentence, e.g.

> (10) Just you go tae sleep (T. McGrath and Boyle, 1977: 21).
> (11) Away you an' staun up at the front door (T42/20).
> (12) "Gaun you in." (T6/35).

The interrogative. Cause is often queried by *how* or *whit wey* 'what way', e.g.

> (13) 'Sure!' said Shuggie. 'We'll take thum back up wi us an you kin ask ur.' 'How me?' said Aleck. (Spence, 1977: 49).
> (14) "Macgreegor, whit wey ha'e ye gotten yer guid breeks a' twistit-like?" (T28/10,11).

Emphasis. In Central urban Scotland, the word *see* is used to isolate the theme of a sentence on first mention. The subject noun phrase is extracted from the main clause to stand as the object of *see*, its place being filled by an appropriate personal pronoun. This structure perhaps originates with asyndeton of (*do you see* - Noun phrase - Recapitulatory pronoun):

> (15) See the three i thaim? they knock lumps oot i each other. (W. E., see 3.4).

The opacity of this idiom is illustrated by sentences like the following:

> (16) 'See the smell aff it when its jist been laid!' (T34/6).

The common idiom *see you* is not interpreted as having a subject *you*, and is not reflexive, e.g.

> (17) "See you, Judas, you're gettin oan ma tits!" (T15/24).

Introductory *see* extends to other structures in sentence initial position, e.g.

> (18) "but see when ye've got a few i these cheap wines in ye" (T15/45,6).
> (19) "Ah thoat Ah'd went aff ur afore, so Ah did. But see noo? Ah've went *right* aff ur." (Hamilton, 1976b: 24).

The verb *know* is similarly, but less commonly, used with a following *-ing* clause, e.g.

> (20) honess / pals / like / no been born / a cleg / s e bess (T58).

The word *sut* - see (1) above - is an emphatic form of *so* as a pro-form, especially in rhyming exchanges with *nut* as in that example.

Ellipsis. The non-past tense forms of *be* are frequently elided following

---

40 *Parkies* 'park attendants'.

there (both as a deictic and as a dummy subject), e.g.

> (21)   Cos there Wee Junior, he wis up at probation (W. E. see 3.4).

In the West of Scotland, *be* can also be deleted following *here*, e.g.

> (22)   HERE A FORM - NOO BEAT IT QUICK! (Figure 9).

Verbs of motion are frequently elided, giving quasi-verbal uses of prepositional adverbs, especially *away*, e.g.

> (23)   So he's awa' back up to heaven (T46/8).
> (24)   Away you an' staun up at the front door (T42/20).

Tags. Millar and Brown (1979) identify a tag particle *e* /e/ in Scottish speech, used following positive statements to elicit confirmation, e.g

> (25)   Your name's Willie, e? (Millar and Brown, 1979: 27).

This particle can be fronted as a marker of interrogation, e.g.

> (26)   E you've got a new bike? (Millar and Brown, 1979: 32).

A corresponding tag *e no*, which cannot be fronted, occurs following negative statements, e.g.

> (27)   He disnae like pictures, e no? (Millar and Brown, 1979: 32).

These tags are perhaps more common in children's speech. In the West of Scotland, there is a commonly used tag of the form (*so* - Pronoun - Operator), which is used to reinforce a positive statement - see (19) above. This also occurs in HibE, where there is, in addition, a corresponding negative form (*so* - Pronoun - Operator - Enclitic negative particle). This can be heard occasionally in Glasgow, but there is also an alternative (*neither* - Pronoun - Operator), e.g.

> (28)   Don't answer nothin incriminatin, says the sherrif ... And
>   neither ah did, neither ah did (T64/31-4).

A common tag is *but* meaning 'however', e.g.

> (29)   'Aye, sandpies it wis. Looked great. Tasted horrible but.'
>   (T34/19).

2.4.2 The verb phrase

A number of verbs which are irregular in St E have regular past tense and past participle forms, e.g. *seed*, *gied* 'gave'. Increasingly common, however, are past tense forms used as past participles, e.g. *went*, *wrote*, *took*, *fell*, *came*, *did*, *saw*. Sometimes it is the past participle form which is generalised, e.g. *done*, *seen*. The past tense and past participle inflection of regular verbs is /ɪt/, /t/ or /d/ depending on the preceding segment. In Glasgow, /ɪt/ is heard only after plosives, e.g. *landit*, *likit*, *skelpit* 'spanked'. /t/ is heard after /l/, /r/ and nasals, e.g. *killt*, *battert*, *kent* 'knew'. Otherwise the form is /t/ or /d/ depending on the voicing of the preceding segment, as in St E. The inflection of the present participle is commonly /ɪn/.

In the non-past tense, *has*, *is* and to a lesser extent inflected forms in /s, z, ɪz/ are used with subjects other than third person singular, if the subject is a full noun phrase, e.g.

> (30)   I'm gaffer o'er the boys that makes the hot asphalt (T27/8).

When the non-past is used as a narrative tense, inflected forms (but not *has*, *is*) occur with all types of subject, e.g.

> (31) "Naw!" I goes, near screaming, you know? (Hamilton, 1976a: 12).

The verb *be*. In the West of Scotland, a form *mur* occurs for *be* with first person singular subject, in the non-past tense. This is found under emphasis, thus avoiding the awkward sequence *Ah am*, e.g.

> (32) if Ah dae it, if Ah mur stealin (T8/14,15).
> (33) "Aw, yir jokin," I goes. "Aw naw Ah'm urnae," he says. (Hamilton, 1976a: 22).

Mur appears to be a blend of *am* and *are*. Notice that the need for emphasis is often produced by contrast with a sentence containing *you are* in the preceding context.[41] The form *was* occurs in Scots with second person subjects in the past tense, e.g.

> (34) 'an they'll luck at ye as if ye wiz a Dalek or sumpn' (T68/4-5).

Several verbs which are stative in St E are dynamic in Scots, e.g. *think, forget, remember* and *want*:

> (35) "*Ah'll* dae it agayn fyiz ur wantin tae see it" (Hamilton, 1976b: 27).

A number of verbs have different case structures associated with them in Scots than in St E, notably *learn* which admits an indirect object, *look*, which admits a direct object, e.g.

> (36) Everybody says ah need ma heid looked going aboot wae him. (T. McGrath, and Boyle, 1977: 24).

and *learn*, which need not take a direct object, e.g.

> (37) A offerred - bit a room in kitchen isny much better (Kelman, 1973: 43).

Modal and auxiliary verbs. Auxiliary *do* has a stressed form *div* in the non-past tense, with all persons except the third singular, e.g.

> (38) 'They hink y're sayin: "Tak me tae yer leader!" so they div.' (T68/5).

Auxiliary *have* is sometimes followed by a second *have*, which is always weak or enclitic, and is sometimes written *of*, e.g.

> (39) Ah would rather they had've been on the committee (T1/34,35).
> (40) 'Ah wouldnae of came if Ah had of knew,' he insisted. (Pryde, 1947: 24).

This is also found in AmE, and in Ulster, where Adams (1948) suggests that it may be a survival of O E *ge-* before the past participle. If so, it can only have entered Scottish usage through HibE. In Central and Southern Scotland, a double modal *will can* is in common use, e.g.

> (41) "Moan. Mibbe wull kin stoap im daein ehihin stupit." (Hamilton, 1976a: 6).

Infinitival complements are often introduced by *for to*, especially when

---

41   Cf. the rhyme between *nut* and *sut*, above.

51

intention is expressed, e.g.

(42) "Ah'm going for to give youse a prophecy." (T15/18).

2.4.3 The noun phrase

Singular forms of nouns are used for collective plurals after numerals, e.g.

(43) a hundret poun (T8/16).

and also after *their*, including the reflexive *theirsel*, e.g.

(44) they young yins nooadays iv goat their heid screwed oan (T35/5,6).

Personal pronouns. In the West of Scotland, and increasingly elsewhere in Central Scotland, there is a second person plural pronoun *youse*, often written *yiz* when unstressed, e.g.

(45) "By the way, boays. Youse urnae thinkin a cumin roon, ur yiz?" (Hamilton, 1976a: 8).

The nominal form of the first person singular possessive pronoun is often *mines*, with an -*s* by analogy with the rest of the paradigm, e.g.

(46) "Yir no tae touch it, awright? ... Kiz it's mines!" (Hamilton, 1976b: 24).

The third person reflexives are commonly *hissel* and *theirsel(s)* with possessive forms of the pronouns.

Determiners. The definite article is used in ScE with exophoric or homophoric reference before various categories of nouns where other varieties of English have no determiner, including trades, e.g.

(47) Good joab A hid tae oan the long distance. (T35/14).

and institutions, e.g.

(48) Landit up in the hoaspital way it tae. (T35/14,15).
(49) 'Ah've seen um with ye at the burroo. Nice wee fella!' (Spence, 1977: 147).

The also precedes the names of various periods of time, with the sense of 'this', including all those which take *to-* in St E, i.e. *the day*, *the night*, *the morn* or *the morra*, and also *the noo* or *the now*. *The* is also common before *both*, e.g.

(50) "and gets stuck right intae im wi thi baith a is hauns" (Hamilton, 1976a: 13).

The Scots forms of the deictics *these* and *those* are *thir* and *thae*, often written *they*. Only the latter is heard in Glasgow. *Them* as a deictic determiner occurs as early as 1935 in the West of Scotland (Research Committee of Glasgow Local Association of the Educational Institute of Scotland, 1935: iv). Scots has an additional distinction in the deictic system. *Yon*, which also takes the form *thon* by analogy with the rest of the paradigm, expresses a further degree of conceptual or physical distance, and is unmarked for number, e.g.

(51) We got yon way we'd started just going round to the wee school (Hamilton, 1976a: 2).
(52) "Heh, Ah hope he gies us wan i yon stories, eh?" (T15/10).

2.4.4 Modification

Adverbs. As in other non standard varieties, manner adverbs are often formed without the addition of a suffix in Scots, e.g.

> (53) yi canny talk / <u>right</u> (Leonard, 1976: 36).
> (54) Ah wid huv arranged the furniture <u>different</u>. (T. McGrath and Boyle, 1977: 52).

There is a suffix -s which occurs with certain sentence adverbs, e.g. *mebbies*, *whiles* 'sometimes', *nae wunners* 'no wonder'. In some cases, restrictions on the position of adverbs are different from St E, e.g.

> (55) he got paid overtime for just checking a bunch of boys (Hamilton, 1976a: 2).[42]
> (56) Up he goes again, flying almost this time (Hamilton, 1976b: 28).

Relative clauses.[43] Scottish speakers commonly use the relativiser *that* with personal antecedents, e.g.

> (57) An auld man at wis drunk goat taen intae the polis boax (W. E., see 3.4).

That also occurs in non-restrictive clauses, e.g.

> (58) Jock Allan (that has done so well in Embro) was a herd (T25/14,15).

The relativiser can be deleted even in subject position, e.g.

> (59) What a rare story that was ... about auld Johnny Clerk ... said, 'Can ye tell me, man ...' (T66/1-4).

This is particularly common in existential sentences, e.g.

> (60) But there is no trade unionist will defend ... (T1/40,41

K. Brown (forthcoming) found that Scottish speakers use *which* almost exclusively in non-restrictive relative clauses with sentential antecedents, e.g.

> (61) What it is, they're pullin the midgies oot, which we used tae dae (T5/12,13).

Two types of subordinate clause are regularly linked by *and* to the super-ordinate clause in Scots. The subordinate clause often expresses a circumstance which ought to preclude the situation expressed in the main clause. The first type is a verbless subordinate clause of the form (*and* - Objective personal pronoun - Subject complement), e.g.

> (62) I'll soap in yer eyes ye - and it rationed! (Tait, 1942)

or of the form (*and* - Objective personal pronoun - *with* phrase), e.g.

> (63) charging up to the hut like King Billy as if he's just seen the Pope - and him with his back turned at that (Hamilton, 1976b: 18).

---

42 *Check* 'reprimand'.

43 *What* is occasionally found as a relativiser in the West of Scotland, e.g. 'like the other birds what takes Dexedrine, she disnae know whit she's dain!' (Patrick, 1973: 52).

The second type is a non-finite -*ing* clause, again with a personal pronoun in the objective form as subject, e.g.

> (64)   as if it was our fault that a lassie was gawky enough to
>   break her arm, and us being good enough to give her a game
>   (Hamilton, 1976b: 21).

2.4.5 Other points

Some other points of non-standard grammar are commented on as they arise in texts, below. Since it is modelled largely on speech, the dialect literature naturally includes many colloquial forms apart from those considered non-standard, for instance *us* with singular reference, e.g.

> (65)   geez peace, / pal! (T62/9-10).

or the avoidance of *that* as a complementiser - see (51) above.

3.0 The texts

The transcriptions in this chapter are from the hour-long cassette tape which
accompanies this volume, and which can be obtained from the publishers. (For
copyright reasons, only a limited number are available). A wide range of
speech genres are represented, from public speaking, to radio phone-ins, to
friendly conversation. These texts illustrate more or less natural speech
within the limitations of the Observer's Paradox, in a variety of styles.

The first two speakers exemplify the use of St ScE in public speaking. The
first has a working class and the second an upper middle class accent. In
order to show the similarity between these speakers at the phonemic level, a
few lines of each are transcribed in Abercrombie's (1979) model of St ScE
(Figures 2 and 4). To show the differences at the level of phonetic realisation, a narrow phonetic transcription of a few lines is also given (Figures
3 and 5). Narrow phonetic transcriptions are given for three further speakers,
a young upper middle class woman, a young working class man, and a middle-aged
working class woman. In most of these, an impressionistic transcription of
the intonation is also given.[44] Subsequent transcriptions are in St E or in
a modification of the local orthography, with some phonetic details, in the
notes to each text, of unusual variants and those which are not well documented
elsewhere.

3.1 Public speech, Jimmy Reid

3.1.1 Trade union campaign

The following is part of a televised speech made by Jimmy Reid at a trade union
meeting on 10 August 1971, that is, in the run-up to the successful industrial
action of that winter (see 1.9). The speech comes at a crucial moment in the
campaign, when Reid and other shop stewards are mobilising the workforce to
reject the findings of a government enquiry and to take industrial action in
defence of the shipyards. It is clearly vital at this juncture for Reid to
convince the men that the enquiry is biased, that the yards are viable, and
that the workers have the intellectual authority to challenge the official
view. He makes use of quotation, sarcasm and humour to expose the interested-
ness of the official arguments, and draws on the ideology of the Left, and the
authority of the Labour movement, for an alternative view. His delivery is
lively, with continually varying intonation, rhythm and loudness, as well as
varying sentence length and complexity. He uses a number of socially marked
variants, while speaking basically in St ScE.

---

44 I am grateful to Paul Johnston for help with the segmental part of these
    transcriptions. Any mistakes which have crept in are my own.

TEXT 1   ᴏ꞉ᴏ

Now, for too long we have tolerated such policies and such practices. For too
long, they've been getting away with it. And at last a section of the workers
have rejected and repudiated such social, economic an political theories, and
have reasserted the dignity of working men, to establish that they've got
5 rights; that they've got commitments, and privileges, and principles; and
they are going to utilise their ability and capacity to resist these measures;
to fight and to unite around them their brothers an sisters; so that in win-
ning this victory - and that's what we should be speaking about today - it is
not a narrow victory for the U.C.S. workers, but a victory for the British
10 working people, that can reverse the whole trend that's been so obvious in
our country for the last years ... ...

   That's not a White Paper! This is supposed to be the result of a most ex-
haustive examination by experts of the situation of shipbuilding on the upper
reaches of the Clyde. I tell you, my twelve year old daughter could've bet-
15 tered it, as a result of three or four visits to the yards on the upper
reaches. There's no analysis. There no substantiation. There's contentions.
And it seems to us, that in point of fact, this is not a White Paper, it's a
dollop of whitewash, that was constructed in order to justify the preconceived
position of this government relative to the U.C.S. Because it takes a summa-
20 tion of statistics, by and large, from the inception of the U.C.S. They met
for five weeks - five weeks - and incidentally, they were not in constant
session. They probably had about a dozen meetins. A dozen meetins? To examine a situation of such complexity? They brought on Lord Robens in the last
week. We never saw Lord Roabens. He was brought on for a bit of window dress-
25 ing, as an ex-Labour minister, that might give an aura of Labour movement re-
spectability to the findings of this committee. We have said before, of course
Lord Roabens is finished in the Labour movement as a result of his associations
with this committee. Cos it was a hatchet job. (Applause).

   Davies told us in Glasgow, that he didn't want shipbuilding experts on the
30 committee, because they would have to be, almost by definition, competitors
of the U.C.S. who had a vested interest in ending the U.C.S. But he says,
"Ah can assure you, they had access to shipbuilding experts" - who presumably,
were competitors of the U.C.S., who had a vested interest in destroyin the
U.C.S. (Applause). If they were givin evidence, Ah would rather they had've
35 been on the committee, in the front line, in public glare, rather than surreptitiously giving evidence through the back door. Competitors they may be,
with a vested interest, as Ah've said, in the destruction of Upper Clyde
Shipbuilders. What does it amount to?

   Nobody will argue that if you take the statistics of the U.C.S. from its
40 inception, that these statistics aren't damning. They are damning. But there
is no trade unionist will defend the record of the U.C.S. from about nineteen
sixty-eight to halfway through nineteen sixty-nine, for reasons which Joe
touched upon. The money was squandered - compensation given to the previous
owners. Too many of them, too many of these previous owners, who had brought
45 shipbuilding on the upper reaches of the Clyde to the sorry state they were
in, as a result of their neglect, were represented on that Board. And I'm
sayin this to you quite bluntly: the record of the shipbuilding families of
the Clyde - that's the owners - is such that they shouldn't be allowed to
manage a Bingo Hall, let alone an industry vital to this community. (Applause)

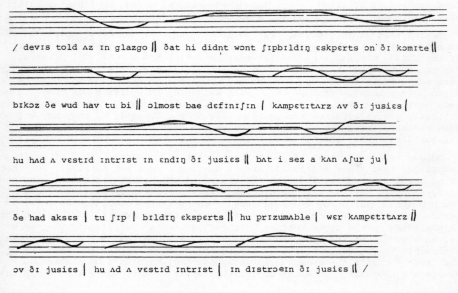

Notes

The pronunciation of *a* as /e/ (e.g. 2) is emphatic, as is trilled /r/, e.g. *rejected* (3). A tap [ɾ] for intervocalic /t/ occurs quite frequently, e.g. *political* (3). /w/ for /ʍ/ occurs in e.g. *white* (17) and *whitewash* (18). Cacuminal [ş] appears in e.g. *reaches* (16) and *contentions*(16). Notice that the word *meetins* repeated in 22 has [ʔ] in the first instance and [tʰ] in the second. Speakers generally use a more rather than a less prestigious variant in repititions. There are several non-standard syntactic forms: deletion of the copula (*there no*, 16), *that* in a non-restrictive relative clause (18,25). In the latter, the antecedent is human. Also a zero relativiser in subject position (41), and a double *have* construction (*had've been*, 34-35).

Class-tied features include the lowered and retracted realisation of /ɪ/, the occasional glottal(ised) realisations of voiceless plosives, the pharyngeal realisation of /r/ in *glare* (35), the lenition of /θ/ in *through* (36), and the downgliding diphthongs in *glare* (35) and *door* (36). On the other hand, the realisation of /u/ is not extremely fronted except following /j/. There are also a number of approximant /r/. There is a clear /l/ in *surreptitiously* (35-6), and these occur elsewhere in the text. At some points - *line* (35), and *may* (36) - an unusual form is produced, perhaps under the influence of other nearby words which are heavily stressed. Notice that vowel length is determined by stress and emphasis.

The characteristic local intonation contour is used sparingly. Rising movement from a non-low position is used in the significant repitition in 32 - 34. The sentence is thus marked as a continuing part of the discourse, with ironic effect, as it is clearly the clincher of the argument. This may also serve to hold off the impending applause.

/ devɪs told ʌz ɪn glazgo ‖ ðat hi didn̩t wɒnt ʃɪpbɪldɪŋ ɛskpɛrts ɒn ði kɔmɪte‖

bɪkɔz ðe wud hav tu bi ‖ ɔlmost bae dɛfɪnɪʃɪn | kʌmpɛtɪtʌrz ʌv ði jusɪɛs |

hu hʌd ʌ vɛstɪd ɪntrɪst ɪn ɛndɪŋ ði jusɪɛs ‖ bʌt i sez a kʌn ʌʃur ju |

ðe had aksɛs | tu ʃɪp | bɪldɪŋ ɛkspɛrts ‖ hu prɪzumʌble | wɛr kʌmpɛtɪtʌrz ‖

ɒv ði jusɪɛs | hu ʌd ʌ vɛstɪd ɪntrɪst | ɪn dɪstrɔeɪn ði jusɪɛs ‖ /

Figure 2: Phonemic transcription of T1/29-34.

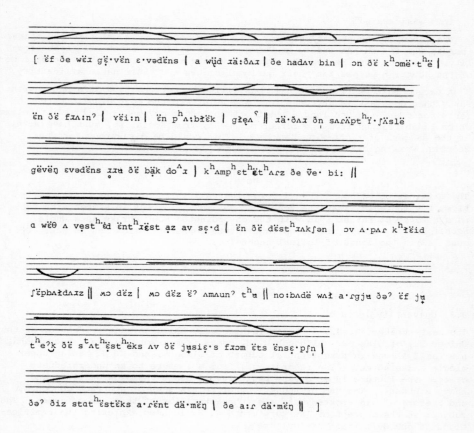

Figure 3: Phonetic transcription of Tl/34-40.

3.1.2 Election campaign

It is interesting to compare the transcript above with part of a published speech by Reid (1976b: 123).

TEXT 2

Above all the Scottish working class and the Labour movement has got to face up to the demands of the nationalist movement in a principled manner. The pioneers of the Labour movement were always in favour of a Scottish parliament. At the Labour Party conference in 1948 - when that party lurched disastrously to the right and created the climate for the return of the Tories in 1951 - Herbert Morrison argued for dropping the demand for a Scottish parliament.

This was carried.

The Labour movement has paid for this wrong decision. Just like the aris-
tocrats who framed the Treaty of Union, Labour leaders cannot obliterate rea-
10 lity. All they did then was to create a vacuum in relation to the aspirations
of the Scottish people for their national rights and their national identity.

A vacuum must be filled, and it *was* filled by nationalists in a Nationalist
Party that does not in any conscious way relate to the most dynamic potent
force for change in Scotland - the Scottish Labour movement. And a Nationalism
15 which is abstracted from the Labour movement, from Socialism, must have within
it the dangers of right-wing populism. This could be disastrous for the
Scottish working class and the Scottish people as a whole.

Notes

The elimination of non-standard forms leaves a colloquial type of St ScE. Notice, for instance, that the verb *have got to* (1) agrees in number with *the
Labour movement* rather than with the co-ordinated noun phrase as a whole.
Have (got) to normally replaces *must* in the sense of obligation in ScE. Cf.
must (12)in the sense of logical necessity.

3.2 University lecture

The next speaker, W. H., is a man in his early thirties, and a lecturer at the
University of Glasgow. Although W. H. comes from a working class background,
his family lived in a residential suburb of Glasgow, and W. H. has an upper
middle class accent. The recording is from a lecture to an undergraduate
class. The lecture is at a very basic level, hence the slow delivery and
heavy emphases. The use of hedges, concrete examples of abstract concepts,
and rhetorical sign-posting are also characteristic of this speech genre. The
subject is the concept of 'culture', and W. H. is here exploring the ramifications of one definition of 'culture'.

TEXT 3

I want to say something about sub-cultures at this point. I'm still talking
about (4) though. The quotation from Lotton that I gave you a moment ago referred to social class sub-cultures. Now, of course, not all sub-cultures can
be defined in class terms, and I simply want to draw your attention to the
5 complexity of the relation between class and a sub-culture. For instance, we
might talk of a criminal sub-culture, which would certainly cross simple class
boundaries. Indeed, I imagine that the most successful criminals are the ones
who manage to absorb themselves most fully into respectable middle and upper
middle class societies.

10   In general, the term 'sub-culture' refers to a group of people within the
larger culture who share certain understandings based on common experience.
And you can obviously apply this notion of sub-culture very widely. We talk
naturally, for example, about immigrant sub-cultures existing within the national culture of Britain. On a much smaller scale, we might talk about a
15 patient sub-culture in a hospital, where patients share certain understandings
based on common experience, involving breaking the rules for instance, in re-

lation to things like smoking, or whatever. And this example, I think, lets us
approach one of the most crucial issues for education, namely the extent to
which a sub-culture is or is not sympathetic to the dominant culture. Because
20 from an educational point of view, sub-cultures become particularly interesting
when they are perceived as being hostile or indifferent to the values associated with education.

Transcriptions

/ ʌ wɔnt tu̜ se sʌmθɪŋ ʌbʌut ‖ sʌb kʌltʃʌrz ‖ at ðɪs pɔent ‖ aem stɪl ‖ tɔkɪŋ
ʌbʌut' ‖ for ‖ ðo‧ ‖ ðɪ' kwoteʃn froṁ lɔtʌn ‖ ðat ae ‖ gev ju ʌ momɪnt ʌgo ‖
rɪfɜrd tu soʃʌl klas ‖ sʌb kʌ́ltʃʌrz ‖ nʌu v kors ‖ nɒt ɔl sʌb kʌltʃʌrz kan
bi‿dɪfaend ɪn klas tɛrmz‾ ‖ and ae sɪmple wɒnt tu drɔ jur ʌtɛnʃn tu ‖ ðɪ
kʌmplɛksɪte ‖ ɔv ðɪ rɪleʃn bɪtwin ‖ klas ‖ and ʌ sʌb kʌltʃʌr ‖ 'fʌr ɪnstʌns ‖
wi maet tɔk ɔv ʌ krɪmɪnʌl'sʌb kʌltʃʌr ‖ ʍɪtʃ wud sɛrtɛnle ‖ krɒs ‖ sɪmpl̩
klas bʌundʌrez ‖/

Figure 4: Phonemic transcription of T3/1-7.

[ɪ̩ndid æ̩i ɪ̩mæ·dʒən ðət ðɪ̩ most sëkse̩ːsfüˡ kʰɹɪmɪnʌ̍ɫ·z ‖ aɪ ðɪ wʌnz hɐ
mæ̈nëdʒ tʰü əbzɔːᴵb ðɛmse̩·ɫvz moᵁst fülë ‖ ɪ̩ntʰü· ɹɪspɛktʰɪ̩bl̩ mëdˆɫ ‖ and
ʌpəɾ mëdˆɫ ‖ kʰlæs sʌsa̩e̍ətȩ̈z ‖ ɪn dʒȩ·nəɾəɫ ‖ ðɪ tɛːɪm sʌb kʌltʃʌɪ ‖ ɹɪ̩fë·ɪz
tʰü̈ː ‖ ə gɹ̩ü̩pʰəv pʰipʰʌˡɫ ‖ wɪ̩θɪ̩n· ðɪ lɑːᴵdʒəɪ kʰʌltʃʌɪ ‖ hü· ʃȩ·ɪ sɛɪʔtn̩
ʌndəstæ·ndëŋz ‖ be·ᴵstʰ ‖ ɔn kʰomən ëkspiːɾɪ̈ëns ‖ ænd jü kən ɔvɪˆslë pɫ
ʌpʰɫa·e ‖ ðës noᵁʃn əv sʌb kʰʌlt·ʃəɪ ‖ ve̩ɾë wɾ·edlë̈ ‖]

Figure 5: Phonetic transcription of T3/7-12.

Since the intonation is monotonous, all contours ending in falls, this is
not included in the transcriptions. The speaker has several RP-like features:
/tʃ/ rather than /tj/ in *culture* throughout, clear /l/ where this is clear in
RP, merger of /ae/ and /ʌi/ - cf. *societies* (9) and *widely* (12) - and upgliding
diphthongs for /o/, e.g. *most* (8 but not 7), and for /e/, e.g. *based* (11) but
not *share* (11). Speitel (1975: 38) notes that /e/ rarely reaches a full diphthong with Scottish speakers. The /r/ is realised as a tap mainly intervocalically, but also in *upper* (8). There appears to be distinction between /ʊ/ as
in *fully* (8) and /u/ as in *group* (10), and between /ɔ/ as in *draw* (4) and /ɒ/
as in *cross* (6). It is not clear whether there is a distinction between /æ/
and /a/. Before /r/, *larger* (11), there is a realisation [ɑ̈], with [æ] elsewhere. The realisation of /æ/ is sometimes quite raised, as is the first element of /ae/, both 'Kelvinside' characteristics.

On the other hand, the speaker preserves post-vocalic /r/ (though this is
sometimes almost deleted). He has /ɛr/ where RP has /ɜ/ and some Scottish
speakers have Abercrombie's /ë/, e.g. *term* (10), and of course /er/ where RP
has /ɛə/, e.g. *share* (11). Vowel length is related to stress, but is also
conditioned by the following consonant, / n, l / being added to the environments of the Scottish Vowel Length Rule. The speaker is thus identifiable as
Scottish, but it is only the tendency to lengthen stressed vowels which links
him with Glasgow rather than Edinburgh.

3.3   Interview, L. G.

It is useful to compare W. H. with a younger speaker of the same class, in
this case a female student in her early twenties, L. G.   This is also a more
casual style of speech.   The recording was made in the present writer's office,
and L. G. is chatting about people she knows, first one of her teachers at
school, and then a friend.

TEXT 4

So she was one of those little ladies that was, ye know, quite, quite extrovert in the sixties, you know, quite interesting.   Something that didn't happen very often, ye know, kind of running away from home to go and live with
this chap.   She had two children, and then, very boringly, ten years later,
they decided to make an honest woman of her, kind of thing, ye know.   So they
ended up getting married when she was teaching at my school.   It was kind of -
the kind of hat went round the staffroom, asking for collections for Linda's
wedding, and everyone kind of thought, "But she's married, she's married already."   And everyone kept calling her - the chap she was living with, her
husband.   My friend Rosemary used to keep saying, "Your husband said such and
such," and every time she said this, Linda used to kind of cringe away, you
know, wondering, "Shall I tell them, or shan't I?" kind of thing.   But everybody knew, except Rosemary, who was very naive, at this time.

   She has now turned extremely extrovert herself.   She went to Edinburgh
University, and smashed in on the social scene of the Drama Department.   She
now spends all her time making - yes, the the Drama Department.   She spends
all her time making clothes for them.   She's in their wardrobe department.   An
she wants to be their designer for next year.   She's into designing clothes.
She designs things that are hideously impractical to make, one of these people,
you know.   An she goes around - she's got an Edwardian hairstyle;   she kind of
comes down at the sides, an up to the top an then tied in a knot, with combs
stuck all over the place, and feathers sprouting out the top.   No kidding.
She goes about with feathers kind of sticking out the top, an if she's in a
really extrovert mood, she wraps pearls around it, the knot at the top.   An
she wears floompy dresses, an she comes mincing around.

   Ah remember going in to see her at her part time job in the summer, which
was in a restaurant, kind of serving in the bar an washing up after lunch, an
this kind of thing.   And we went in, and we just sat down to wait for her, an
she came mincing out of the back shop - mince, mince, mince - in her baggy
boots with her high heels, an her exquisite Cadise suit, with her feathers
sticking out the hair, kind of, "I've only got a few more dishes to wash and
then Ah'll be out," an anything less like a dish washer is hard to imagine.
An she just kind of minced out the kitchen with these little wet paws at the
end of this extremely expensive suit going, "I've just got a couple more
dishes to wash."

Notes

Shall is considered 'proper' in St ScE, and is used with all persons and numbers.   *Shan't* (12) is particularly formal.   The usual alternatives would be
won't I, or more colloquially, *will I not*.   *Designer* (18) and *designing* (18)
have /ae/.   Cf. following /n/ as a length environment in the speech of W. H.
(3.2), and see 2.1.2.   *Pearls* (24) [p^{n}ɛɹəɫz] has an epenthetic vowel.

[sʌ ʃi wəz wʌn ɔv ðɔz ɫ̈etʰɫ̈ leːdëz | ðë? wəz | jë nọ | kʰwɹ̩itʰ ‖ kʰwəitʰ ɛm |

ɛːkstɹọvë·ɹtʰ ën ðë sɪːkstʰɪz | jë nọ | kʰwəi? ɪːntʰɹɛstëŋ |

sʌmθëŋ ðë? dɹ̩dn? hæ̈ːpʰën | vɛ·ɹë ɔːfën | jụ nọː ‖ këind ʌv | ɹʌnëŋ ʌwɛɹ fɹəm hoːm ‖

tʰø̈ tʰø̈ go n lë̈ːv ‖ wëθ ðës tʃæːpʰ | ʃë hæd tʰˠ tʃɹɫ̈dɹ̈ën | n ðɛn | vɛ·ɹë boːɹ̈ëŋɫ̈ë |

tʰɛ̈n jɪɹz leitɹ | ðë disäidëd tʰɛ̈ mekʰ ʌn ọnëstʰ wu·mën ɔv ë̈ɹ | kʰə̈ind ʌv θëŋ |

jë no ‖ so | ðe ɛndëd ʌpʰ gɛtʰëŋ mæːɹ̈ë̈d | ʍën ʃë wëz tʰitʃëŋ (ë? mɹ̈·e sku·l ‖]

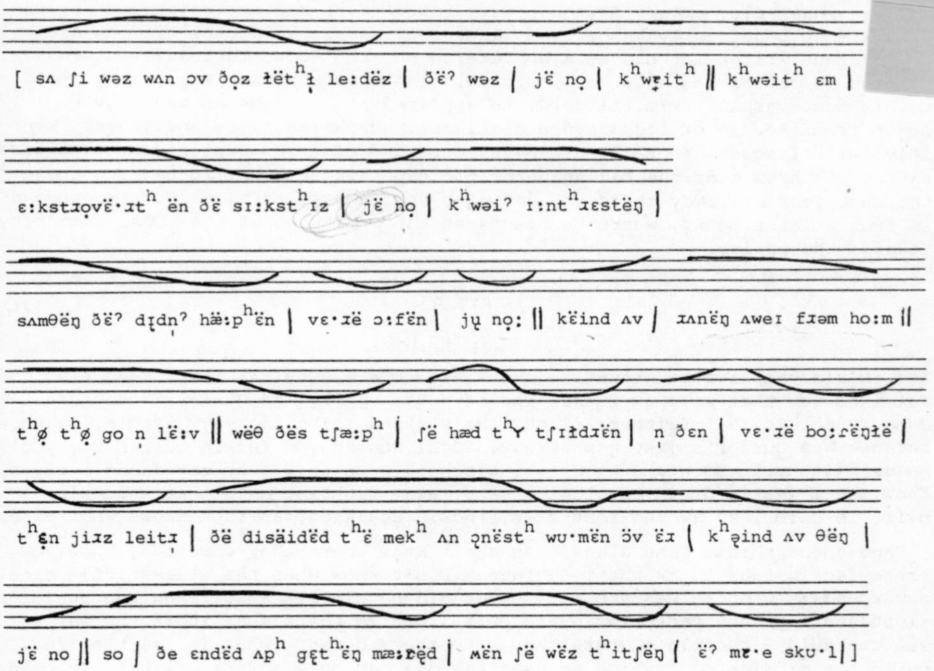

Figure 6: Phonetic transcription of T4/1-6.

It is immediately clear that L. G. is much further from RP than W. H. The
only extensions of the basic St ScE system are the diphthongisation of /e/,
e.g. *away* (3) but not *ladies* (1), and possibly a distinction between /ʊ/, e.g.
woman (5) and /u/, e.g. *two* (4). From this and the preceding transcription
(Figure 5), it seems that Abercrombie's (1979) implicational scale for additional distinctions in St ScE (see 2.1.2) may not hold for Glasgow speakers.
/ae/ and /ʌi/ are distinct - cf. *quite* (2) and *my* (6). L. G. shows a great
deal of variability in her realisation of /ɪ/, from [ɪ] as in *interesting* (2),
through [ë] as in *little* (1) to [ɛ̈] as in *live* (3). Velarised /l/ and [?] for
/t/ occur freely. The length of vowels is determined by stress, as with more
localised speakers, and the local intonation contour predominates.

3.4 Interview, W. E.

The next speaker, W. E., is a young working class man, in his early twenties,
from an inner city area. Although very intelligent and articulate, W. E. had
been almost continually unemployed since leaving school at the minimum age.
The present writer met him at a conference on 'the Scots language' in Glasgow,
and the recording was made in my office. The speech style is probably close
to his most casual style. Indeed, he appeared not to have another style.
Apart from the use of localised and stigmatised variants, he speaks very rapidly, with frequent phonetic assimilations, and numerous expletives. The first
extract is from near the beginning of the tape, where W. E. is talking about
the behaviour of rowdy children, and glue-sniffing in particular. The second
is from a later point, where he discusses the attitudes of the local community
towards the police.

TEXT 5

a. Wee Junior

And it's a complicated situation, ye know? The wey things are. Know how
faimlies get that wey, aw fuckin ins an oots. Well, Wee Junior, because -
John isnae his real faither, right? He's kinna loath tae say onythin, ye know,
because Wee Junior's jist gonnae say, "Och, who're you fuckin talkin to, you're
5 no ma faither." So Wee Junior gets his heid. An he's away oot daein everythin
Know, he's gettin divin aboot wi a gang, away fightin, he's goat - fuckin
cairryin chibs, an aw the rest i it, fuckin staikies, an fuck knows what else.

And these things come alang. Ah don't know where they come fae, know, aw
these fuckin fags an aw that. Things. Don't know when the glue-sniffin came,
10 never had it when Ah was a boay. Never did nothin lik that. And Wee Junior's
jist gaun roon the backs, or where ever. But Ah think what it is the day -
see the auld - the place where they keep the midgies? What it is, they're
pullin the midgies oot, which we used tae dae, an buld a fire, right? Ye buld
a fire, place where the midgies are, an jist sit aroon. We yist tae jist sit
15 aroon, mebbe smoke - Ah never smoked an that, but. But noo they're intae,
fuckin, the glue; they're gaun oot their heid wi it.

b. The authorities

Well, it aw depends. Likes i up in Barrafield, Ah was tellin ye, ye've
goat nearly aw broken faimlies, right? An everybody's gettin their money aff
i - oh - everybody's gettin their money aff i the Social Security, right? or
20 the Broo, or whatever. An aw these people are aw the enemies. Because every
cunt official's the enemy - teachers, Social Security, polis, an every cunt
like that. Because when ye're waantin anything, ye're needin anything, they're
comin up an they're pryin in, an they're tryin tae put ye doon. Ah mean, ye
walk in - there's me. Ye walk intae a Social Security oaffice, Ah mean, ye're
25 jist, ye're a load i rubbish tae them. Jist a loat i keech, ye know? Nothin.

An everybody's goat the attitude: they're aw the enemy. So when the weans
get pickt up, it's no the weans' faut, it's the polis's faut, or some cunt, ye
know. Except when it's their weans that get battert wi some other weans.
Then it's "they wee bastarts up the road."

Notes

Pullin (13) has /ʌ/. *Up* (27) has [p']. *Backs* (11) is short for *back courts*.

Phonetic transcription

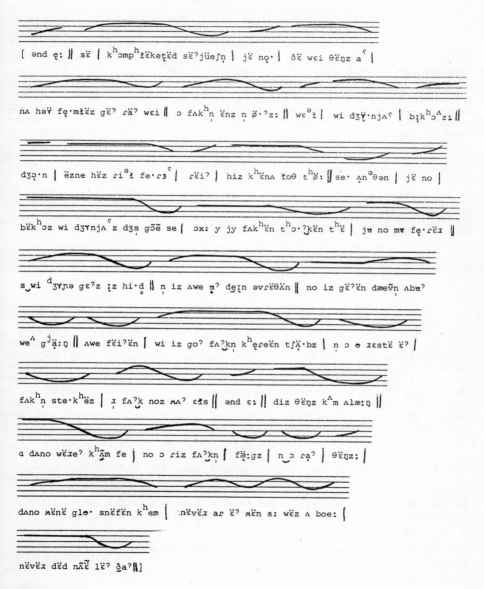

Figure 7: Phonetic transcription of T5/1-10.

Many localised features are in evidence in this transcription: lowered
and retracted /ɪ/, advanced and lowered /u/, glottal(ised) realisations of
voiceless plosives, pharyngeal realisations of postvocalic /r/, merger of /ʒ/
with /r/ and of /ʍ/ with /w/. Deleted initial /ð/ also occurs, e.g. in *their*
(18). /θ/ is not lenited in this extract, but cf. *think* (11). /e/ is not
merged with /ɛ/ before /r/, e.g. *cairryin* (7) - for the realisation of /e/ cf.
faimlies (2). The realisations of /a/ are also fronter and higher than might
have been expected.

Many unusual forms here can probably be attributed to speech rate, for instance the lenition of /d/ to [ɾ] in *had it* (10) and the assimilation of /nj/
to [ɲ] in *Junior* (5). The reduction of [Vnʔ] to [Ṽ] as in *gonnae* (4) and also
tryin tae [tʰɹãẽʔe](23) probably also depends on speech rate; cf. the reduction of [Vhn] to [Ṽ] in *nuthin* (10). However, the occurrence of /d/ for initial /ð/ as in *these* (8) and also *then* (29) is not unique to this speaker.
(See, for instance 3.7 below). The development of a /j/ glide between a velar
plosive and /a/ in *gang* (6) (as in N HibE and South West Scotland) is also
interesting.

As in Figure 3, vowel length is conditioned by stress, but this speaker also
lengthens some continuant consonants, e.g. /z/ in *oots* (2). The intonation
contours include many of the localised type with low rising terminals. High
rising terminals occur in sentence tags, but not in the *wh-* question in 4.

3.5 Conversation, Mrs. P.

The next speaker, Mrs. P., is a middle aged, working class woman from the inner city. The recording was made by Ann Tierney, who was tutoring Mrs. P. in
an adult literacy scheme. The tape was made in A. T.'s house without Mrs. P.'
knowledge, but when it was revealed she gave her permission for it to be used.
The quality of the recording is poor, but the style is extremely natural. One
consequence of this is the varied intonation. Mrs. P. is telling how her son
and his fiancée went to a dance in place of herself and her husband, and how
the fiancée won a beauty contest.

TEXT 6   ◷

Mrs. P. So he worried aboot me, because he says, well, if anything happens
to him, Ah cannae work or anythin, he says, so Ah'll need tae get a good security. So somebody goat us in touch wi these Forester people, so they came
up tae the house tae see him, so he took an insurance policy out on hisself,
5 ye see, but Ah couldnae get intae it because Ah wasnae healthy enough.

A. T. Yeah.

Mrs. P. So that even when he retires, he gets a pension, ye see, off this
policy.

A. T. Yeah.

10 *Mrs. P.* Pays it through the bank every month. But it's security for me -

A. T. Aye.

Mrs. P. That's the point. Aye. See, it was cos he's worried aboot that. So, well, wi us bein in that, ye get tickets through for aw the big dances an it doesnae cost ye anything; your ticket's free. So when Ah felt no too bad, Ah
15 went tae aw the dances, right enough, but last year, Ah was - just had an operation on ma wrist, an the book came in, an the faither says, "There nae good wi us," - he gets angry, right enough - "there nae good wi us lookin at the book," he says, "You're no able to go anywhere; you cannae go to any dances, an Ah wouldnae go withoot ye." So he threw the book away in the bucket, ye
20 know.

So Joseph jumped up, he says, "How does he know anythin aboot it, ma?"

Ah says, "Well, Ah don't think Ah'd be able to go, Joe."

So he looked through it. Ah says, "Here, listen, you an Morag could get oor tickets."

25 He says, "D'ye think that would be okay?"

Ah says, "Long as we get your Da tae phone them an explain that Ah'm no able tae go." So he done that.

An he says, "Aye, we'll send your son an his girlfriend the tickets," ye see? So they went away to the dance, but she didnae even go preperred for any-
30 thing like that; she just went wi an ordinary dress an everything on.

A. T. This was when she won it?

Mrs. P. Aye, that night. So they came roon -

A. T. She's a nice-lookin girl.

Mrs. P. Aye. They came roon askin for people tae enter, an Joe says to her,
35 "Gaun you in."

She says, "Ah'm no enterin nothin like that."

He says, "Ah stuck a ticket on her back, ma," (laughter) - ye know how ye get a ticket?

A. T. Aye.

40 *Mrs. P.* An he says, "Ah shoved her in." Cos she's a bit kind i shy, ye know. An she won it. An she got forty pound - cheque. She gave five poun to charity. She got a forty pound cheque, and she got forty poun tae buy herself a dress, an twenty poun tae get herself a herrdo. So that was quite good.

A. T. (?)

45 *Mrs. P.* Aye. So she'd tae go an enter for Miss Strathclyde, but she didnae won it. She didnae won at the show. But she come in -

A. T. Aye.

Mrs. P. second - thurd - that time. But she stull won it for a year, so she gets tae aw the dances free.

Notes

The *Ah* of *Ah cannae work* (2) is Mrs. P. *The faither* (16) is her husband, i.e. the father of the family. *Need tae* (2) is assimilated to [niʔë]. This is common, as is *gaun* (35) 'go no' and the loss of /t/ finally after /s/, e.g. *last* (15). *When* (7) has /w/. *The* occurs as [rë] (13) and [ë] (17). *Point* (12) is [poẽʔ]. After /w/ as in *won* (46), /ʌ/ for /ɪ/ is general in Scots.

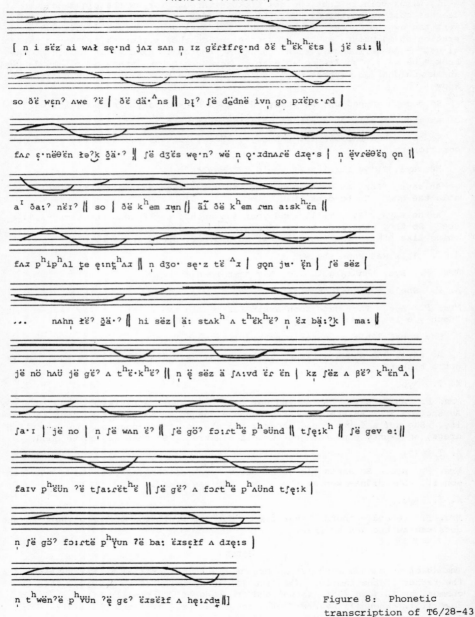

Phonetic Transcription

Figure 8: Phonetic transcription of T6/28-43

Localised features here include glottal realisations of /t/, and glottal
(ised) realisations of /k/. Notice the lowered and retracted /ɪ/, advanced,
and sometimes lowered, /u/, and centralised /a/. The realisation of /e/ in
stressed syllables is usually [e], while the realisation of /ɛ/ is usually
[ɐ̞]. There is a merger before /r/, e.g. *preperred* (29). Vowel length is conditioned by stress. The local intonation contour is the basic unmarked contour, with high rising terminals in sentence tags and in the yes-no question
in 37-8. The reported speech of the son's fiancee, where she modestly rejects
the idea of entering the contest, is uttered quietly, and on a low pitch, and
is unfortunately almost inaudible on the tape.

3.6 Interview, A. G.

This recording was made with the help of Ann Tierney in the home of the speaker,
A. G., a retired engineering worker and Labour Party activist. This is a
careful style with few non-standard items, although the accent is working class.
A. G. is gamely keeping up this rather limp conversation with a brief account
of family life when he was a child.

TEXT 7   ◠◡

Ma parents - ma father Ah never had much time for. Ma father was a heavy,
very heavy drinker. And he worked at - he was a hard worker, but he never had
much time for his children. He was one i these sort i Victorian - he thought
it was the woman's duty to bring up the children an tae look after the children. If he handed in the money on a Friday, it was her job tae feed them,
pay the rent, and look after their welfare. His joab was tae provide the
money, and he spent most of his weekend drinking. He was a very heavy drinker.

But Ah admire my mother, because she was very hard working, loved her children. But she never got a lot of happiness out of her life, because she'd so
O many mouths tae look after, so many children tae fend for, that she'd a very,
very hard life. Young people nowadays, young mothers, they don't realise how
difficult it must have been in these days for parents, specially wi the mother,
who was more a - just a piece i property. She wasn't an individual; she
wasn't allowed to have any social sort of inclinations of her own. She wasn't
5 allowed any social time. Her job was to see that the children were looked
after, put tae bed, got up for school in the morning, and fed, and that was
her job. She'd no - she'd never any time for social occasions. Fact, Ah
think ma father would've'a resented her having any social life whatsoever.

Although, she was a great church-goer, and she was a member i the Church
O Women's Guild, but that was - it used tae be in these days, women didn't work,
so that the Church Guild was always in an afternoon, because, as Ah say, women
didn't work in these days. But that was her only interest that I ever knew
of, was the Women's Guild, and the church. Then she went tae the service and
- on a Sunday.

Notes

Initial /ð/ is deleted in e.g. *the* (5). /d/ also occurs for initial /ð/ e.g.
in *the* (6). Medial /ð/ is [ɾ] in the first instance of *father* in 1, but is
deleted in the second instance. /r/ is deleted before [ʔ] in *sort* [sɔˆʔ] (3),
[sɔt] (14). Notice the double *have* in *would've'a* (18). There is an absence
of [ˤ] for /r/, [ɾ] for /t/, and merger of /ð/ with /r/ initially.

3.7 Interviews, Radio Scotland

The following collage of street interviews was recorded by Haig Gordon and
broadcast by Radio Scotland as a postscript to Stewart Conn's production of
J. McGrath's *The Game's a Bogey* (see 5.3.4). The speakers are all clearly
working class Glaswegians, but they vary in their degree of casualness. Speakers G and H are women. The speakers are making some very animated comments on
unemployment, housing, and the inadequate response of the medical profession
to problems such as alcoholism and depression.

TEXT 8

A. Nowadays there's actually nothing ye can go tae. Ah mean, the yairds are
aboot run doon, sae there's nothing else aboot here. They're pullin this whole
place apart, know? Mean, even if they dae offer ye a joab, hauf i the joabs
it's no even worth your while takin a joab, like, know.

5 *B.* If Ah've nae money, Ah wouldnae beg. Ah've never begged, an Ah never wull.
Ah'd rather steal. An Ah've done it before. Ah'm doin it now. Ah'll do it
again. Cos ma family'll no go hungry.

C. Ye're fullin in application forms aw the time, ye know. Then they check
ye up through the Employers' Federation, an if ye're - 've got a bit i a rad-
10 ical or anythin like that, ye know, in the unions, ye don't get a joab. So
ye're stuck wi therteen poun ninety a week.

B. If A can get a joab aboot seventy poun a week, that would jist, that would
jist do me. Because what Ah get aff i the Labour Exchange, it's only aboot
half i that, if it is that. Then Ah've goat tae make up masel. Usually if
15 Ah dae it, if Ah mur stealin, likes i for, as Ah sayed, ma rent an things like
that, it's mebbe aboot a hundret poun, two hundret poun, mebbe less, mebbe
more if Ah'm lucky. But it's roughly, at an average, it would be roughly
aboot - if Ah taen it ower, say, a period i a year, be roughly aboot seventy,
eighty poun a week, ye know. So if Ah'd a wage that could cover that, Ah'd be
20 okay. Ah wouldnae need tae steal.

A. Ma wife's got a job. That's the only wey we're survivin, you know. But
otherwise we wouldnae be able tae live, you know, cos prices i things are jist
sky high.

C. Ah have tae travel. Ah cannae get a joab here. Ah have tae travel. Ah
25 cannae get a joab up at Sullom Voe because there a big waitin list in Bellshill
Probably half the people that's oan the waitin list are employed, ye know. Ah
was up there at the Employment place, up the sterr, askin them, sayin, "Can ye
no gee it up a bit?" But Ah have tae go tae the end i the queue.

D. Ah'm a painter. But the thing's in Glasgow now, it means to get a paintin
30 job, which means travellin all over Glasgow; then again, that details bus
fare (laughter), ye know what Ah mean. Well, Ah'm separated; Ah'm still payin
maintainance; so it doesn't leave me much, by the time Ah pay digs, keep masel
You just can't do it nowadays on the cost i livin, ye know. Mean, ye know,
jist tae come fae here tae mebbe tae Cardonald or - that's twenty pence there
35 an twenty - that's forty pence jist tae sign the Broo. Ah mean what Ah'm
gettin is twenty three poun a week. That's me to support maself, an the rest
i it, ye know. It's jist gettin worse, Ah think, ye know. There is, well,
Ah mean, painter's job, but it means too, as Ah say, travellin, an people
sometimes don't want tae travel from their home tae get a job, ye know. But

40 Ah think that'll have tae be the stage in the future, jist have tae take jobs
    elsewhere, ye know, because Govan - Govan's jist dead.

    E. It's lik the bloody seige i Stalingrad, so it is. Aw the empty spaces!

    C. Ah've been away for five years. Jist come back in February, an it's ter-
    rible. Ah'm disgusted wi it. They say put your litter in a rubbish bin.
45 Where's the rubbish bins, ye know (laughter). They put these plastic wans up
    an somebody comes up an puts a dog end in it, an it melts!

    A. Aw the life has went oot i this community, specially roon aboot Govan, cos
    see when they're takin aw these tenements away, they're leavin it liein for
    long enough. An then they've discovered too late, it's easier to sand blast
50 and redevelop the houses than it is to pull them away. An they've done it aw
    too late. Cos Ah lived in a - Ah'd a great wee hoose, jist over in Sharp
    Street, an they took that away. That was a san stone building. They took
    that away, an ye're in hooses noo - they say they're redevelopin them aw noo,
    an that's - but, as Ah say, they've discovered that too late.

55 *E.* Same as in the city, they're stickin them oot miles away oot intae the
    schemes: they're only bloody barracks. There was a scheme we stayed in,
    Pollock: they've only opened up a shoppin centre now. That's been up for the
    last therty year. Ah think there was only aboot - see at the most, to cater
    for aboot forty, fifty thousand people, there was only aboot a dozen shoaps.
60 It's travel aw the time, an wi the buses, the expenses oan the buses, it's
    slaughter noo.

    B. Ah've heard it said aboot this errea that they're takin aw the anti-social
    tenants oot i everywhere else, an puttin them in the wan errea, where they can
    watch them. Whether that's true, Ah don't know. But Ah mean, it seems tae be,
65 for every wan good family, you've goat aboot fifteen bad yins.

    D. For a young chap here, his only ambition is tae get out of it, ye know.
    Or there he jist gets the same as the rest i us, ye know, unemployed, livin
    fae week tae week wi no hope, no moral - morale, like ye know. And Ah don't
    see any future for any young person here.

70 *B.* When Ah got intae trouble when Ah was ten years of age, it was for money,
    an it was only for coppers. But now, at ten years of age, they're runnin aboot
    wi knifes - aboot here anyway. They're runnin aboot wi knifes an swords an
    God knows what else. 'Ve started very young about here. Seems tae be a dif-
    ferent breed entirely. Seem tae be wilder. They're breakin intae places,
75 it's only to destroy them, burn them down, things lik that, ye know.

    F. Ah worked in the yairds for five year, but it was gettin that bad, ye know.
    Ye were gaun in, ye were daein nothin. It was borin, actually, ye know. Ye
    were actually turnin intae an alcoholic; actually takin drink in an drinkin
    it. That was how borin it was.

80 *G.* Ah found my doctor tae be most unco-operative an most unhelpful. Ah went
    tae him on several occasions an told him that ma husband had become totally
    alcoholic. Ah tried tae explain tae him jist how badly it was affectin the
    home life; it was affectin ma nerves; it was affectin him as well. And Ah
    found the doctor to be just totally indifferent tae the whole situation. He
85 much preferred to hand you a bottle of tranquillisers.

    H. Ah was takin the tranquillisers. They were makin me drowsy, ye know. They
    were makin me, Ah'd be walkin along the street an ye would think Ah had a drink
    in me; Ah'd be staggerin. So Ah jist got, Ah jist stopped takin them an tried
    tae do without them. He started giving me sleepin tablets, but, as Ah sayed,

90 it was just makin me worse.

    G. Ah know ma husband got insurance line from his GP every other week, for a day off, two days off, a week off. Anything at all, he went to his doctor an got an insurance line. An really, at the root of the problem was: excess drinking. And it actually took something like six years before an outside,
95 an outsider - ye know one of these Panels that they go to if they're havin too many insurance lines - and they then pursued it. An eventually he was referred for psychiatric care. But that was after - I could never count the number of insurance lines he got from his GP. An Ah don't think the was ever any discussion aboot alcoholism.

100 *E.* This is a thing that Ah violently disagree wi, this family income supplement. This is the tax payer subsidisin the employer, because the employer isnae peyin a luvin wage.

    A. If you can get a joab, fae - mean, sweepin the streets, if there's enough money in it, ye'll take it. It's as simple as that. But there's no really
105 much - they're no gien them - anythin gaun aboot at aw.

    E. Ye're gonnae go back tae the auld - the totties an purritch. This is what it's gaun back tae, the wey this - even the Labour government theirselfs, the wey they've let it run doon.

    I. Tenement buildings then were tight, but it was never as bad as this. Ah
110 mean, we're gaun back tae the nineteen therties. This is no nineteen seventy nine. This is - might as well be nineteen therty. Because this is the wey it is here.

    B. Ma mother an father were poor. They never had money. Ma mother never had money tae ma father died, an she got insurance. That was aw. But tae me, they
115 went through life poor, but Ah'm no gonnae go through life poor. As Ah say, Ah would rather steal. Mean, when Ah was a wee boay, many a times we've went withoot supper, because ma mother an father didnae have any money. But ma father would - he would try an borrow it aff i somebody; couldnae get it. But Ah wouldnae. Ah would - we'll never go shoart, cos Ah would jist go oot
120 an steal it. They were wullin tae jist sit back an take it. They were wullin tae jist - resigned tae their lot, sort i thing. But Ah wasn't. Ah'd tae go up an dae somethin.

    E. But you take it - jist at the back i the church there, there was Harland and Wolff's, in there. Ower there, that was a wee dry dock, Henderson's.
125 There was another wee wan up the road there, Pointhoose, built the tugs. The wan further up, Harland and Wolff's, the shipyard, hit was closed; Stevens' was closed; Flemin an Fergusson was closed; Barclay Curle's is closed; the Elderslie dry dock, hit's closed. Only Rab Butler opened this Govan dry dock up again. There a man wi a bit i go. There, take the docks an aw. There's
130 Yorkhull Dock, Queen's Dock, Prince's Dock, an the wee dock that the Hielan boats sailed oot i.

Notes

Sullom Voe (25) is an oil terminal in Shetland. The other places mentioned are in or around Glasgow. Notice the idiom *took that away* (52), which suggests that the buildings were somehow misappropriated rather than physically demolished. *That* (76) means 'so'. *Tae* (114, first case only) means 'until'. *Maintainance* (32) has the stress on the second syllable. *Empty* (42) is [ɛmʔɪ] -the loss of /t/ after /p/ is general in Scots. *Knifes* (72) and *theirselfs*

(107) have the voiceless fricative retained before the plural inflection, which is usual in ScE.

Speaker E, who is apparently an elderly man, has almost consistent cacuminal realisations of /s/ and /z/, and in one word, *sailed* (131), he has /ʃ/. Speaker D, like the two female speakers, uses few items differing from the standard in lexical incidence. He is evidently paying attention to his speech style, and produces several slips of the tongue. Curiously, his pronunciation of *future* on both occasions, (40 and 69) has /j/ deleted. The female speaker G is the least localised. She uses [ʔ] only for /t/, and produces twice as many *-ing* as *-in*. She deletes initial /ð/ only once, in *the* (84, first case only). The second female speaker, H, has [ʔ] also for /k, p/ before nasals.

Speakers A and E produce between them three examples of unrounded fronted variants of /u/: [ɨ] in *pull* (50) and [ɛ̈] in *aboot* (2, first case only, and 58). The word *aboot* seems to have been transferred to the class of words which take /ɪ/ when unstressed. All of the male speakers except A have some [ˤ] realisations of postvocalic /r/. Most have a few [ɾ] for intervocalic /t/. There are a number of ejective realisations of voiceless plosives finally in intonation contours, mainly /k/ in the word *week*. There are occasional examples of /w/ for /ʍ/, e.g. *where's* (45). Most of the male speakers delete initial /ð/ in a number of items, while B and E also have occasional /d/, but only B has /r/ for /ð/ initially. Speaker B (if indeed this is one speaker) is probably the most localised in terms of the frequency with which he used stigmatised variants, and in particular those, like /r/ for /ð/ and [ˤ] for /r/, which are not found with all working class men. Another characteristic which he shares with W. E. (3.4 above) is a marked lengthening of /z/ and other continuants finally in intonation contours.

3.8   Classroom discussion

The following discussion was recorded by Kenneth Brown in Whitehill Secondary School in Glasgow. The speakers are four girls of average ability aged around 14 or 15. They are discussing a poem, "Work" by D. H. Lawrence, with the guidance of a worksheet, to which they refer from time to time. The situation is a rather artificial one, and for much of the time the girls say to each other the things which they would normally say to the teacher, and they circulate the teacher's role amongst themselves. Here the discussion becomes lively as one of the girls takes a stance in defence of modern life, and against the Luddite position implied by the poem and explored further in the worksheet. The speech style is strongly localised but not very fluent. A further transcription from the same tape can be found in Kenneth Brown (1981).

TEXT 9

A. What do you think's the best? Manufacturing - Ah mean, lik, know how - lik we're luvin in the Furst Wuruld, right? Where we jist get money, go intae a shop an buy what we want. Well, the people in the Thurd Wuruld - d'you think -

5   *B.* Poor.

A. Are poor. An they need tae make their own things. What d'you think's the best? Well, not necessarily bein poor, Ah mean, jist makin their own stuff?

C. Well, Ah prefer factories (laughter).

A. You're jist ...

10 *C.* Naw, Ah dae. Ah wouldnae - Ah don't like makin ma ain stuff -

D. Ah know, some people don't -

A. Naither dae Ah, Ah don't -

D. Some people aren't really good at makin their own clothes. If you manufacture somethin then -

15 *C.* Everybody's gettin a choice.

B. Ah, but then if you're poor, an you've goat tae make your ain claithes, you've had practice at makin your ain claithes.

D. Aye, that's right, cos (?)

B. (?) make them quite good.

20 *C.* Well, Ah don't like makin ma ain stuff. Ah like jist tae buy it, ye know, fae factories.

A. But you see, we're - we wouldnae be able tae make clothes as good as the people in another country that lived wi out machines, d'ye know what Ah mean? We're luvin with machines, right? But we wouldn't be able tae make clothes as 25 good as the people that lived in a country that didn't have machines, d'ye know what Ah mean?

D. Mmhmm.

C. Naw.

A. Lik that, know how -

30 *B.* Like, hand-weavin's stull the best.

A. Mmhmm.

C. Aw aye. It would last longer an aw that -

B. The best standard.

C. but it might no look as good (laughter). Well, it might no look as guid.
35 It's stuff that they make theirsels.

B. Ah know, but if they have lots i practice in it, they'd be better than we
are in it.

A. Ah know. A good, a good ...

B. Good standard.

40 *A.* Good standard i makin things, ye know, havin (?)

B. Ah mean, people that can dae that, they don't need machines.

D. There's a loat i things that machines cannae make, that humans can only
(?) handle it.

C. Ah, but they would (?) machines an aw, but. Ah mean, the people have goat
45 tae know what tae dae afore they put it - put use tae the machines. Mean, it's
lik a calculator, right? Mean, you've goat a calculator, but you've goat tae
know what tae feed intae this calculator. Mean, the calculator doesnae dae it
aw itself. Mean, you've goat tae know what tae feed intae it. It's the same
as that. Mean, let's say you've goat a sewin machine; you'll need tae cut
50 oot the pattern and that an aw, an draw oot a pattern first. So ye're sort i
daein it yourself there.

Notes

The girls are speaking very rapidly, especially when trying to gain or hold
the floor, and there are frequent phonetic assimilations and deletion of re-
coverable sentence initial items, e.g. *what do you think* [ʔdju hɛŋk] (3-4).
There are numerous items differing from the standard in lexical incidence, and
a free use of [ʔ] for /k/, and deleted /ð/ initially. There are even occa-
sioal pharyngeal realisations of postvocalic /r/, e.g. *poor* (7); and a vocalised [ɤ] for /l/ in *people* (23) (cf. Cockney).

3.9 Conversations, Radio Clyde   ⚉

The following series of items are from programmes on the local radio station,
Radio Clyde, presented by Tiger Tim (Tim Strevens). The programmes are made
up of popular music, chat, and listeners' phone calls. There is also a female
stooge called Maggie, whose voice is heard from time to time. The phone-ins
follow a regular format. After Tiger Tim has exchanged greetings with the
caller, he asks a few personal questions, usually the age of the caller, where
he/she lives, and what he/she does for a living. He then asks about the caller's leisure activities. The length of the conversation varies according to
whether an interesting topic emerges from these questions. There is often a
quiz or some other item in which the caller is invited to participate, and the
exchange ends with the caller being given the chance to mention, or dedicate
a record to, his/her friends and relatives. Many of the callers speak in a
fairly casual style, and as many of them are working class Glaswegians, this
is often quite localised, although non-standard items, including those involving lexical incidence, tend to be avoided. Tiger Tim has a very wide style
range, from a style as localised as most of his callers, to a formal 'broadcasting' style which includes some forms unusual in colloquial St ScE. This
occasionally leads to difficulties of communication with callers.

3.9.1 Tiger Tim and Billy Sloane

The first item is an exchange between Tiger Tim and another DJ, Billy Sloane,
about a forthcoming programme.

TEXT 10

Tim: Through the wonders of the modern electric wireless, I have here with me
in the studio right now, preparing for his show - see, he's not on until
twelve, but he's already here doing it (he's also preparing for his show) -
Billy Sloane. Bill, you did meet Pete Townsend, then?

5 *Bill:* Yes, I had the great distinction of meeting the god of modern rock.

Tim: Was this an ambition of yours?

Bill: Yes. Yes. He's always been my hero, an the chance tae get - gettin the
chance tae interview him for therty minutes seemed less of a chore, an more of
just a dream come true, if ye know what Ah mean.

10 *Tim:* No, but anyway (laughter). Thank you.

Bill: Thank you.

Tim: Were you disappointed at all?

Bill: No, not in the least. Ah mean, Ah think the guy is a musical genius,
an, ye know, Ah think he said enough in that interview, as ye'll perhaps hear
15 tonight, to indicate that there's life in the old dog yet.

Tim: Yes, well, I would perhaps hear it if I listened, but eh ...

Bill: (groans) (slapping noise, laughter)

Tim: I'll be listening!

Notes

Billy Sloane is the more localised of the two, with, for instance, more tap realisations of /r/, and more lowered variants of /ɪ/. But in other ways his speech is more formal than Tiger Tim's, for instance in the use of non-local-ised clichés like *life in the old dog yet*, and a slower and less fluent deliv-ery. That is, both speakers are responding to the situation as a rather for-mal one, but in somewhat different ways.

3.9.2 Tiger Tim and Doreen

The following is part of a conversation between Tiger Tim and a caller, a working class woman with a young family, who has just given the correct answer in a quiz which involved identifying a song played backwards.

TEXT 11

Tim: What gave it away for ye? Was it the wee bit at the start where she goes "ooh-ooh ooh-ooh"?

Doreen: Naw, Ah think it's jist actually her horrible voice.

Tim: Oh, you're a fan! Yes. Can you give us a quick "ooh-ooh, ooh-ooh"?

Doreen: Ooh-ooh ooh-ooh.

Tim: Yes. Was that you or the baby?

Doreen: That was me!

Tim: Oh, it was you! Doreen -

Doreen: Mebbe Ah've goat a touch i wind, right enough! (laughter).

Tim: You've won yourself a prize. Would you now like to say hello to someone?

Doreen: Well, tae ma Mum, whose lookin after ma young - my - ma wee daughter jist now; Mrs. Brown, Cairnhill Circus. An ma young sister, Alison, and, oh anyone else that knows us. Ah don't really know who tae mention.

Tim: Okay -

Doreen: Ma brother, and ma sister-in-law, Catherine and Tom, and ma Auntie Ellen.

Tim: Yes?

Doreen: An Ah think that's aboot all (laughs).

Tim: Right, Doreen, thanks very much for taking part. You've won the prize. We'll get it off tae ye -

Doreen: Oh, an Ah forgot tae mention ma husband! (laughter)

Tim: Oh, don't forget tae mention your husband, for goodness' sake. What's his name?

Doreen: John.

Tim: John. An what does he do for a living?

Doreen: He's - works for an engineering company.

Tim: I see. Is he working just now?

Doreen: Well, actually, he's off on the Panel.

Tim: Is he?

30 *Doreen:* He's got a bad back jist now.

Tim: Oh, I wonder why! (laughter) Doreen, thanks very much for calling -

Doreen: I wouldn't like tae tell ye! (laughter)

Tim: Thanks for callin, Doreen.

Doreen: Okay, then. Thank you.

35 *Tim:* Bye-bye.

Doreen: Bye-bye.

Notes

On the Panel (28) means receiving Sickness Benefit. Doctors' Panels were superseded in 1948.

Tiger Tim's style here is much more localised than in T10. The style of the caller is comparable to that of speaker G in T8. Her accent is fairly localised, but there are few dialectal forms. *Ma young sister* (12). for instance, is a more formal alternative to *ma wee sister*, but not so formal as *my young sister*.

3.9.3 Tiger Tim and Jimmy D.

The caller in this extract is a working class man, probably in late middle age. After a lengthy chat, he is asked to give his opinion of a record played earlier, and to sum up the opinions of other callers, which involves him in making funny noises: fabby-doo is the code for 'good', mm-mm (high falling intonation) for 'indifferent', and a raspberry for 'awful'.

TEXT 12

Tim: We're talking now to Jimmy Davidson. Hello, Jimmy.

Jim: Hello, Tiger.

Tim: How are you?

Jim: Not bad, thanks.

5 *Tim:* Do you work for a living, Jimmy?

Jim: Well, unfortunately, I'm disabled.

Tim: Are you really?

Jim: Yeah.

Tim: So are you in the house most of the time?

10 *Jim:* Mostly, yes. For the last therteen years to be approximate.

Tim: Is it? Aw, that's a shame. But still. What dae ye do tae pass the time?

Jim: Well, Radio Clyde, obviously.

Tim: Oh yes, of course!

15 *Jim:* And television, and Ah like to correspond a lot.

Tim: Do you?

Jim: Yeah.

Tim: So you're able to, actually to do a lot of things?

Jim: Well, it's not a physical handicap, Tiger. It's - it was actually -
20 it's agrophobia, and I took it after an operation therteen years ago, an Ah
haven't got rid of it since.

Tim: I see. So ye don't get out very much at all, then.

Jim: Very seldom.

Tim: What happens when ye do go out?

25 *Jim:* (intake of breath) Well -

Tim: Or is that a silly question?

Jim: Jist one big sort of panic stations to get back up the stair again -

Tim: Honestly?

Jim: to the house as fast as possible.

30 *Tim:* Ah think people that don't suffer from that disease, Jimmy, they find
it -

Jim: They've no idea.

Tim: They find it very difficult to understand. Ah think it's one of those
things that ye must experience yourself.

35 *Jim:* Too true, Tiger. And - one other thing, ye know, as you say, people
don't realise it until they themselves have been affected by it. And it's
hard to live with, and it's hard to fight down, ye know, what - Ah mean, against
other people's, what they think of you.

Tim: Yeah.

40 *Jim:* They think ye're just lazy an don't want tae do anything. Whereas, in
comparison, before Ah took this, Ah was a very active an versatile worker.

Tim: Sure. So tell me, Jimmy, how far have you actually managed tae get when
ye go out the house? What's the furthest ye've ever been.

Jim: (gasps) About therty yards.

45 *Tim:* Is that right?

Jim: Yeah.

Tim: Aw. An ye just sort i panic an then turn roun an get back up the sterr
again?

Jim: That's about it, yes.

50 *Tim:* Isn't there any sort of treatment that ye can get for this?

Jim: Yes, there is, but unfortunately, you have to travel to get to it, and
eh ...

Tim: Yeah, that's Catch Twenty-two, isn't it?

Jim: Ye know, Catch Twenty-two. Ah have heard that there is some hospitals
55 which will send out an ambulance, ye know, but I haven't found one that'll do
this yet.

Tim: Would you be able to get into the ambulance an mebbe go to the hospital,
then?

Jim: Well, Ah would have to face up to that, ye know, if it arose, like, ye
60 know. But Ah jist wouldn't know at the moment, Tiger.

Tim: That's a shame. Jimmy, is it -

Jim: Not to worry. Ah mean Ah'm cheerful enough.

Tim: No, you -

Jim: Ah'm resigned to it. And that's a - Ah think that's a big step in itself,
65 you know, not resignin oneself to it.

Tim: Ah think in one respect, that it's good that ye can do that, but Ah think
in another respect, that it would be nice that if ye didn't resign yourself
one hundred per cent, an ye stull had a wee bit i hope that ye could get over
this sort i thing.

70 *Jim:* Oh no - yeah - oh, definitely, that's - that is true. And ye know, Ah
always make a go, and always have a try, irrespective of what happens when Ah
do try, ye know.

Tim: Yeah. Jimmy, Ah'll keep ma fingers crossed for ye.

Jim: Thanks very much.

75 *Tim:* It's nice tae have ye on the programme. What about that record we played
there? Did ye like that?

Jim: Yes, Ah thought it was fabby-doo.

Tim: Did you!

Jim: Yes, I did indeed.

80 *Tim:* Ah. So you think it's gonnae be a hit single, do you?

Jim: Yes, quite possibly so, yes.

Tim: Fine. What about the rest of the panel?

Jim: Well, there was two fabby-doos, three mm's, and - don't laugh, because
Ah've not got ma teeth in (laughter) - one, two (attempts to rasp). Ah can't
85 do it. (Rasps). Is that better?

Tim: Yeah. That's what it sounds like, ye've not got your teeth in. Do it
again for us.

Jim: (rasps)

Tim: Aye, ye get that kind i broad spectrum of sounds when ye do it without
90 your teeth (rasps).

Jim: Naw, that was - yeah, that was jist ma lips.

Tim: Yeah (laughter).

NOTES

The caller here is speaking very carefully and in a style similar to that of
Speaker D in T8. Like him, he tends to stumble as a result. He contradicts
himself in lines 64-5, and produces what appear to be blends - *in comparison*
(40-1) (cf. *by comparison, in contrast*) and *make a go* (71) (cf. *have a go,
make a go of*) - and a hyper-correction, *to be approximate* (10). Tiger Tim's
style is similar to that in T11, with the consequence that overall his speech
is probably more localised in this exchange than that of the caller. Notice,
for instance, that he prefers *yeah*, while J. D. prefers *yes*, and that, while
J. D. uses *stair* (27), Tiger Tim, in echoing this utterance, uses *sterr* (47).
Thakerar (1981) discusses a similar phenomenon, where speakers converge on
each other's speech to the extent that they pass each other going in opposite
directions. He demonstrates that the speakers are actually converging on group
stereotypes.

3.9.4 Tiger Tim and Maggie

The next item is a short exchange between Tiger Tim and a female presenter on
the programme, who has just finished giving marks to a number of records on
the basis of the callers' 'fabby-doos' etc.

TEXT 13

Maggie: Well, that one did fairly well. Two fabby-doos, three mm an one
(rasps). A twenty.

Tim: A twenty. Ah like the way she says that. So that means ...

Maggie: That we have a tie tonight, both with twenty four: "And the loving
goes on," Earth Wind and Fire, and The Who, "You better, you bet."

Tim: But you want me to play The Who, because you saw them last Sunday, an I
didn't.

Maggie: It was actually Saturday, but yes.

Tim: Oh, Saturday.

Maggie: Yes.

Tim: But you're still rubbing it in.

Maggie: Yes, I am indeed. Aw, they were great!

Tim: Were they?

Maggie: They were wonderful.

Tim: The highlight of the year?

Maggie: Yes.

Tim: It is only February.

Maggie: So far, so far.

Tim: I keep saying that.

Notes

Line 2, *a twenty*: high falling intonation.

Tiger Tim's style here is similar to that in T10, and to Maggie's here.
Localisation is minimal.

3.9.5 Tiger Tim and the Famous Five

The final item in this section is part of a conversation between Tiger Tim and
a group of schoolgirls, probably younger than those in T9, who are participating
in a spot where listeners sing along with a record. The girls are from a village to the south of Glasgow. They are very confident on the telephone, which
results in a varied conversation, with questions, instructions and exclamations
from the callers as well as from Tiger Tim.

TEXT 14

Tim: Now, the thing is that every week on the Sing-one-for-you spot, we like
to give talent a chance, an bring new people on for you. However, last week,
we had five young ladies on, singing at the one time along with their favourite
record of the time, which was Adam and the Ants and "Dog eat dog." They
5 called themselves 'the Famous Five' from Neilston, an would you believe it, I
got so many cards an letters sayin, "You've got to get them back again" (laughs
Mind you, Ah did get a few cards sayin, "You've got to get them!" However,
they are here. Hello-o.

Sheila: Hello.

10 *Tim:* Who am I speaking to?

Sheila: Sheila.

Tim: It's Sheila.

Sheila: Yes.

Tim: Of the Famous - actually, last week, if I remember correctly, we only
15 had four.

Sheila: Yes, but we've got five tonight.

Tim: We have the full five this time.

Sheila: Yes.

Tim: The full quota is with us. I see. Now which one wasn't here last week?

20 *Sheila:* Anne.

Tim: Anne. Is Anne there?

Sheila: Yes. D'ye want to speak tae her?

Tim: Yes, why not?

Sheila: Right, here she is.

25 *Tim:* Thank you.

Anne: Hello.

Tim: Hello, Anne. How are you?

Anne: Fine. How are you?

Tim: I'm fine. Did you happen to hear your friends last week?

30 *Anne:* Yeah. Ah was baby-sittin an Ah heard them.

Tim: I see. And were you feeling a bit left out of it all?

Anne: A wee bit.

Tim: Do you think that your contribution to the Famous Five is something special?

35 *Anne:* Ah don't know, cos Ah've never done it before.

Tim: Well, we're going to find out now, aren't we?

Anne: Yeah.

Tim: Yes. What are ye -

Anne: What -

40 *Tim:* Pardon?

Anne: Nothin.

Tim: What were ye goin tae say?

Anne: Nothin.

Tim: You were going to say something. Come on!

45 *Anne:* Naw, you say first.

Tim: All right, Ah'll say it first. I was going to say, what are ye gonnae sing for us?

Anne: "Help."

Tim: You may -

50 *Anne:* By the Beatles.

Tim: Yes, I know who it's by!

Anne: Yeah.

Tim: Ah was just goin to say, again, that you may need help after it, depending -

55 *Anne:* You're right.

Tim: Depending on how well you sing. Last week, you had your biscuit tins an guitars an flutes, an all sorts i things. Have you got them with you this week?

Anne: Yeah.

60 *Tim:* Oh no! [Music, the girls singing along; jingles imitating audience response]. Well, it's a bit mixed there. We have a mixed opinion from the audience. But eh, what else can I say except (rasps). Naw, actually, it was - it was as good as it was last week. That's as far as Ah'm allowed tae commit myself. Who's on the phone line now?

65 *Chris:* Aw, this is Christine.

Tim: Oh, hello, Christine.

Chris: Hello.

Tim: How are you?

Chris: Pardon?

70 *Tim:* How are you?

Chris: Aw Ah'm fine, thanks.

Tim: How does it feel to be a superstar, because you do realise that you are the first act ever on the Sing-one-for-you spot to be invited back two weeks in a row?

75 *Chris:* Ah know. It feels great. We feel really famous.

Tim: What? Yeah, well, you are the Famous Five, after all.

Chris: Ah know, we are the Famous Five.

Tim: Why do you think that you appeal to the masses?

Chris: Because we're daft.

80 *Tim:* Yes, Ah'll agree with that.

Chris: Ah-huh. We're really daft, aren't we?

Tim: Ah'll tell you something, would you like to say hello to someone?

Chris: Well, can Ah tell you somethin first?

Tim: Yes, you tell me something.

85
Chris: We came up to see you today, but ye weren't in.

Tim: Where? Here at Radio Clyde?

Chris: Ah-huh. We came up.

Tim: Aw, what a shame.

Chris: Round about three o' clock. An we were all sad, because ye weren't
90 there.

Tim: The whole five of you?

Chris: Ah-huh.

Tim: Am I glad! No I'm not! I wisht I had been there. Would I have man-aged to get a (kissing noises) kissy kissy?

95 *Chris:* Oh yes. We would've given you lots i kisses.

Tim: Aw, that's the gemm. Well, perhaps we could make another date some time.

Chris: Ah-huh?

Tim: Yeah, Ah was - the thought occurred to me there that perhaps we could
100 actually have you live in the studio doing this.

Chris: Ah-huh. Live in the studio! That would be great.

Tim: But perhaps not (laughs). Ah'll have to think about that one.

Chris: D'you really mean that?

Tim: No.

105 *Chris:* No?

Tim: Yeah, Ah mean it that Ah'll have to think about it.

Chris: Ah-huh.

Tim: What I do really believe is that the audience need a rest for a couple
i weeks at least.

.0 *Chris:* Need a rest?

Tim: So that they can recover from this - madness.

Chris: Ah-huh. But we'll always come back on an cheer them up again.

Tim: Yes, this is true. Unfortunately.

Chris: Ah-huh.

.5 *Tim:* Christine, who d'you want tae say hello to?

Chris: Well, can we all have this wee shot each, please?

Tim: Why not?

Chris: Okay. Ah'd like tae say hello tae ma Mum an ma Dad, Fiona, Alex, an
ma Uncle Archie, an aw ma other relations in Tenby, an Crawford an Glen.

20 *Tim:* Great.

Chris: Okay? Cos they'll be listenin just now.

Tim: Thank you.

Chris: Here's Anne.

Notes

You say first (45) is a children's idiom, picked up wrongly by Tiger Tim in
his reply. *All sad* (89) means 'very sad' (not 'all of us'). *Wisht* (93) is
perhaps a West of Scotland form: cf. *oncet* 'once' and *twicet* 'twice'. *Nothin*
(41) has /h/, but is repeated (43) with /θ/.

The girls use considerably fewer stigmatised forms than the speakers in T9,
either because they are from a higher class, or because they come from outside
the conurbation, or both. Tiger Tim's style swings between his most formal,
which he uses half-jokingly, as if interviewing a celebrity, and a quite localised style, which he produces, for instance, in response to localised forms
from the girls, such as *nothin* (41).

3.10 Comic narrative, Billy Connolly

The following are extracts from a story told by Billy Connolly at a concert in Airdrie (near Glasgow) and recorded live by Transatlantic Records. Although this is a stage performance, the narrative is unscripted, and can be regarded as spontaneous speech. Connolly began his career as a musician, but he is now admired as a raconteur (and recently also as a playwright). He excels in naturalistic dialogue and in characterising situations from the viewpoint of a working class Glasgow man.

"The crucifixion" is one of Connolly's best known stories. It is an account of the crucifixion as prophesied by Christ in a Glasgow pub. The first part below describes the scene at the Last Supper, with Judas as an insecure and unpopular little man, of the type known as a 'nyaff', trying to catch the eye of the charismatic Christ, known to his friends as 'the Big Yin', in recognition of his personal prestige. (This name is now applied to Connolly himself, particularly in Malcolm McCormick's cartoon strip in *The Sunday Mail*). In the second part, the Big Yin reaches the end of his narrative when he is restrained by his drinking companions and rebuked for telling them such a tall story.

TEXT 15   ᘒᑎ
a. The Last Supper

So after a while, they're aw drinkin the wine, an wanderin aboot, screamin an shoutin. They all sat down, because - they sat down round this big table, because they were havin trouble standin up at this point, ye see. So they aw sat doon - ye might've seen the picture, an the Big Yin's haudin oan tae the
5 table - he's steamin! He's feart in case he faws oot that windae at the back!

So they're aw sat doon. They're aw singin songs an talkin an that. An drinkin the wine an terrin lumps oot the breid. An the Big Yin says, "Hey, wait a minute! Best of order here!" Silence.

An the wee apostle's sittin opposite. He says tae the bloke next tae him,
10 "Heh, Ah hope he gies us wan i yon stories, eh? Aw thae stories are magic. Ah lap them up, so Ah dae. See thon wan aboot his faither up in the sky? What a story yon is, eh? Aw-haw! Aw thae punters wi the wings an aw that. What a story! Heh, Big Yin, gies a story!"

"Shut your face!" Bang! And his face was shut. For it is written. He
15 says, "Open yer face." He says, "Right, let that be a lesson tae you."

He says, "Aye, aw right. That's terrible, eh?"

He says, "As a matter a fack, Ah'm not goin to give youse a story today. Ah'm going for to give youse a prophecy."

"Ooh! d'ye hear that!" says the Wee Yin. "D'ye hear that? Prophecy, eh?
20 Nae bother tae the Big Yin, eh? Prophecies an everythin, jist lik that, eh? Whit's a prophecy anyway?"

Big Yin says, "Look, a prophecy tells ye what's gonnae happen the morra."

Says, "What aboot the three therty the morra?"

The Big Yin says, "See you, Judas, you're gettin oan ma tits."

b. The resurrection

25 "As if Ah could dae anythin aboot it, they roll a big stone in front i the
door. An ye know me, Ah'm that skerred i the dark tae. But in the mornin a
couple i chinas i mine - unknownst tae youse, ya bunch i scruff - turn up wi
the good gear oan, the wings an everythin - couple i ferries, like, ye know -
roll the stane away - ye never know the strength i these people - roll the
30 stane away, get me oot, an say, 'There ye go, Big Yin, away up tae the sky an
see your faither.'

So Ah'm up in the sky an Ah'm sittin on a cloud wi ma Da, an Ah'm lookin
doon, an Ah can see ye aw, sittin in the boozer. Ye're aw sayin, 'Where's the
Big Yin?' 'Ah don't know.' 'Did you go up?' 'Ye're kiddin.' The door's
35 gonnae open - bang! - an Ah'm gonnae walk in. An you're gonnae say, 'You're
no the Big Yin.'

Ah'm gonnae say, 'Aye, Ah am.'

Ye're gonnae say, 'Well, where's the holes in your hauns?'

An Ah'm gonnae say, 'There they are.'

40 You're gonnae say, 'They're no holes.'

Ah'm gonnae say, 'Okay. Haud up fingers. Cop your whack for the chib mark
under the semmit!'"

Jist then, John stauns up an says, "Aw wait a minute, Big Yin. We like
you. We've always liked ye. An we know that you chipped in merr for this
45 kerry-oot than anybody else. But see when you've got a few i these cheap wines
in ye, your patter's rotten, so it is."

From Billy Connolly, "The Crucifixion",
Billy Connolly Solo Concert (Transatlantic
Records, TRA 279, 1974).

Notes

Doon (4) is pronounced [dɨ̩n]. *Apostle* (9) is /ʌpostḷ/. The loss of /t/ after
/k/ as in *fack* (17) is general in Scots.

Lines 17-18 capture the self-consciousness of a working class man making a
speech in front of an audience to whom he is known personally - the non-standard grammatical items *youse* and *for to* are emphasised. The dialogue is char-
acterised throughout by liberal use of all the most stigmatised phonetic variants - [ˤ] for /r/, /r/ for initial /ð/, and cacuminal /s, z/. Also, the
realisation of /e/ tends to be lowered finally, e.g. *dae* (11) as well as before
/r/. These two latter features are probably produced by the articulatory setting, with protruded lower jaw, which Connolly adopts throughout the dialogue.
Only the angel, however, has /d/ for initial /ð/.

's

̶ ̶ ̶ otype' is widely used, following Labov (1972), to designate
sociolinguistic varieties or variants of which there is a high degree of consciousness in the speech community and which are part of the conventional wis-
dom of the community with regard to language. Linguistic stereotypes can not
be expected to be accurate or up-to-date, but they do normally have an empirical
basis. When features become stereotyped, they may then begin to die out in
natural speech, as speakers are embarrassed to find that they are parodying
themselves. On the other hand, speakers may use stereotypes as such, putting
them, as it were in quotation marks, in order to send out a clear signal of
group identity. The middle class scottisisms discussed by Aitken (1979) are
of this kind, as are the non-standard grammatical items in T15/17-18.

The texts which follow illustrate the use of stereotyped Glasgow English
in comedy and light entertainment. T16, T17 and T21-4 can be heard on the tape
which accompanies this volume. The characters and situations in these pieces
are often themselves stereotypes or parodies. Materials such as these, which
reach large audiences, not only utilise stereotypes, but may, on occasion, be
their source or means of dissemination. It is not clear how one would inves-
tigate this, but it is certainly the case that popular artistes and comedians
often have catch-phrases associated with them which may be based on local dialects or accents (cf. Mackie 1978: 76ff). It is not possible within the scope
of this volume to do more than glance at a few items representative of the
comic portrayal of Glasgow English. Many of the texts in Chapter 5 are also
humorous or constructed around a few well-known local variants, and indeed any
writer, in recreating a variety, makes a selection of linguistic items of which
he/she is more or less consciously aware.

4.1 Will Fyffe

In the early part of this century, when Glasgow was known for the radical politics of its workforce, the area was frequently referred to as 'the Red Clyde.'
It is this radical image, combined with the Glasgow man's reputation for heavy
drinking, which is portrayed in Will Fyffe's "I belong to Glasgow." Although
this is one of his best known numbers, Fyffe was not in fact from Glasgow, but
from Dundee, in the East of Scotland. The song and monologue are supposedly
based on an actual encounter which Fyffe had in Glasgow's Central Station. The
main theme is that a hard-working man has a right to get drunk without being
pilloried for it.

TEXT 16, "I belong to Glasgow"

Ah've been wi a few i ma cronies,
One or two pals i mine,
We went in a hotel,
We did very well,
5 Aye, an then we came out once again.
An then we went intae another -
That is the reason Ah'm fu,
We had six deochandoruses,
Then sang a chorus,
10 Just listen, Ah'll sing it tae you.

I belong to Glasgow,
Dear old Glasgow town.
But there's something the matter with Glasgow,
For it's going round an round.
15 Ah'm only a common old working lad,
As anyone can see,
But when I get a couple i drinks on a Saturday,
Glasgow belongs to me.

There's nothing in bein teetotal,
20 And saving a shilling or two,
If your money you spend,
Ye've nothing to lend -
Isn't that all the better for you?
There's nae harm in takin a drappie,
25 It ends all your troubles an strife,
An it gives ye the feeling,
That when you land home,
Oh, ye don't care a hang for your wife -

Heh, heh, that's the feeling ye get, mine ye, and I always say that the man's
30 the man that takes a good drink, he's a man. He's a man. Because when ye're
teetotal, when ye're teetotal - ach when ye're teetotal, ye've always got a
rotten feeling that everybody's your boss.

People, you don't realise yet that I stand here as the representingtimpim,
the representative of the man who made the country what it is today, the working
35 man. Fellow workmen, I have been deputed, deputed, not only deputed, but asked,
to speak on behalf of the British working man. Now, these caputilists, these
blooming capuputilists, millionaires, where did they get their millions from?
Us. Yet these are the people, the rich, the people wi the money, an what do
they do? What do they do? What do they do? (Hic). Us. Yet these are the
40 people, the rich, they're the very first tae turn round and condemn a poor
workin fella - why? Because they see that poor fella goin home on a Saturday
night after a hard week's work just a wee bit drunk. (Hic). Is he not entittled? Is he not entittled as well as them? Yet they laugh at him, they
condemn him, they do. They laugh, they point the skinger of forn at him. They
45 say, "Look, look at that common labourer. Intosticated. Absolutely disgraceful.
Under the affluence of inkohol. Disgraceful." Why? What's the poor fella
tae do? Heavens, he's got tae get home. What about the rich people themselves?
It's all right for them, they've got big fast motor cars. They can go past
sae quick, you don't know whether they're drunk or sober. But mine you, I
50 know, I know, because -

I belong to Glasgow,
Dear old Glasgow town.
But there's something the matter with Glasgow,
For it's going round an round.
55 Ah'm only a common old workin lad,
As anyone can see,
But when I get a couple i drinks on a Saturday,
Glasgow belongs to me!

From Will Fyffe, *I Belong to Glasgow*,
(World Records / EMI SH200, 1975; first
recorded, 1929).

Notes

What do they do? Us (39) puns on *do* 'swindle'. *These are the people* (39-40) would clash, in current Glasgow idiom, with the football chant *we arc the people*.

The speaker is portrayed as having slurred speech as a result of being drunk. Hence the mispronunciations of *capitalists* as *caputilists* (36), *entitled* as *entittled* (43) and *intoxicated* as *intosticated* (45); and the spoonerisms *skinger of form* (44) and *affluence of inkohol* (46), with the additional happy pun on *affluence*. There are a number of cacuminal /s, z/ which may be part of the stereotype of drunken rather than of localised speech. The only features associated (stereotypically) with Glasgow are glottal realisations of /t/ and fronted realisations of /u/. Fyffe does not attempt to imitate the Glasgow intonation pattern. Postvocalic /r/ is deleted in *labourer* (45).

4.2   Stanley Baxter

4.2.1   "The Professor"

In the past, one of the favourite arguments of those who wished to suppress non-standard varieties of English was that they lacked the universal intelligibility of St E. Although local dialects, and even accents, do potentially present problems of communication to non-speakers, this is often exaggerated, both from hostility to the dialect as a means of communication, and from local pride in its distinctiveness. The supposed unintelligibility of Glasgow English is the running joke in a series of sketches featuring a character called 'The Professor', created by Alex Mitchell for the Glasgow comedian Stanley Baxter in the 1950s, and performed by Baxter on stage and radio, and latterly on television. The Professor is an outsider to Glasgow who sets himself up as an authority on its customs and language, but who invariably misinterprets everything he hears. His mistakes are clear to the audience, because the dialect is not, of course, unintelligible at all. The text below is an edited version of one of these sketches, broadcast by Scottish Television in January 1980.

TEXT 17   ⚭

Thank you, thank you so much, you're most kind. And may I say how exhilirating it is to sojourn once more in this charming citadel of tradition and culture. By a happy chance, my arrival coincided with the ancient and picturesque festival of Hogmanay, or as it is termed in the native patois, "Ra big booze up."
5 It was my good fortune to meet with a gentleman who invited me to accompany him to the sacred Hogmaniacal rites in a residence in the remote southern terrain of the city, known as "Ra Sooside." When I suggested that it might be expedient to engage a taxi cab, my new found friend mentioned a lady's name. "Nora," he said, "Nora blidy chance." Before I could question him as to the
10 lady's identity, he made certain obscure references to snow and to the Yukon. "Snow faur," he stated. "Yukon hoof it." Then we commenced to walk to our destination.

When we reached the residence that was to be the scene of the ceremonies,
I was more than a whit surprised when the gentleman who had conducted me there
15 revealed to me that not a few of the guests were of Chinese ancestry.   "See,"
he said, "he is Hauf Foo, he is Nearly Foo, and he is Bung Foo."   A guest who,
with delightful informality, was reclining on the floor was designated "Foo
Asawulk."   A few minutes later, the bells that signified the demise of the old
year rang out.   The merry sound called forth a spate of good wishes from the
20 assemblage to a Mister Wananaw.   "A good new year tae Wananaw," they sang.

But ere the clamour of the bells died away, the singing stopped, and the
guests became silent.   Awe-struck, they stared at the doorway.   There stood a
mysterious lady.   She had obviously braved the torrential rain in order to at-
tend the Hogmaniacal ceremony, and she was soaked to the skin.   Addressing the
25 gathering, she disclosed her identity.   "I am Drookit," she stated.   Immediately, the gathering hailed her as a goddess.   "Goddess," they cried, "Goddess
months since she had a waash."   In her lilting tongue, she wished me well in
the haunting words with which I now bid you farewell, "Och awan, och awan, och
awan get knoatit."   Delightful.   Thank you so much.   Good evening.

Notes

Hogmaniacal (6) is a nonce formation on *Hogmanay*, the Scottish New Year cele-
brations, with a pun on *maniac*.   *Nora* (9) is *not a*, plausible with raised /ɔ/
and tap [ɾ] for /t/.   This punning spelling is also used for *no(t) the*.   *Yukon*
(11) is *you can*.   *Snow faur* (11) is *it's not far*.   *Hauf Foo* (16) is *half full*.
Foo Asawulk (17-18) is *full as a whelk*.   *Wananaw* (20) is *one and all*.   *Goddess*
(26) is *God it's*.   *Och awan get knoatit* (28-9) is *oh, (go) away and get knotted*.

The Professor is portrayed as an RP speaker, with a few St ScE characteristics, such as postvocalic /r/;   and as an elderly man with an unusually formal
turn of phrase which is old-fashioned.

4.2.2 "Parliamo Glasgow"

In his "Parliamo Glasgow" sketches, also for Baxter, which first appeared in
1960, Mitchell continued the same type of joke as in "The Professor."   These
sketches originated as a parody of a television programme, "Parliamo Italiano."
The audience are shown supposed Glasgow words, divided up so that part resem-
bles a foreign or foreign-seeming word.   When the item is completed and read
aloud, it is revealed as a phrase or sentence in the dialect.   Part of the
humour lies in the pompous glosses and fatuous etymologies which are given.
Again the unintelligibility is an artefact, achieved by orthographic devices,
in particular the elimination of word boundaries.   As mentioned above, this
has been much imitated.   An early precursor is Bill Tait's (c. 1940) cartoon
caption, "Yaffayat? Whityatyaffa?"   'Are you off a yacht? What yacht are you
off of?'   The text below is from a sketch written for a pantomime in the King's
Theatre, Glasgow, with the capitalised items displayed to the audience.

TEXT 18

Woman: Oh, I'm so excited! I've found a man who looks up to me!

Man: A man who looks up to you? Where did you meet the midget? Oh, I know,
he's raweewanwirrawalliz.

Woman: In the name o' heaven! What kind of word is *that*?

Man: You should know it. It's used in your native city. Give me the book.
(Takes up Parliamo Glasgow book). Parliamo Glasgow, Lesson 1. Here we are:

      RAWEEWANWIRRAWALLIZ

The small gentleman with the artificial teeth. Now, if we remove certain syllables - thank you, ladies - we have the important word:

10   WANWIRRA

A gentleman arriving home late will use this word as he explains to his wife
that he had:

      WANWIRRAPALZ

When she learns that he has been socialising with his friends, she may well
15 add two other words to *wanwirra*, and so we have:

      JEWAANTWANWIRRAHEID?

Of course, if these two additions are removed,

      WANWIRRA

can be used in a complimentary sense. Thus, when a young gallant enthuses at
20 the sight of a well-built maiden, he will add two words to give us the graceful tribute:

      AFANCIRAWANWIRRABOADI

   And so we come to lesson 2. This demonstrates vividly how freely Glaswegians
have borrowed from the Japanese language. To a gentleman who is partial to a
25 refreshment we apply the old Japanese phrase:

      HEKINTAKA NOFASKINFU

To this we may add:

      FORMOSA

Woman: Formosa?

30 *Man:* Yes:

      FORMOSA RATYMEEZBUNGFU

The wife of the bibulous gentleman may begin her protest with the Japanese
word:

      SAMURAI

35 adding a Gaelic word to form the accusation:

      SAMURAISTOCIOUS

Her husband Sam may wish her to be silent, using yet another Japanese word:

      DATSUN

To this he appends the word *uffarat* to emphasize his request:

40   DATSUNUFFARAT

One can understand the lady's annoyance as she beseeches her mother to:

      HONDA

This is used in conjunction with another Japanese word which completes the
sinister command:

HONDAZATPOKURMURRA

Her mother hands her the poker and the husband quails when his wife utters the dread word:

HITACHI

making it even more menacing with the added word *geisha*:

GEISHA HITACHI

Suddenly, her mother lapses into Spanish with the advice:

OLE

She directs her daughter Sarah:

OLE INTYIMSERA

The warlike mother continues in Spanish, urging her daughter to chastise the husband further. She cries:

SENOR

SENOR FITUPIZBAHOOKI

Let's look at Lesson 3 now. Ah, this deals with romance. A young gentleman enamoured of a maiden will start with the Arabic word:

AWSHIZZA

He adds a word to complete his love-cry:

AWSHIZZASMASHUR!

But a friend may not approve of his choice of sweetheart, and will caution him with a word derived from the Italian:

BAGATELLE

He precedes this with *awshizza* and inserts the letter *y*, and so reveals the stern warning:

AWSHIZZABAGATELLYE

But the ardent wooer might reject this frank assessment of the young lady and declare:

WHIRRAPERRA

This word refers to the maiden's physical attributes. It is most often heard in the graceful compliment:

WHIRRAPERRABRISTULZ

Should the young lady reject her admirer's addresses, she will probably borrow two words from the Serbo-Croat language. First:

WIDRATNO

and second:

MAKYIBOAK

And so we have:

WIDRATNOMAKYIBOAK.

Notes

The capitalised items can be read as follows: *the wee wan wi the wallies* (3),
with /r/ for /ð/; *wan wi the pals* (13), i.e. a drink; *(do) ye waant wan wi
the heid* (16), i.e. a blow with the head; *Ah fancy the wan wi the boady* (22);
he can tak an awfu skinfu (26), i.e. of alcohol; *for most i the time he's
bung fu* (31); *Sam, you're ay stocious* (36) - in fact *ay* has /ʌi/, not the /ae/
of *samurai*; *that's enough i that* (40), with /d/ for /ð/; *haund us that poker,
mother* (45); *gie us a hit at ye* (50), with [ʔ] for the /z/ of *us*; *oh, lay
intae him, Serah* (54); *send yer fit up his bahookie* (58); *aw, she's a smasher*
(63); *aw, she's a bag, Ah tell ye* (69); *whit a pair i bristols* (75), with
[ɾ] for /t/; *would that no mak ye boak* (82).

Punctuation has been altered slightly from the original.

4.2.3 "Parliamo Glasgow" song

The following song was written for Baxter by Hector Nicol, also for pantomime,[45]
and after the fashion of "Parliamo Glasgow."

TEXT 19

        Geeza punna burra furra murra,
        Geeza baura choklit furra wean,
        Seeza tenna fags, huv yezonni tottie bags,
        Tae pit ratotties in til Agit hame?
    5   Pirrit oanaslate, Ahl pye ye zeftar,
        Azzawa tae seera panti mime.
        Anif yuzkin say ramorra,
        Orrabest an itznae borra,
        Yezkin parliamo Glasgow orratime.

Translation

Give me a pound of butter for my mother; give me a bar of chocolate for the
baby; give me a ten of fags; have you any potato bags, to put the potatoes
in till I get home? Put it on account, I'll pay you later. I'm off to see the
pantomime. And if you can say 'tomorrow', 'all the best' and 'it's no bother',
you can 'parliamo Glasgow' all the time.

Notes

Azzawa (6) 'I is away' is a solecism. *Aw the best* (8), a farewell, and *nae
bother* (8) 'no problem' are idiomatic local utterances. Two phonetic variables
which are prominent here, as in T17 and T18, are tap [ɾ] for intervocalic /t/
and changes affecting initial and medial /ð/.

---

45 This poem has appeared in print before, and I have seen a cutting of it,
    but have been unable to trace the source.

4.3   Rikki Fulton

When he plays a local character, the Glasgow comedian Rikki Fulton usually
portrays him as gauche and provincial, or as what a Glaswegian might call 'ignorant' or 'thinks he's gemm'. He puts across a brash cheerfulness of which
the main linguistic correlate is a tendency to hypercorrections and mispronunciation. The sketch below was written by R. S. Andrews, and this is a transcript of Fulton's rendering of it for Scottish Television. Like "Parliamo
Glasgow", this is a parody of an established television genre, in this case the
cookery lesson.

TEXT 20, "Dirty Dicky Dandruff"

Aw, hello there, housewives, an welcome once again tae Durty Dick's Motorways
Caff, for another gander at how tae cook up the muck - the mess - the meals
that we serve oot to wir clientele. Now, this week I'm goin tae - for tae show
you how tae prepare one of my unique home made pies, or, as they are known on
the M1, the foot an mouth specials.

Now, wir first requirement tonight is a bakin bowl. Here we have a bakin
bowl, and that's the sheep's heid which I will tell ye aboot later. Goad, it
looks lik a wummin Ah used tae go oot wi. Now, intae this bowl I have placed
a kinna hauf pound of flour, a cupful of waater, and a big daud i butter. And
after that, of course, ye have to - oh, by the way, just - Ah might just di-
verge for a monument - Ah've had a couple i cheeky letters about me no waashin
ma hauns before Ah've handled edible foodstuffs. So, well, fair's fair, Ah
mean, a bit i hygeine never hurt anybody, ye know what Ah mean. So Ah'd just
like tae tell ye, before Ah came on the air Ah gave the offending appendages
a good scrubbin wi soap an waater, an Ah waasht ma hands as well.

Anyway, now, in here, as I say, we've got this mixture that we're goin tae
sort i - give it a good knead, because it needs a good knead, if anything needed a good - (sneezes). Jings, Ah hope Ah'm no comin oan for a cold.
Wance ye've goat it intae a kinna consistency tae tim out oan tae the thing,
so that ye can roll it intae a pastry - fortunately, my assistant chef, Clarty
Claude, has made up some pastry for me. Would you see us the pastry, Clarty,
please. Ya mug, ye. Right intae the sink, there, look at that. Never mind,
Ah'll wring that oot. Heh, Clarty, how many times've Ah told you no tae pit
your Y-fronts in wi the dinner dishes? That's ridiculous that, could ruin the
elastic.

Now, here we have this bit of pastry - jist hing on a sec, would ye? (Stamps
on a cockroach). Now we put this in the bottom of a pan, like so. And now,
of course, we require the filling for the pie. I may say - Goad, these bloody
big cockroaches, trip ye up as soon as look at ye. Away, ya durty beast!
Gaun ye! Now, throughout the ages, Ah mean, folk have - flyin tonight, eh?
(Swipes at a cockroach).

Now, we should have something really scrumptious in here tae pit in the pie.
Aw, heh, Clarty, that is ridiculous. (Another pair of Y-fronts is found in
the freezer). Got tae watch what ye're - by the way, I perhaps should tell you
that - Ah wouldnae worry aboot that, it's next door's. (A dead cat is found
in the freezer). Here we have the very best kind of scrumptious pie-filling -
get away, ya durty beast, gaun ye! (Swipes at a cockroach). Listen, if you
don't get - heh, we might as well use these. (Puts cockroach in pie). Well,
it's protein, ye know what Ah mean. Now, this is the best kind of pie-fillin,

40   cos this is the kinna leftovers that auld Jessie, the cleaner, has picked up in
     her travels.   Aw, aw, aw, heh, Clarty, you've been makin your rock buns a bit
     too hard have ye no?   (A pair of dentures is found attached to a rock bun).
     Look, that might come in handy later oan.   Now, we take the pie-fillin and we
     put it intae the - dear God help us! - and we pit it into the pie there and we
45   scrimle it aboot there, and we pit the sheep's heid right oan the tap.   (The
     sheep's head is uncleaned and complete with horns).

         Now, we want tae marinate this in a little white wine, and this seems tae
     be quite good stuff.   Ah, it's no bad that.   (Takes a mouthful and spits it
     into the pie).   That's aboot the right amount, a moothful and a hauf.   Now, we
50   cover this whole thing with another daud of pastry, just lik that, and this is
     where mebbe the teeth'll come in handy, crimp the edges, just tae make it nice
     and neat.   And ye bung this in the oven, for anythin up to two oors, or until
     such times as it blows up.   Of course, like any other good chef, I already
     have one cooking, and I'll go and get that now from the oving.   And we - oh
55   ya!   (The dish is hot).   Here, here we have this delicious delicacy which is
     guaranteed tae pit hairs on your chest, and make you run faster than the Bionic
     Wummin.

         Well, that's all for this week, chinas;   I do hope that you'll look in again
     next week, when I'll be making the humble Scotch salmon and turning it into an
60   Italian treat which they call 'salmonella'.   Bon appetit.

Notes

Gaun ye (30, 37) and *oh ya* (54-5) are conventionally suppressed oaths.

Next door's (35) is short for *the people next door's* with postponed possessive
marker.   *Picked up in her travels* (40-41) is a colloquial idiom - her travels
have been around the kitchen.   The *Bionic Woman* (56-7) is a television character.

    Fulton does not follow the script very closely, and it is therefore not
surprising that he also substitutes dialectal for standard forms, and vice versa
On the whole these substitutions tend to balance each other out.   He interpo-
lates *chinas* (58), one of his own catch-phrases.   The hypercorrection *oving*
(54), the nonce word *scrimle* (45), and the deliberate mispronunciations *monumen*
(11) 'moment' and *marienate* (47) are also his own.

4.4 Advertisements, Radio Clyde   oΩ

Small advertisers often use the local speech variety as a means of identifying themselves with the area. Roadrunner Motorcycles and Masterfreeze (a frozen food chain), both have adverts on Radio Clyde which try to give the impression of local people, with whom the listeners can identify, just on their way to, or just returning from, their premises.

4.4.1 Roadrunner Motorcycles

The Roadrunner adverts are constructed as dialogues in which one speaker recommends the shop, and the other acts out the desired enthusiastic response of the listener. In T21, the speakers have 'Kelvinside' accents, and in T22, working class Glasgow accents. The Roadrunner is a television cartoon character, which makes a 'beep beep' call. 'Roadrunner' is also the name of a well known brand of motorcycle tyre.

TEXT 21

A. Hello, Frank. What's the big rush?

B. Oh, Ah need to get home in less than an hour tonight.

A. An hour? I'll be home in less than fifteen minutes, and I stay further away than you do.

B. How can you manage that? What with traffic, an getting out of the car park, an so on?

A. Och, it's easy. I was down seeing the free video films with my son, at Roadrunner Motorcycles in Clydebank on Sunday - ye know the place that has that 'beep beep' advert on radio. Well, I bought myself a lovely little Kawasaki Z200, which gives me about a hundred miles per gallon, gets me to work in no time at all, and no worry about parking meters. And what with a free helmet, gloves, and qualified driving instructions, it must be the best thing I've done in years.

B. What makes do they stock?

A. Aw, Kawasakis, Hondas, Suzukis, Yamahas - they've got them all down there.

B. What do you call that place again?

C. (Beep beep). Roadrunner Motorcycles, Dunbarton Road, Clydebank.

Notes

Stay (3) means 'live permanently' in St ScE. *Than you do* (4) is formal - *do* is not normally present as a sentence pro-form in St ScE. *Per gallon* (10) is also formal - cf. *to the gallon*.

   The raised [æ] is very much in evidence here, sometimes reaching [ɛ] e.g. *park* (6). The realisations of /ʌi/ and /ae/ are rather inconsistent. Speaker A has the 'Kelvinside' [æːᵉ] in *qualified* (12) and *driving* (12), and [ӓɪ] in *time* (11), but /ae/ in *my* (7) and realisations closer to /ʌi/ than /ae/ in the /ʌi/ words *cycles* (8) and *miles* (10). Speaker B has /ae/ in the /ʌi/ word *tonight* (2). Both combine these real or supposed upper middle class variants

with glottal realisations of /t/, and with the local intonation pattern, in a
way typical of the stereotype. Cf. also *hour* (3) with an epenthetic vowel.
They both speak in high pitched voices, which is again stereotyped, Kelvinside
men supposedly being effeminate.

TEXT 22

A. Haw, Jimmy, any idea where this place Roadrunner is?

B. Aye, it's jist up the road a bit, used tae be the auld Regal Cinema. Hey,
what's your hurry?

A. Aw, they've goat this daft oaffer oan. They're sellin full face helmets
5   for fifteen quid - that's aboot hauf price. And they gie ye a free pair i
gloves when ye buy wan.

B. But that seems a good place for motorcyclists. The boay was thinkin i
gettin a wee bike.

A. Aye, well he'll no need tae buy a helmet, cos ye get a free helmet an
10 gloves when ye buy a bike there, an ye'll get qualified drivin instructions
for nothing.

B. When are they open?

A. Aw, that's the lights cheynged. Eh, they're open every day includin
Sunday.

15 *C.* (Beep beep). Roadrunner Motorcycles, Dunbarton Road, Clydebank.

Notes

Full (4) is /fʌl/. *The boay* (7) means 'my son' - names of members of the family take the definite article in Scots.

Both speakers here are heavily localised, but Speaker A uses a wider range
of stigmatised variants, including /w/ for /ʍ/ in *where* (1), and deletion of
/ð/ in *this* (1), which makes him sound the younger of the two. He preserves
/e/ before /r/ in *pair* (5) and *there* (10), and lengthens /z/ in *is* (1). Cf.
W. E. (3.4). The opening greeting, *Haw, Jimmy*, is a stereotype.

4.4.2 Masterfreeze

The Masterfreeze adverts use a working class female voice speaking very excit-
edly about the latest bargains at Masterfreeze. A local linguistic item which
is heavily stereotyped here is the construction with *see* which focuses the
theme of a sentence. Since the function of this is to establish the common
ground of an exchange, and the *see* fragment takes 'open' (high rising) intonation, the effect here is to give the impression that these are not monologues
but one side of a dialogue, of which the other side belongs to the listener.

TEXT 23

See Marshall's Chunky Chickens? See Masterfreeze? See forty-nine pence a
pound? See me? No wonder Ah'm crowin. That's the price i Marshall's Chicken
at Masterfreeze this month. Forty-nine pence. Could ye credit it? There's
dozens more bargains besides. And a great competition too. Ye could win a
5   Pye fourteen inch portable tele, a Moulinex foodmixer, a Goblin Tea's Maid, a
scores of Chunky Chickens to be won at all branches. See me. See Masterfreeze

Notes

The opening sentence here is badly formed grammatically. Four noun phrases
have been fronted indiscriminately as thematic elements, and moreover, the
sentence *see me, no wonder Ah'm crowin* has been embedded between the other *see*
fragments and the main clause to which they relate. It is also unacceptable
to end an utterance with *see* fragments.

TEXT 24

See cakes? See ma man? He loves them. Specially when they come from Masterfreeze. And Masterfreeze have a special offer on Tiffany's cakes. Oh, ma
mouth's waterin already. Sponge roll wi raspberry filling, chocolate sponge,
ginger cake, sponge sandwich wi orange or lemon filling, chocolate or coffee
sandwich, or walnut sandwich. Oh, Ah'm puttin oan weight jist sayin it! But
who cares! When each i these big, oven-fresh cakes costs only thirty-nine p.?
See cakes. See ma man. See Masterfreeze.

Notes

Raspberry (3) /raspɪre/ and *sandwich* (4) /saŋwɪdʒ/ have their St ScE forms.

4.5 The English press

One final stereotype which is worth including here as a last minute addition
is the 'dictionary dredging' approach to writing Scots. Scottish writers would
probably not see the Glasgow dialect as a candidate for this treatment, which
represents Scots as highly divergent lexically. This text was a leading article in *The Guardian* in the run-up to an important Glasgow by-election.

TEXT 24a, "Feeling foreign up the sporran"

MR ROY JENKINS, SDP candidate at the Glasgow Hillhead byelection, has been
sharply criticised for attempting to use the ancient Scottish word "hoddendoon"
which means frustrated, in a constituency speech. It has even been suggested
that this is not the sort of word Mr Jenkins habitually uses, and that he has
5   deliberately smuggled it into his vocabulary to ingratiate himself.

Though Mr. Jenkins has not replied publicly to these charges he is said by
usually reliable sources to be feeling extremely ramfeezled by them and even
to have been driven at times into a state of loundering kippage. The allegations, Mr Jenkins is believed to have told friends, amount to nothing less
10 than a humgruffianly humdudgeon, designed to create the maximum possible mixter
maxter of argle-bargle, flyte and collieshangie.

Mr Jenkins is understood to attribute the circulation of such calumnies to
"a rickle of camstairy clishmaclavers, gilpy-like gaberlunzies and murgeoning
rintherouts" in rival political parties. In a speech to be delivered in
15 Hillhead later this week, he is expected to describe the allegations as "simply
the flaffing, fuffing and flichtering of fozy fikes". And he will advise
Hillhead voters not to attach so much as a firlot, forpit, or mutchkin of cre-
dence to such "gumplefoisted and wanchancy" attempts to beflum the people of
Hillhead.

20 Reports that Mr Jenkins had been overheard expressing the hope that "the
de'il might nirl the noops" of those guilty of such miscalling, and even that
they might be smitten with the braxy, were authoritatively discounted yesterday. And late last night an SDP spokesman said accounts of Mr Jenkins resentment should not be exaggerated. "Candidly," he added, "he disnae give a plack
25 about it, Jimmy."

(Sassanach readers seeking elucidation are referred to Chambers Twentieth
Century Dictionary, Edinburgh, £8.95, though in view of its definition of the
word Jenkins - "a society reporter; a toady" - this may not be much used by
the SDP.)

From The Guardian, 19 January 1982.

Notes

The Scots items selected are mostly literary or old-fashioned. Only lexical
items - not dialect word forms or syntax - are included, and indeed the writer
relies, as he states, on *Chambers Twentieth Century Dictionary*. Many of the
items were coined on phonesthetic principles between the seventeenth and nineteenth centuries, and reflect a taste in word formation which is no longer
fashionable. The quaint and bitcny tone is reminiscent of Kailyard literature.

LITERATURE
5.0 The texts

The texts in this chapter are taken from published sources, and are mostly
works of literature. After section 5.1, which illustrates some varieties related to Glasgow English, the texts are loosely grouped according to genre -
the novel and short story, drama, poetry and song, journalism and reminiscence.
The intention, however, is to cover a wide range of linguistic variation in
different contexts, and only incidentally to show the range and quality of
Glasgow writing.[46]

The series in which this volume appears is based on the realisation that
literary texts often provide richer specimens of a variety than do the speech
styles which can be captured in recordings. This is not only because of the
tendency of localised speakers to edit out non-standard lexis, lexical incidence and grammar when speaking to class-outsiders. There is also the fact
that many local words, idioms, and conversational clichés are used only occasionally when the opportunity is provided by a specific situation. The creative writer can, however, reproduce the situation along with the appropriate
linguistic choices; sometimes by means of the appropriate linguistic choices.

The St E written in Glasgow, and in Scotland generally, differs little from
St BrE except when colloquial, as, for instance, in T2, T69 and T70. The texts
in this chapter have therefore been selected predominantly from dialect writing.

5.1 Varieties related to Glasgow English

5.1.1 George Douglas Brown, *The House with the Green Shutters*

First published in 1901, this novel is set in Ayrshire, in a small town usually
identified with Ochiltree, near Ayr. Although there are some puzzling incon-
sistencies and idiosyncracies, the Scots forms which appear in the dialogue
are judged by McClure (1972) to be broadly acceptable as local dialect forms.
G. D. Brown was in reaction against the sentimental view of Scottish life presented by the 'Kailyard' novelists. His portrait of a small town shows a dom-
ineering and inarticulate bully, the Gourlay mentioned in the text, ruined by
his inability to keep up with progress. His fall is watched with vicious glee
by his male contemporaries, who form a kind of 'chorus'. In the passage below,
they have been discussing Gourlay's inordinate pride in his house, and com-
menting unfavourably on his choice of a wife. Johnny Coe recalls how the two
came to be married.

TEXT 25

"I ken fine how he married her," said Johnny Coe. "I was acquaint wi' her
faither, auld Tenshillingland owre at Fechars - a grand farmer he was, wi' land
o' his nain, and a gey pickle bawbees. It was the bawbees, and not the woman,
that Gourlay went after! It was *her* money, as ye ken, that set him on his
feet, and made him such a big man. He never cared a preen for *her*, and then

---

46 For a thematic selection, arranged for schools, see Thomson (1981). One
area which has not been covered here is television drama.

when she proved a dirty trollop, he couldna endure her look! That's what makes
him so sore upon her now. And yet I mind her a braw lass, too," said Johnny
the sentimentalist, "a braw lass she was," he mused, "wi' fine, brown glossy
hair, I mind, and, - ochonee! ochonee! - as daft as a yett in a windy day.
10 She had a cousin, Jenny Wabster, that dwelt in Tenshillingland than, and mony
a summer nicht up the Fechars Road, when ye smelled the honey-suckle in the
gloaming, I have heard the two o' them tee-heeing owre the lads thegither,
skirling in the dark and lauching to themselves. They were of the glaikit kind
ye can always hear loang before ye see. Jock Allan (that has done so well in
15 Embro) was a herd at Tenshillingland than, and he likit her, and I think she
likit him, but Gourlay came wi' his gig and whisked her away. She doesna lauch
sae muckle now, puir bodie!

> From George Douglas Brown, *The House with
> the Green Shutters*, ed. J. T. Low (Edin-
> burgh: Holmes McDougall, 1974), 36-7.

Notes

Embro (15) is Edinburgh. Notice *loang* (14), Scots *lang* 'long'. Such spellings
occur throughout the novel. McClure (1972: 160) suggests that ⟨oa⟩ may represent a down-gliding diphthong in forms like *oald* 'old' and *moar* 'more'. The
problem with spellings like ⟨loang⟩ is that the words do not normally take /o/.
Cf. the similar *awoe*, usually /ʌwɔ/ 'away' in Trotter (1901: 24). Speitel
(1975: 40) points out that there is an overlap in ScE between the realisations
of /o/ and /ɔ/, and in the transcriptions in Chapters 3 and 4, it was sometimes
difficult to decide between the two in words which can take either. The ⟨oa⟩
then may represent a raised variant of /ɔ/.

Notice the denseness of Scots lexis and lexical incidence in this text. The
morphology includes the Scots forms *-na*, enclitic negative particle, and *-it*,
verbal inflection, but cf. *-ing* throughout, and *themselves* (13). The syntax
is St E. This pattern of selection between standard and non-standard forms at
different linguistic levels is typical of Scottish literature, despite the use
of Scots here to represent a speech variety. The literary register of Scots
influences Glasgow writers to different extents up to the present time, and
makes it impossible to use the evidence of earlier texts negatively to establish the non-existence of forms. Traditional spellings, in particular, may or
may not conceal localised variants.

5.1.2 Tom Leonard, *If Only Bunty was Here*

Literary Scots, now often known as 'Lallans', has enjoyed a great vogue in this
century, especially as a medium for poetry. Its use in the novel and in drama
is limited by the demands of verisimilitude, but even here it has its place,
for instance in treating historical subjects. There is a small coterie of
writers and other enthusiasts who view Scots as a minority language and potentially a medium for mass communications in an independent Scotland. This and
other aspects of the Scottish literary scene are satirised in Leonard's radio
drama, *If Only Bunty was Here*, a sequence of sketches centring on a Glasgow
writer. To quote a spurious review on the back cover,

We must be grateful to Mr. Leonard for drawing out attention to
the Stephen Daedalus manqués of the post-war council housing estates. Rejecting the earnest "decency" of their upper lower
working class backgrounds, they eschewed existentialism and provocative blasphemy with their then innovatory Bic pens.

The scene below parodies the radio genre of the phone-in. Leonard gives the
following directions for the Newsreader ('Some Notes on the Cast', p. 2):

As he is meant to be a satire on some of the more lunatic elements
in the Lallans movement, a bit of exaggeration wouldn't go wrong.

TEXT 26

*A trio of gruff male voices bawl out "Wonderful Radio Twa" to the same tune as
the "Wonderful Radio One" refrain.*

MAN. Mony couthie folk are thocht tae hae gien up the ghaist the nicht, whan
thir plane plummitit -
5 *He is interrupted by a phone ringing, and picks it up.*
WOMAN. [*On phone.*] Is that Leon Trotsky?
MAN. Wha?
WOMAN. Is that the Trotsky phone-in programme? I've a question for Mr Trotsky.
MAN. Naw, laddie. This is wonderful Radio Twa yir on tae. There's naebuddy
10 here ca'd Trotsky. I think ye must hae got the wrang nummer.
WOMAN. I'm not a "laddie" - I'm a woman!
MAN. A whit?
WOMAN. I said I'm not a "laddie" - I'm a woman!
MAN. [*Shouting.*] I'm a man, dae ye hear? A great big hairy Scoatch man! Lea'
15 me alane!
WOMAN. This isn't "Candid Camera" by any chance is it?
MAN. Lassie, I wadna ken wha yir "Trotsky" is, nor I wadna ken whit yir "Candid
Camera" is. I happen tae be the chairman o' the Radio Twa Bannock-an'-But-
an'-Ben Preservation Society. Mind how ye spell it!
20 WOMAN. Oh, I'm terribly sorry if I've got the wrong number here. Just as a
matter of interest, what does your society do?
MAN. Ah weel, that's a secret between me an' ma fellow bannock-an'-but-an'-
ben preservers. But if ye're ever in a conversation whaur ye say "bannocks"
or "but-an'-bens" or "mealie-puddins", an' the chiel listenin' tae ye rolls
25 up his left troser-leg an' says, "Aye. Ding them doon!" - ye're in the
company of a bannoock-an'-but-an'-ben preserver!
WOMAN. I think I've heard a lot of your members on the radio, now that I know
who you are. As I say I'm terribly sorry - I thought this number was the
one given in Radio Times for the "Phone-in to Trotsky" programme. I wanted
30 to ask Mr Trotsky what effects he thought a revolution might have on our
beautiful English language.
MAN. Damn yir beautiful English language! It took me twal' year at a fee-
payin' schule tae learn tae talk it, then six - sorry, saxteen year wi' the
Bannock-an'-But-an'-Ben Society tae learn tae talk like this! Get aff the
35 line, ye ignorant bitch - I've got a centeenial ode tae feenish!

From Tom Leonard, *If Only Bunty was Here,
a drama sequence of totally undramatic
non-sequiturs* (Glasgow: Print Studio
Press, 1979), 13-14.

Notes

Candid Camera (16) is a television programme. Notice the correction into Scots in 33. *Gien up the ghaist* (3) 'given up the ghost' is a calque of a St E idiom. This happens quite often in Lallans. *Couthie* (3), *Scoatch* (14), *bannock* (18) and *but-an'-ben* (18-19) are Scots stereotypes. Some purists insist that *Scotch* can only modify non-human nouns, preferring *Scots* for human ones. Several of the Scots items here are probably obsolete in Glasgow speech - *twal'* (32), *saxteen* (33) and *ghaist* (3). *Chiel* (24), a stereotype of Northern Scots, exemplifies the eclecticism of Lallans.

5.1.3 "Hot Asphalt"

This is a Scottish folksong portraying the Irish immigrants of the nineteenth century, many of whom found work building roads. Glasgow itself and its Kelvingrove Museum are mentioned in the song.

TEXT 27

Oh, good morning til youse Glasgow boys, I'm glad to see youse well,
For I'm just as self conceited as any tongue can tell.
Oh, I've got a situation, or, a begob a fancy job,
I can whisper I've the weekly wage of eighteen bob.
5   It's a twelvenonth now come Easter since I left Glenory town
Along with my brother Barney for to mow the harvest down,
Ah, but now I wear a garnsey and around my waist a belt,
For I'm gaffer o'er the boys that makes the hot asphalt.

All the boys I have in under me outside and in the yard
10 Have the nerve to turn round, say I work them rather hard,
But if they rise my dander I give a murdrous shout,
Sure you'll see these lazy shakrins how they stir the tar about.
  In come a bobby to me the other day, he says "Now, McGuire,
  You might let me light my dudyen at your boiler fire."
15 For he placed hissel in at the fire, his coat tails up sae neat,
"Oh," says I, "my decent fella, for you'ld better mind your beat."

Says he, "My lads, I'm down on you, I have your bloomin' marks;
Sure I take you for a lot o' Tipperary barks."
Man I drew out from my shoulder and I hit him such a welt,
20 For I knocked him in the boiler full of hot asphalt.
  We pulled him from the boiler and we placed him into a tub,
  Among soap and warm water it is there we did rub and scrub,
  Oh but devil the bit of the tar come off till it got as hard as a stone
  Wi' the rubbin' and the scrubbin' sure you could hear the poor bobby
25   groan.
Wi' the rubbin' and the scrubbin' sure he catched his death o' cold,
For scientific purposes his body it was sold,
Into the Kelvingrove Museum he's hangin' by the belt,
An example to the boys that makes the hot asphalt.

From Norman Buchan and Peter Hall, eds.,
The Scottish Folksinger (Glasgow and
London: Collins, 1973) 147-8.

Notes

Youse (1) was perhaps not yet current in Scotland when the song was composed. Apart from one recorded occurrence in Scots, *dudyen* (14) is a HibE item. *Begob* (3) is a HibE stereotype. *Into* (28) for *in* occurs in O Sc, but in modern dialect is found mainly north of the Forth.

5.2   The novel and short story

As the largest city in Scotland, Glasgow naturally figures as a setting in many
works of fiction. Extensive lists of Glasgow novels can be found in Burgess
(1972). Not all of these portray working class characters, or make use of the
local dialect. Some of the best-known of those which do are represented here,
along with a number of recent texts, including short stories.

5.2.1   J. J. Bell, *Wee Macgreegor*

J. J. Bell's *Wee Macgreegor* and its sequels are sequences of loosely linked
short stories which first appeared in the Glasgow *Evening Times* in 1901. Wee
Macgreegor is a cheeky kid of primary school age who usually gets what he wants,
and gets away with his innocently naughty pranks, because he is so 'cute' that
nobody can deny him anything. The language is idiomatic, without, for instance,
an exaggerated denseness of Scots lexis, but with few indications of geographical origin within Central Scotland. Most of the items in the·Glossary are
general in Scots.

Bell (1933: 8) writes:

> I am well aware that I have been suspected of eavesdropping on
> tramway cars and elsewhere, and of furtively lurking in close-
> mouths, and in sundry other places, in order to gain my knowledge,
> such as it is, of the Glasgow, or Lowland, dialect; but the truth
> is that, just as I have never deliberately "studied" a fellow-
> creature, I had never made any effort to "learn" the speech of the
> people of the period. While I was familiar with the older men in
> my father's factory, who used the vernacular as a matter of course,
> I feel certain that I acquired little or nothing there. Indeed, I
> cannot doubt that from the lips of my paternal grandmother, a
> lady of the old school, who died when I was seven, fell all the
> quaint words and phrases - many of them embodied in nursery rhymes
> - into my memory, there to lie quiet till the years should bring
> a use for them.

This would push the speech model back into the early part of the last century.

The passage below is from a story in which Wee Macgreegor lords it over
another boy, who dares him to climb a lamp post, knowing that the paint is wet.
His father conspires with him to hide the mishap from his mother, but the tur-
pentine with which they try to remove the paint turns out to be black lacquer,
and they are caught in a terrible mess. The mother is furious, but allows
herself to be mollified by the touching attempts of each to take the blame upon
himself. By the end, Wee Macgreegor is even pushing his luck to see if he can
go to the McOstrich party.

TEXT 28

"Dod, ay," said John agreeably. "We mauna interfere wi' his lessons. Are
ye gaun yer messages noo, Lizzie?"
"Aye. I'll no' be lang. I'm vexed I didna get them done afore ye cam'
hame, but I wis gey thrang the day, an' Mrs. M'Ostrich cam' in an' blethered
hauf the efternune. She's gaun to ha'e anither pairty, but she's no' askin'
Mistress Purdie."
"She's askin' Macgreegor, though."
"Macgreegor 'll get, if he's a guid laddie....Weel, I'll awa' afore the

shopes shut. Luk efter wee Jeannie, if she waukens, an' hear Macgreegor his
10 spellin's, if he's ready afore I come back....Macgreegor, whit wey ha'e ye
gotten yer guid breeks a' twistit-like? Pu' them roon' at the knees, an' see
an' learn the meanin's furbye the spellin's."
She hurried away, and silence reigned for a little in the kitchen.
John resumed his paper, but ere long he glanced over it at his son. He felt
15 that all was not well with the youngster.
"Are ye wearit, ma mannie?" he asked kindly.
"Naw."

"Are ye no' weel?"
"I'm fine," replied Macgregor in a voice that belied his words
20 Three minutes passed, and John took another glance.
His son was holding the lesson-book to one side, and appeared to be examining with much minuteness the knees of his knickerbockers.
"Are ye no' comin' to sit aside me the nicht, Macgreegor?" John inquired,
dropping his paper and stretching out a big inviting hand.
25 Macgregor hastily resumed his studies.
"Come awa'," his father went on. "I dinna like ye sittin' there as if you
an' me had cast oot....Are ye no' comin'?"
The youngster shook his head; then gulped slightly.
John got up and went over to where the penitent sat. "Macgreegor, ye best
30 tell us a' aboot it," he said gently. "Whit's vexin' ye, ma wee man?"
After a little while Macgregor explained his unhappy plight, easing at the
same time his stiffened limbs.
"Puir laddie," said his father sympathetically. "It wis a dirty trick to
play on ye," he added indignantly.
35 "I wiped ma haun's on his heid," Macgregor observed with some satisfaction,
"an' I wud ha'e gi'ed him a bashin', if a daft auld wife hadna come oot an' - "
"It's a peety it wisna yer auld breeks," said John reflectively. "I doot
yer Maw'll be sair pit aboot....I wonder if we canna get them cleaned afore
she comes hame. If I had a wee drap terpentine noo, I wud try it."
40 "There terpentine in the wee press ablow the jaw-box," said Macgregor
eagerly. "She wis cleanin' ma auld breeks wi' some the day."

From J. J. Bell, "Green Paint" in *Wee
Macgreegor* (London: Nelson and Sons,
1933), 70-73.

Notes

The apostrophe as in *M'Ostrich* (4) was formerly the usual way of writing the
abbreviated *Mac-*. Notice *pairty* (5) rather than *perrty*. *Like* in *twisted-like*
(11) is a mitigating particle used in Scots following adjectives and past
participles, and as a sentence tag. *Ye best* (29) 'you had best' is colloquial.
Several open class quantifiers in Scots do not take *of*, thus *a wee drap terpentine* (39).

5.2.2 McArthur and Long, *No Mean City*

No Mean City is probably the best known Glasgow novel. It is the prototype
for Burgess's (1972)'gangland' category. One of the writers, Alexander
McArthur, was a baker, who took up writing as a career. The other, H. Kingsley
Long, was a professional writer who collaborated with him. A few items of
local slang are known only or mainly from this novel - *nit the jorrie* 'leave
the girl alone', *breadsnapper*, *clabber jigging* and *hairy* 'hatless girl' ('girl'
in Agutter, 1979).

The portrait of slum life presented in the novel is unrelievedly harsh and
sordid. The central protagonist, Johnny Stark, the 'Razor King', lives only
to maintain his macho image, and comes to a predictably bad end via alcohol,
violence and prison, taking with him his formerly respectable wife and her
respectable lover, and incidentally brutalising a series of young women. His
brother and schoolfriends, who try to raise themselves above the grinding poverty of the slum, meet only disappointment and humiliation. The novel has
been through many reprints, and is still available. It compares unfavourably
with, for instance, Michael Thelwell's *The Harder they Come*, which tells a
similar story in a Jamaican setting. The tragedy of a broken society, the
crushing demands of a traditional culture, and the animal sexuality of the
central character are absent in *No Mean City*. One can only suppose that it
remains popular because it presents a picture of Glasgow which readers wish
to believe.

In the first extract below, the unfortunate Lizzie disappoints her girlfriend Mary in order to go out with Razor King. In the second, his brother
Peter, who no longer lives at home, calls into the house and finds Razor King
just rising from his bed, and their mother out assisting at a birth. An unusually lengthy conversation follows.

TEXT 29

Mary Halliday, a girl of twenty-two, sallow, but well-built and not ill-looking,
called at a quarter-past seven and was immediately informed in chorus of
Lizzie's date with Razor King.
  "An' what wull I do?" she demanded indignantly. "Go out on my tod (alone)?"
5   "Be sensible, for Jesus' sake," retorted Lizzie sharply.
  "Oh, sensible!" railed Mary, looking round for sympathy. "What do you make
of that, eh?"
  "Don't be daft awthegither, Merry. It's only just for this evening. Ah'll
be seeing you again all right an' then we might baith manage to get a click
10 somewhere, eh?"
  With her hands clasped over her handbag in front of her, Mary looked at
Lizzie suspiciously and Lizzie hurried on, hoping to escape argument and further protest.
  "Come on an' see me away, Merry. I'll no keep you long."
15 Rather sullenly Mary nodded and followed Lizzie out on to the landing.
Half-way down the stairs to the narrow close Lizzie paused, caught Mary by the
elbow and spoke to her with earnest impressiveness.
  "As sure as Ah'm going down they sterrs wi' you, Merry, I didn't know I
was going out with Razor King until I met him at the Coffin Building alang
20 there. I was all put about when I met him. I didn't know he was such a nice
fella, Merry."
  Mary became more cordial as she listened to this explanation which was half
an apology, and she began to think of Johnnie Stark with less resentment.

"Ah wull say," she agreed, "that he never uses the razors on lassies. Mebbe
25 he's no sae bod. But better you than me, Lizzie, for aw that. Ah would take
my time if I was you."

From Alexander McArthur and H. Kingsley
Long, *No Mean City* (London: Corgi Books,
1973; first published 1935), 77-8.

Notes

Notice ⟨err⟩ spellings in *Merry* (8) and *sterrs* (18). *Click* (9) is contemporary
slang for a date. Cf. more recent *lumber*. *Bod* (25) is a misprint for *bad* in
this edition.

TEXT 30

"You're lookin' grand," Johnnie went on evenly, "collar and tie and aw!
You should have said you were coming. The lassies wid have stayed in for ye,
nae doot. And Ah wid have bin in ma paraffin, tae. Ah widnae be surprised if
the Donaldson woman wid have put off bairnin' for a wee while so that Mither
5 cud be here tae greet ye instead of helpin' to bring another breadsnapper intae
the world."
"Aw, to hell with your kiddin', Johnnie! I was just out from the warehouse
to see a customer for Mr. Morgan, and being not far from here I thought I wid
look in to see Mither before I went back. So she's away to the Donaldson wo-
10 man? There's some will never learn sense. Eight of a family already and she
forty-four of five if she's a day....She should ask some of the lassies what
tae do to stop accidents, or mebbe how to poison that drunken old man of hers."
Johnnie began to rub his hair vigorously with his towel and he replied at
jerky intervals.
15 "Education, Peter - we're no' aw so educated as you. You'll be for labour
these days, mebbe - socialism by slow degrees - more schooling for the kids -
an' less kids for the schools - what wey should the workin' classes have families they canny afford? I know - dumb brutes like yon Donaldson - folk who
havenae the sense or the guts tae hold a respectable job - only the one plea-
20 sure in life, breeding fodder for the capitalist cannons. Oh, ay! Ah've heard
it aw. Ah can almost talk the language."
"If Ah'm anything," his brother retorted. "Ah'm a Communist, but Ah'm no'
interested in politics at all. For all I care Donaldson and the like of him
can go on havin' kids till he's played out. I'm only saying I wouldny be for
25 having a big family myself."

ibid, 90-1

Notes

The authors comment on the term *in ma paraffin*(3) elsewhere in the novel (ibid:
28):

> In the language of the Gorbals, he was "well put on" and proud
> of his "paraffin". There was actually a paraffin dressing on his
> sleek black hair, and, perhaps there may be some association of
> ideas between slumland's passion for smoothed and glistening crops
> and its general term for a smart appearance.

Bairnin' (4) in the sense of 'giving birth' appears to be a solecism. The
word *bairn* 'child' is now normally replaced by *wean* in the West of Scotland.
Rather strangly, the joking term *breadsnapper* (5) is the one most commonly
used for 'baby' in the dialogue of the novel. *Who* (18) is less colloquial than
that as a relativiser.

5.2.3 Helen Pryde, 'The McFlannels'

Helen Pryde's 'McFlannels' stories first appeared as radio sketches. The
McFlannels are a young working class couple with small children, who are anxious to get on in life, especially the wife, Sarah. In her speech, Sarah is
considerably less localised than her husband, except when angry or upset. In
the passage below, the family have just moved into a slightly larger house, and
are trying to sleep in the first night. One of the children is frightened by
a little dog which has come in without anyone's knowledge. Willie, the husband,
tries to put the child back to bed. In the morning when the animal is discovered, Sarah objects to encouraging it, but of course, she is won over, and the
family keep it. Notice how Sarah's more proper speech is a way of trying to
manipulate the rest of the family, by maintaining a social distance from them.

TEXT 31

'Look, son,' he said. 'There's naeb'dy here. Come on away back tae yer
wee beddie-baw.'
   'No! I don't want to hear thon noise again.'
   'Whit kinna noise wis it?'
   Matt cleared his throat and gave what nobody recognized was a fairly good
imitation of a dog barking in its sleep. Husband and wife looked at each other
in the flickering matchlight. 'Ach, ye've been dreamin'!' said Willie. 'There's
nae sich noise. Sure there isnae, Mammy?'
   Sarah, bone-weary, ached for bed. 'Ach, come on.' said she. 'He can sleep
at the foot of our bed to-night. He'll be all right to-morrow night when wee
Peter's here and they're both in the bed. It's him being sleeping on the sofa
that's upset him. Come on, son. Come on, Willie.'
   Because it was Saturday the household was late in rising the next morning.
Willie was on 'short time.' The four of them were seated at breakfast when
the door creaked. Matt jumped in his chair.
   'What's up with you now?' demanded his mother.
   'The door!' murmured Matt, wide-eyed. 'The door's opening!'
   And so it was, slowly, and for no apparent reason. Then gradually, about
six inches from the ground, a small black snout appeared, followed timidly by
a hairy little face lit by two bright eyes.
   'A rat!' gasped Sarah, petrified.
   Polly, from her seat at the far side of the table, saw more than the others
- a lifted, uncertain forepaw, a shrinking little body, ending in a ragged but
plucky tail.
   'Oh, a wee puppy!' she shrieked delightedly.
   'A puppy?' echoed Matt.
   Both of them bounded to the door, but the dog, scared, raced for the shelter
of the parlour and had taken refuge below the sofa before they reached it.
Willie was on the heels of his children. 'Whaur is it?' he demanded. The
three of them peered under the sofa making coaxing noises of all kinds, but the
frightened dog merely growled in response. 'That beast's scared tae daith,'
said Willie, lying flat on his front. 'Serah!' he yelled. 'Bring us a saucer
o' milk.'
   'I'll do nothing of the kind!' came back the indignant reply. 'Kick it
down the stair.'
   'Aw, Serah, ye widnae see the puir beast starvin'! It musta came in wi' the
flittin' last night.'
   'Well, the sooner it's out the better I'll be pleased. Come on you, and
finish your porridge.'

                              Helen W. Pryde, *The First Book of the*
                              McFlannels (London: Nelson and Sons,
                              1947), 32-3.

Notes

Beddie-baw (2) is baby-talk, and *sure* (8) as a marker in interrogation is a
feature of children's speech. Notice *being sleeping* (11), where an *-ing* complement follows the *-ing* form of *be*. *Down the stair* (35) is intermediate between Scots *doon the stair* and StE *downstairs*. *Daith* (31) is one of a small
number of words with /ɛ:/ in O Sc which take /e/ in most modern Scots dialects.
Another is *seat*.

5.2.4 William McIlvanney, *Laidlaw*

The dialogue in this recent novel by a local writer is very accurately observed
down to the details of conversational style. *Laidlaw* is an unusual type of
detective story in which the main interest is not in the pursuit of the criminal, but in the elucidation of his psychology by the intellectual and human-
istic detective, Laidlaw. A young and inexperienced policeman, Harkness, accompanies him, and is the recipient of his observations on this and other subjects. The man whom they are pursuing is a young homosexual who has tried to
rape a girl, panicked, and killed her. He involves his lover, who has links
with a shady character called Mason. Mason is a crooked businessman whose
money has advanced him into the middle class, where he is socially insecure,
and apt to commit *faux pas*. In the first passage below, Mason is warning his
henchman, Lennie, not to antagonise the police. For further discussion, see
1.8.3 above. In the second passage, Laidlaw, with Harkness, is trying to en-
list the support of the underworld. A very tense encounter takes place in the
'snug' or private room of a bar, with a character called Rhodes and his two
bodyguards. Laidlaw and Rhodes each try to dominate the situation without
attacking the other's 'face' in an obvious way. Rhodes' weapon is hospitality;
Laidlaw's is language. Laidlaw wins.

TEXT 32

'Be nice tae the fuzz? Are you gettin' saft, boss?'
Lennie's laughter ran against a silence. He tried again, 'Eh-heh,' like
someone knocking at the door of an empty room.
'You want to find out?' Mason's voice was so gentle it wouldn't have broken
5   a cobweb.
'Whit's the gemme? Ah wis only - '
Mason held up his right forefinger.
'I could beat you with that.'
'But. Listen - '
10   The finger moved down to point at Lennie.
'No. You listen. Wee. Silly. Boy. Any more cheek out of you, and I'll
stop your comic money. You better get brains, son. Even if you've got to
steal them. I don't pay you to be stupid.'
Lennie said nothing, stayed perfectly still, knew himself hanging over the
15   sheer drop of Mason's anger. Mason sat over his desk, staring at it.
'Surrounded with balloons,' he said, fogging the glass top. 'What am I?'
Lennie said nothing. He knew the way Mason sometimes used people like a
mirror in which to examine himself. Mirrors shouldn't talk back.
'I'm a legitimate bookmaker. I've got my shops. I run the business. All
20   right. But you know and I know that I've got other interests. And if we know,
do you think the C.I.D. have no idea? I've got fingers in a lot of pies. If
I get just one of them cut off, I lose the lot. Because the blood'll bring

them to me. And that could be nasty. I've had to arrange some accident-in-
surance along the way. Some people live awful careless. Never underestimate
the polis, son. They're not daft. They're waiting for me. I'd like to keep
them waiting.'
    Lennie stayed silent.

From William McIlvanney, *Laidlaw* (U. K.:
Hodder and Stoughton, 1979, first published 1977), 87-8.

Notes

Fuzz (1) 'police' is probably still recognised by speakers as an Americanism.
Cf. synonyms in 2.3.4 above. *With* (16) 'by' is a hypercorrection of Scots *wi*.

Mason's threats are underlined by the stabbing finger which punctuates *Wee.
Silly. Boy.* (11). At the same time the tone is humorous, and this leaves Lennie
without an appropriate response. If he shows deference by laughing, he appears
to ignore the threat, but neither can he be resentful.

TEXT 33

'Hullo, you,' he said to Laidlaw and sat down across the table from them.
'Ye'll hiv a drink.'
    'A whisky for me,' Laidlaw said. 'With water.'
    'I won't bother, thank you,' Harkness said.
    The blue eyes turned on him like a blowtorch lit but not yet shooting flame.
    'He'll have a pint,' Laidlaw said. 'He's such a fierce drinker. When he
says he won't bother, he means he'll just stick to the beer.'
    'Is he age? John Rhodes asked.
    Harkness began to wonder. As the wavy-haired man nodded through the door
of the snug, Harkness realised that John Rhodes hadn't been making a suggestion,
just stating a fact. They were visitors to his territory. He made the eti-
quette. Harkness became conscious that he and the other two men were just
witnesses at a special kind of confrontation. The tension was that of a contest. Harkness didn't know the rules but he understood that he had already
weakened Laidlaw's position by breaking one of them. He resolved not to be
an embarrasment again.
    The barman brought in the drinks and shut the sliding door as he went back
out. Harkness felt surrouded. They drank in silence for a moment. John
Rhodes was drinking port, Harkness thought.
    'You'll be wondering why we're here,' Laidlaw said.
    'Ah thought ye might tell me.'
    'I think I will. You know there's been a girl murdered.'
    'It wis in the papers.'
    'It's about that then.'
    'I'm not guilty, your honour.'
    The other two men laughed and Harkness smiled. Laidlaw did nothing but
wait.
    'It's about that then.'
    'Ye're repeating yerself.'
    'No. I'm just keeping my train of thought in the face of facetious inter-
ruption.'
    There was a silence. Harkness realised suddenly that the chilly core of it
was 'facetious'. It was a word John Rhodes didn't know. That was why Laidlaw
had chosen it.
    'All right, college-boy. Go on wi' yer story.'

ibid, 96-7

Notes

You'll be wondering why we're here (20) is literally a prediction. Since it does not make sense to predict the present, this is a cue to the hearer to interpret the utterance indirectly. The prediction is one which he (in this case, only he) can confirm or disconfirm. It is actually a question with positive expectation.

This use of *will* is common in ScE and is readily understood as interrogative In fact, as with idioms, it is the literal reading (prediction) which would be marked as unusual. This is a case of what Brown and Levinson (1978) call 'conventional indirectness'. The meaning is clear, so that the FTA of asking a question has really been performed baldly, except that the use of a conventional circumlocution expresses the wish to have been indirect. Conventional indirectness solves a conflict in meeting the hearer's negative face - the speaker does not wish to impose himself forcefully, but at the same time, he does not wish to try the hearer's patience by beating about the bush.

Ye'll hiv a drink (2) is a similar case. Here what is superficially a prediction can be fulfilled by the hearer doing what the speaker predicts he will do. It is actually an imperative, and again this is a conventional locution in ScE. Rhodes apparently intends it as an imperative, but Harkness interprets it in terms of a second convention. When a speaker is offering some small item to the hearer, which doesn't involve the hearer incurring any great debt, the speaker can save the hearer's negative face by appearing to force it upon him. Thus Harkness has, in effect, belittled Rhodes' hospitality. He is also out of line in using the formal *thank you* (4). Notice that Laidlaw does not say this, thereby accepting that he has incurred a debt.

Is he age (8) means 'is he old inough to drink'; cf. *under-age*. Notice *college-boy* (35). All forms of higher education are referred to as *college* or even *school* by many working class Scottish speakers, at least in connection with acquaintances. The word *university* seems to be treated as ideologically alien.

5.2.5 Alan Spence, *Its Colours they are Fine*

This is a collection of short stories, set mainly in Glasgow, and arranged in a rough chronological order from childhood to early adult life. There is a thread of disappointment in the early stories which gives way to lassitude in the later ones. The dialogue is rich in localised and idiomatic language. *Its colours they are fine* is from a song celebrating the Orange Lodge regalia. In the passage below, two young boys are playing in the street.

TEXT 34

The afternoon sticky and hot and the pavement tar soft and melting.   Aleck and
Joe were scraping their initials with their arrows.

(The way the tar opened under the pressure - glistening black scar on the
pavement's dusty grey - initials - names.)

'Tar's brilliant stuff, intit,' said Joe.

'So it is, ' said Aleck.   'See the smell aff it when its jist been laid!
Makes ye wanty sink yer teeth inty it!'

'So it dis.   Ah love smells lik that.'

'The smell a the subway!'

'New shoe boaxes!'

'Rubber tyres!'

'Terrific!'

Joe dug into the tar, wound the arrow till its end was coiled and clogged.

'Looks lik a big toly disn't it!'

They dug out lumps with their hands, kneaded and stretched and smeared it.

'Really dis make ye wanty eat it.'

'D'you remember eatin sand when ye wur wee?' asked Aleck.

'Naw, ah don't think so,' said Joe.   'How, d'you?'

'Aye. Sandpies it wis. Looked great. Tasted horrible but.'

(Mouthful of dirt - becoming mud - grit between the teeth.)

'Jesus!' said Joe. 'How ur we gonnae get this stuff aff?'

Aleck looked at his blackened hands.   'Margarine's supposed tae take it aff,'
he said.

'We could always leave them,' said Joe.   'Cover wursels in it so's we look
lik darkies.'

'Fur gawn tae the jungle,' said Aleck. He picked up his bow and arrows.

'Ach look at that!' said Joe. His arrow had split digging into the tar.
He threw it away, disgusted.

'Never mind,' said Aleck. ''Mon wull go up tae mah hoose'n clean it aff.'

From Alan Spence, "The Ferry", 36-45 in
Its Colours they are Fine (London:
Collins, 1977), 40-1.

Notes

Brilliant (5) is a current superlative.   *'Mon* (29) is a reduced form of *come
oan*. Notice *disn't* (14).   There is also a form *dint* (don't, doesn't), which
occurs only in tags in ScE, like *int*, and also like *wint* (wasn't, weren't).

5.2.6 James Kelman, "Nice tae be nice"

This is an extended narrative in the form of a monologue. The monologue is
particularly interesting in Scots prose, as it forms a transition from dialogue
in which Scots has always maintained a place, to narrative, which has been
almost exclusively in St E up to the 1970s. Unlike many Scots texts which
merely pose as monologues, "Nice tae be nice" contains colloquial forms and
conversational structures - indicating, for instance, orientation towards an
addressee - throughout. The speaker is an elderly widower, prematurely retired because of ill health. A good-natured man whose motto is 'it's nice to
be nice', he is exploited by all and sundry, but never has an ill word except
for those in authority. In the passage below he has just parted from a drinking companion at the end of an evening.

TEXT 35

A left him it his close in wint hame. It wis gittin cauld in A'm beginnin tae
feel it merr these days. That young couple wir in the close in aw in at it is
usual. Every night a the week in A'm no kiddin ye. Thir parents waant tae
gie thim a room tae thirsell. A mean everybody's young wance - know whit A
5   mean? They waant tae git merrit anywey. Jesus Chist they young yins nooadays
iv goat their heid screwed oan merr thin we ever hid in the sooner they git
merrit the better. Anyhow is usual they didny even notice me. It's Betty
Sutherland's wee lassie in young Peter Craig - A knew his faither in they tell
me he's almost is hard is his auld man wis. Still thiv been winchin noo fir
10 near enough six months so mibby she's knoaked some sense inty his heid. Good
luck tae thim - A hope she his. A nice wee lassie - aye in so wis her maw.

A hid tae stoap two up fir tae git ma breath back. A'm no is bad is A wis
bit A'm still no right. That bronchitis! - Jesus Christ A hid it bad. Hid tae
stoap work kis iv it. Good joab A hid tae oan the long distance. Landit up
15 in the hoaspital way it tae. Murder it wis. Still A made it tae the toap. A
stey in a room in kitchen in inside toilet, in it's no bad kis A only pey six
pound a month fir rent in rates. Bit A hear thir comin doon although A hope
it's no fir a while kis A'll git buggir aw bein a single man. If she wis back
A'd git a coarpiration hoose bit she's gone fir good in anywey they coarpira-
20 tion hooses irny worth a f---. End up peying a haunfil a week in dumped oot
somewherr? Naw. No me. No even a pub ir buggir aw? Naw they kin stick thim.

From James Kelman, "Nice tae be nice",
42-7 in *The Glasgow Review* IV: 3 (1973),
42-3.

Notes

Notice *merr* (2) from Scots *mair* 'more'. *Knoaked some sense inty his heid* (10) usually refers to violent methods of instructing children.

There are several categories of noun phrase which normally take the definite article in Scots but not in St E. These include the names of languages, e.g. *the Gaelic*, and the names of diseases, e.g. *the bronchitis*, where these are treated as unique entities. *That bronchitis* (13), then, is comparable to sentences like "That Jim Smith was here." The definite article is also used with names of institutions, e.g. *the hoaspital* (15), and names of trades and occupations, e.g. *the long distance* (14), where there is supposedly only one in a given community. Similarly with the names of members of the family, e.g. *the faither* (T6/16), *the boay* (T22/7).

Translation

I left him at his entrance and went home. It was getting cold and I'm beginning to feel it more these days. That young couple were in the entrance as well, and at it, as usual. Every night of the week, and I'm not kidding you. Their parents ought to give them a room to themselves. I mean, everybody's young once, know what I mean? They want to get married anyway. Jesus Christ, those young people nowadays have got their heads screwed on, more than we ever had, and the sooner they get married the better. Anyway, as usual they didn't even notice me. It's Betty Sutherland's daughter and young Peter Craig - I knew his father, and they tell me that he's almost as tough as his father was. Still, they've been courting now for very nearly six months, so maybe she's knocked some sense into his head. Good luck to them - I hope she has. A nice little girl - yes, and so was her mother.

I had to stop two flights up to get my breath back. I'm not as bad as I was, but I'm still not okay. That bronchitis! Jesus Christ, I had it badly. I had to stop work because of it. Good job I had too, long distance lorry driving. Ended up in hostital with it too. Murder it was. Still, I made it to the top. I live in a room-and-kitchen with inside toilet, and it's okay, because I only pay six pounds a month for rent and rates. But I hear they're being pulled down, although I hope it's not for a while, because I'll get bugger all, as a single man. If she was back, I'd get a Corporation house, but she's gone for good, and anyway those Corporation houses aren't worth a fuck. You end up paying a handful a week and you're dumped out somewhere? No. Not me. Not even a pub or bugger all? No, they can stick them.

5.2.7 Alex Hamilton, "Stretch Marks"

Alex Hamilton has published numerous short stories and poems. "Stretch Marks", an unpublished novel, tells of a Glasgow University student's experiences working as a dustbin-man during the summer vacation. He is befriended by one of the older workers who is made the rather uncomfortable vehicle, in the novel, of a number of lengthy speeches articulating the working class point of view. The passage which follows is part of a monologue at a student party, in which he contrasts the students' affected scruffiness with his own sense of occasion, shown for instance by smoking packaged cigarettes rather than his usual roll-ups. He describes a film in which Jane Russell played a newly released convict anxious not to give herself away. The language forms a very interesting experiment in the fictive representation of speech.

TEXT 36

"See, Jane Russell in that filim wiz gaw noot intae the big, bad wuril deftir
spendin so minny year zinside fur bein a nenimy a saciety an that. Shid get
oota therr wi a coupla dollir zin ur purse an, it thi very best, sum kinna
shitey joab that a nimployir wi a consciunce - ur a neye fur cheap labour,
5   merrn likely - hiz gie dur tae try an get ur rispectible an back oan thi right
track sagayn. Noo, that lassie's gonnae hiv wan helluva hard time makin enz
meet oan whitivir skitteri, wee wages shi getz an, if shi diz smoke, yid think
shid go ootae ur wey tae kee poan buyin thi cheapiss wanz so's shi kin spend
whitivir sperr cash shi hiz goat oan a wintir coat, shoes, may-kup ur a coupla
10 steel reinforced fuckin brassieres tae keep they magnificent tit sa hurs in sum
kinna ordir. Bit diz shi? Diz shi fuck. An how? Kiz wance it's been pointit
ootae ur jiss whit rollin yir ain means tae folk watchin a wummin, it autamat-
iclli's gonnae mean thi same tae hur ivir eftir. Ivri drag a ivri fag that
wummin smokes, son, is a sook fur freedom. A rimindir that whit shiz daein
15 shiz daein noo iza free wummin, oota clink an celabratin; aye, fuckin *celabratin's* thi wurd fur it - celabratin ur liberti bae consciously rifusin tae
buy cheap fuckin shag jiss tae gie intae a cravin. Whit shiz daein's merrn
jiss satisfyin a need fur tabacca: shiz satisfyin a nurge tae turn roon tae
thi wurild, blaw smoke in its wee rid eye zin say tae it: 'Up yours, pal!
20 Ah've ivri right tae enjoy masel iz much iz youse hiv, nif Ah want a smoke,
naebdi's gonnae turn roon an say *therr za fuckin jailbird*, jiss kiz Ah hivnae
inuff cash tae buy a fuckin packit a readies!'"

From Alex Hamilton, "Stretch Marks" (unpublished), 132-3.

Notes

The orthography here is similar to that of the preceding text (T35) for which
a translation is given. But notice the epenthetic vowels in *filim* (1) and
wurild (1, 19). A feature of this text is the unusually systematic treatment
of word division where a word closing with a consonant is followed by one beginning with a vowel, e.g. *wuril defter* (1) 'world after'. Abercrombie (1979:
82) describes this preference for open syllables as a characteristic of ScE.

   Therr (3) /ðɛr/ occurs as a localised form from St ScE /ðer/. *So minny* (2)
'so many' is less colloquial than *that minny*.

5.2.8 Tom Leonard, "Mr. Endrews speaks"

The spoken word is a recurrent theme in Leonard's work, and he is particularly
inventive in finding ways to represent local variants orthographically. Here
he renders a 'Kelvinside' accent. The piece is supposedly a headmaster's address to the school, and is a satire on the trivial preoccupations of the
would-be genteel, and on irrelevant aims in education.

TEXT 37

Now Tem was never one to hev known the dignity of a laudable profession with
a substantial celery, like my own. It was his own fault, of course. Et St
Kevin Berry's he would hev the school motto, "Porridge end the Tawse" inscribed
on all his Eff Two's. But a leck of self-discipline was to prove his downfall
in later years. You know, my feather was gerrotted when I was a child end it
didn't do *me* any herm. No, I stuck herd et my studies, end in the fullness of
time became a gredduate of Glasgow University. End there were no State hend-
outs in my day, one hed to get by on a seck of oats. *(Clears his throat)*. A
seck of oats.

Of course none of you listening to me here this morning will ever go to
Glasgow University, I'm aware of thet. Most of you will be in the hends of
the Glasgow constebulary before very long, end some of you will no doubt make
your appearance in the High Court on a cherge of murder. Now I want you to
hev the honour of St Kevin Berry's in mind when you plead guilty, end under
no circumstances should use the glottal stop. I want you all to say, "Guilty,"
in a clear, well-mennered voice, with no trace of slovenly speech.

From Tom Leonard, "Mr. Endrews speaks",
13 in *Words* 3 (1977).

Notes

The substitution of <e> for <a> wherever this represent /a/ is sufficient to
suggest the Kelvinside accent, with its [æ] realisation of /a/. *Celery* (2)
for *salary* and *feather* (5) for *father* recall the type of pun on working class
speech seen in T17 and T18. In the cases of *herm* (6) 'harm' and *cherge* (13)
'charge' there is a coincidence, unfortunate for the speaker, with localised
forms in /ɛ/. /hɛrm/ is general Scots, and /tʃɛrdʒ/ is a Glasgow form of
Scots /tʃɛrdʒ/. *Porridge* (3), a staple food in Scotland up to the present
century, and still a popular breakfast, is a cultural stereotype. F2 (*Eff
Two's*, 4) is a standard size of school notebook.

5.2.9   Alex Hamilton, "Our Merry"

Non-dialogue prose is a relatively new departure in Scots, and many writers
who have attempted it have approached it from the monologue, retaining enough
of the context or markers of a speaking voice to motivate the use of the dialect. Hamilton's first person narrative here is in colloquial St ScE, with
occasional non-standard forms. This contrasts with the strongly localised dialogue, thus following a rule of code-switching between narrative and dialogue
which is deeply entrenched in Scottish and other dialect literatures, but without allowing the narrator to become alienated from the action. The price of
this technique, which has been employed by several Glasgow writers, is that
the character of the narrator is circumscribed by the type of language assigned
to him. The voice in this text is that of a small boy, perhaps about ten years
old. The linguistic forms are those of speech, but no context for this speech
is artificially intruded into the narrative. The speaker is telling about his
baby sister Mary, whose presence he resents, but nevertheless tries to adapt
to, despite Mary's awfulness.

TEXT 38

Now I can perfectly understand why ma's like that, that worried way, because
it is an awful busy road, there's no getting away from it. In fact, I can
speak on that probably better than most folk because it was really me that
caused all the bother I'll be telling you about in a minute, although it wasn't
5 my fault if you see what I mean. No, that's not very clear. What happened
was that when I was just started school in the babies' class, ma always used
to take me in, and I suppose that's fair enough when you're only a wee bloke
of five or that. Anyway, Merry wasn't born then and ma had nothing else to do
all day, so it was up to her. After I'd been there about six months though,
10 she started not feeling very well in the mornings, so I remember her taking me
out one day up to the corner and going through the drill - mind all that stuff
you used to get about not forgetting to look left and right and that? Well.

I thought this was great, of course. A wee guy like me being allowed to
cross the road on his own, and that one of the busiest roads in the town! And
15 I was good at it too, even if I say it myself, because when the time came that
I nearly got hit it wasn't my fault at all. It was this f'lla on a motorbike,
and the reason I never saw him was he was going too fast. Not that I remember,
of course, but that apparently is what the judge said to him when he took his
licence away for two years. However, I was lucky, and I don't deny it, and
20 whatever I said to her at the time, I was really glad that ma started taking
me back to school again till she went into hospital, and then arranged for
Andy's mother to take me in along with him in the mornings.

"Aw, nivir agayn, Mrs Montrose," I remember her saying to her that first
morning. "Thi doactur says Ah'm lucki Ah didnae hiv a miskerridge."

25   "Aye, Ah know. That road's a cryin disgrace, so it is," says Andy's ma.
"But doan't you worry yir heid aboot enihin, hen. Ah'll see thi wee f'lla
awright tull yi get oot - then by thi time thi additiun's big inuff tae be
gaun tae school itsel, Andy and him'll be that bit biggir inuff tae take it in
in thi moarnins. An that'll save a loat a trubbil, wintit?"

30   Well, *it* turned out to be Merry, and *it* had to be taken to school right
enough.

                           From Alex Hamilton, "Our Merry", 15-28
                           in Alex Hamilton, James Kelman and Tom
                           Leonard, *Three Glasgow Writers* (Glasgow:
                           Molendinar Press, 1976), 15-6.

Notes

Notice *not feeling* (10). The isolate negative particle can take main verbs,
and also adjectives, in its scope in ScE. *Never* (17) with reference to a
single occasion, is general in non-standard BrE. Deletion of *that* as a complementiser (17) is almost obligatory in colloquial ScE. *Wint* (29), like *int*,
occurs only in sentence tags.

5.2.10 James Kelman, "Acid"

As we have seen, narrative and descriptive prose in Scottish literature is
traditionally in St E, often in a quite formal style. Kelman, as well as writing in styles of varying degrees of localisation, also exploits formal St E
for its alienating effect in both narrative and dialogue. In this short piece,
formal St E is juxtaposed with, or, as it were, superimposed on, colloquial
St ScE, with the effect that the narrator seems to be distancing himself emo-
tionally from the incident described.

TEXT 39

In this factory in the north of England acid was essential. It was contained
in large vats. Gangways were laid above them. Before these gangways were made
completely safe a young man fell into a vat feet first. His screams of agony
were heard all over the department. Except for one old fellow the large body
5 of men was so horrified that for a time not one of them could move. In an in-
stant this old fellow who was also the young man's father had clambered up and
along the gangway carrying a big pole. Sorry Hughie, he said. And then ducked
the young man below the surface. Obviously the old fellow had had to do this
because only the head and shoulders... in fact, that which had been seen above
10 the acid was all that remained of the young man.

                           From James Kelman, *Short Tales from the
                           Night Shift*, (Glasgow: Print Studio
                           Press, 1978), unpaginated.

Notes

The syntax of this passage is highly transformed, for instance the passive mood
and the pluperfect tense are much in evidence. *That which* (9) would almost
invariably be replaced by *what* in colloquial ScE. *Fellow* (4) and *large body*
(4) are correspondingly formal lexical choices. *Fellow* has quite different
associations from the localised form *fella* (cf. T38/16). These forms contrast
with the use of *this* (1) with indefinite reference, and with the broken syntax
of 9. Notice how the emotional implications of the relative clause in 6 are
dislocated by the offering of this information in a non-restrictive clause.

5.3 Drama

The 1970s have seen a significant output of Glasgow drama for stage and television, only a small part of which can be sampled here. Many of these plays are notable for attention to code-switching and the appropriateness of speech style to character, but at the same time there is often an inattention to the kind of detail which can be supplied by the actor.

5.3.1 Bill Bryden, *Willie Rough*

Willie Rough is set in Greenock, just downriver from Glasgow, at the beginning of the First World War, when the working class struggle for better conditions was denounced on all sides as unpatriotic. At the start of the play, Willie Rough, an honest and committed man, is trying to get a job in the shipyards. In the course of the play we see him rashly putting his head on the block for his radical politics. He is sent to prison, and the play ends with him again trying, this time unsuccessfully, to get back his old job. Willie Rough's tragedy is that he is unable to move outside of his own milieu once he has grown too large for it. In the scene below, near the beginning of the play, he has just made friends with two other men who show him how to go about bribing the foreman in order to get a job.

TEXT 40

PAT *and* WILLIE *begin drinking, while* HUGHIE *is fetching the rest of their drinks.*

```
      PAT   Ye mairrit, like?
      WILLIE   Aye. I've got two weans.  A boy and a wee lassie.
 5    PAT   I've got five.
      HUGHIE   [bringing the last of the drinks]  He's tryin tae win the Pope's medal.
      PAT   Shut yer face, you!  What's in the paper.
      HUGHIE   The usual.
      PAT   Dae ye think ye'll be joinin up, Willie?
10    WILLIE   Na.
      PAT   How no?
      WILLIE   It's no my war when it does come.  Nor yours, neither.
      HUGHIE   Aye, but ye've got tae go but.  I mean, I didnae start the last wan,
        but I had tae go.  An' look what happened tae me.  I left wan leg in a midden
15      bin in fuckin Africa, bi-fuck!
      WILLIE   But naething cam out o't at aa, did it?  Can ye no see?  What's five
        weans gonna dae 'ithout thir faither?  Ye see...it's aa arranged frae start
        tae finish.  It's been worked out, like.  The time-tables o trains that'll
        tak the boys back an' furrit frae the Front have aa been organised.  Ye
20      wouldnae believe it.  The war's got tae come nou, because folk want it.  An'
        it's no only the politicians, either.
      PAT   Naebody wants war.
      HUGHIE   Naebody wise, onywey.
      WILLIE   You're wrang there.  Just tak a look at thae men ower at the counter
25      there.
      PAT   What about them?
      WILLIE   They'll volunteer tae a man when the times comes.  Some o them are
```

learnin tae march at nights up our way aaready.
PAT Aye. I go mysel'...the odd time.
0 WILLIE Sorry I spoke, then.
HUGHIE Hey, you...Willie, for Christ's sake, ye're no a German spy, are ye?
PAT Och, Hughie, wheesht! [*To* WILLIE] So what dae ye suggest we dae...sup-
posin...just supposin the war braks out? Take a fortnight's holidays an' take
the weans tae Rothesay for a dip?
5 WILLIE Stay where ye are. Here in Greenock, where ye belang. Sure, we've
got tae try our hardest tae prevent this imperialist war: [*rhetorically*] but
if it starts, as start, God help us, it surely will, it's our duty to oppose
it. Out of the crisis of the war we must find the means to bring an end tae
capitalism.
0 HUGHIE A Red Flagger, for fuck's sake!
PAT Hey! Keep the heid, Willie. Ye sound like wan o they manifestos, or
somethin' lik that. Drink up. It might never happen.

From Bill Bryden, *Willie Rough* (Edinburgh:
Southside Press, 1972), 23-4.

Notes

Like (3) is a mitigating tag, similar to *as it were*. *Can ye no see* (16) is
the usual ScE word order (cf. *can't you see*). *Aa* (16) and *nou* (20) are *Scots
Style Sheet* (1947) spellings (see 2.2 above), and *frae* (17) is literary (cf.
fae). The dialect here includes a number of forms, e.g. *naething* (16), *cam*
(16), *tak* (19), *braks* (33), which are now rarely heard in Glasgow. This may
be an influence of literary Scots - cf. the use of *Scots Style Sheet* spellings
- or the language may be deliberately old fashioned in keeping with the period.

The transition to speech-making in Willie's final speech above is a cue for
code-switching, but the move to St E is modified by the fact that the inter-
locutors remain the same. Rhetorical features such as inversion - *as start...
it surely will* (37) - and the invocation of the Deity, (37), are mixed with
dialectal or colloquial forms. The use of *must* in the sense of moral obligation, (38), is formal. This is generally avoided in colloquial ScE.

5.3.2 Roddy McMillan, *The Bevellers*

The late Roddy McMillan was primarily an actor, and *The Bevellers* is one of
only two plays which he published. It depicts a day in the life of a small
craft workshop. A new apprentice, a naive and mild-mannered boy, has been tak-
en on, and this is his first exposure to the often crude, foul-mouthed and
repressed world of the adult working man. In the first passage below, a young
woman, Nancy, comes into the workshop at lunchtime in search of her boyfriend,
and encounters one of the other men, Rouger, instead. The verbal fencing between them ends in her seduction, which the apprentice has the misfortune to
witness and to interrupt.

In the second passage, there is a heated exchange between the manager, Leslie,
and the foreman, Bob, played by McMillan himself in the original production in
the Lyceum Theatre, Edinburgh. The manager has chosen a very bad time to try
to assert his authority in the workshop, as the men are handling an enormous
sheet of plate glass, one of them with an injured hand. The foreman gives offence by his use of crudities, but his habitual use of broad dialect to the
manager also implies confrontation. For further discussion, see 1.8.2 above.

TEXT 41

ROUGER Ye no set the date yet?
NANCY I think the calendar's stopped.
ROUGER Whit, ye mean tae say Charlie's no sweatin tae get ye signed up?
NANCY You ask too many questions.
5 ROUGER Nae offence. Jist thought ye wanted tae air yur feelins.
NANCY Aye, but ah don't want tae broadcast them.
ROUGER Right. Ah heard nothin. Well, that's that. Wull ah open the door fur
ye then?
NANCY Ye in a hurry tae see me aff noo?
10 ROUGER Naw, naw. Ah like talkin tae ye. In fact ah like you.
NANCY Save it, Santy. How can you like me, ye don't even know me?
ROUGER Well, the cat can look up the queen's drawers, can't it?
NANCY That's enough! Excuse me!
ROUGER It's jist a wey o speakin. Ah've seen ye stacks o times, an' in ma
15 ain wey ah've liked ye. Havenae said much tae ye, but then ah don't know
wherr ah stand, dae ah?
NANCY Ye stand wherr ye've always stood, big-yin, right oot in the rain.
ROUGER That's no exactly fair, is it? Ah mean, fur a' you know, ah could be
wan o the nicest fullas in the city.
20 NANCY Ah'll never know anythin' aboot that.
ROUGER Up tae you. Wer ye supposed tae see Charlie?
NANCY Aye. Said he'd see me at the front o the work at a quarter past.
ROUGER He must have left late. He sometimes dis a bit o trainin wi the weight
therr. Maybe he forgot.
25 NANCY Trainin fur whit? The Possilpark Olympics?
ROUGER Gettin his strength up. Ah mean, a lovely girl like you.
NANCY Flattery'll get ye nowhere.
ROUGER Naw, genuine. Ah think you're a lovely girl.
NANCY The compliments are bowlin me over.
30 ROUGER Ah mean it. Terrific body, smashin face, the lot.
NANCY Don't let *him* hear ye sayin that.
ROUGER He'll never hear it unless you tell him.
NANCY You're dead crafty, aren't ye?
ROUGER Strike me dead, ah mean it, genuine. If ah wis Charlie, you'd be right
35 up on the old pedastal fur ma money.
NANCY Ah used tae think you wer a dead-head. Gettin quite romantic in yur
ould age.
ROUGER I'll say it again, you don't know me, Nancy. Sit doon a minute, an'
if ye'll no fly off the handle, I'll tell ye whit ah think.

From Roddy McMillan, *The Bevellers*
(Edinburgh, Southside Press, 1974), 48-9.

Notes

Wherr (17) /ʍɛr/ is a localised form from St ScE /ʍɛr/. Cf. *therr* 'there'.
Genuine (28) is a protestation of sincerity (cf. *honest*).

TEXT 42

Just then, LESLIE *hurries down the stair.*

LESLIE Hold it, Bob. Hold it, boys.
BOB Hold it? We've jist got tae hold it. We cannae drap it on the fuckin flerr.
LESLIE No need to use that language in front of young boys, Bob.
BOB These young boys have got words we've never even heard o. Whit's the panic?
LESLIE You didn't forget that bowl, did you?
BOB Christ, is that a' ye want tae ask? We're staunin here wi this thing in wur hauns, an' you're worryin aboot some stupid article that some half-arsed cowboy'll use for a chanty in the middle o the night.
LESLIE You don't have to be so crude.
BOB It's lyin ower therr. Gie it a wipe, an' it'll be champion.
LESLIE You managed to get the mark out?
BOB Aye, aye. Noo, will ye kindly take a walk up these sterrs an' leave us in peace?
LESLIE You might be the foreman here, Bob, but you are talking to the manager.
BOB The manager that didnae gie me much co-operation when I was askin fur yur ideas a wee while ago. It wis up tae me, ye said. A'right, then, it's up tae me an' ah'll see the job done. Away you an' staun up at the front door an' scratch yur arse.

LESLIE *leaves.*

ibid, 64-5.

Notes

Radio Scotland broadcast a performance of *The Bevellers* on November 13, 1980, produced by Tom Kinninmont. The play was 'cleaned up' for radio. In 3 *bloody* was substituted for *fuckin*, which weakens the exchange which follows. Also, Leslie was provided with an exit line, "All right, Bob keep you hair on." Again, while this may have been necessary, it weakens the effect. At 18 the relativiser was omitted. This change means that Bob's opening sentence is a main clause, rather than a subordinate clause depending on the closing sentence of Leslie's speech. There is therefore less reliance on Leslie's precedent of talking about himself in the third person. That is, the modification is towards a more explicit confrontation. Together with Leslie's exit line, this strengthens the character of Bob at the expense of Leslie.

5.3.3 Tom McGrath and Jimmy Boyle, *The Hard Man*

This play is a largely biographical account of the criminal career and prison experiences of Jimmy Boyle, the character Byrne, a small-time Glasgow criminal, convicted of murder, whose harsh treatment and subsequent rehabilitation in an experimental prison have attracted a great deal of attention to the penal system in Scotland. The play ends with him totally degaded but still defiant, in solitary confinement prior to his transfer to the New Special Unit in Barlinnie Prison in Glasgow, where he wrote *A Sense of Freedom*, collaborated on this play, and acquired a reputation as a sculptor.

Byrne and the other characters speak directly to the audience, and short scenes are acted out with a minimum of props and costumes. In the original production in the Traverse Theatre in Edinburgh, the part of Byrne was the only one which was not doubled. McGrath (personal correspondence) comments on the language of the play that:

> it is essentially dramatic language which, while it gives the
> impression of being naturalistic, is written primarily for its
> percussive value in the play....the actors were dissuaded from
> trying to deliver it naturalistically.

He points out in particular the "loosely metrical quality" of Byrne's speeches, and the use of refrains like "rats aroon the backs." At the same time, the local dialect is well observed, especially the syntax. The passage below is Byrne's first direct speech to the audience, with the scene which follows.

TEXT 43

My name is Byrne. Johnnie Byrne. I was born in the Gorbals District of Glasgow. You've read about me in the newspapers and heard about me in pubs. I'm a lunatic. A right bad lot. What the Judge always calls, "A menace to society". I'm speaking to you tonight from a Scottish prison where I am serv-
5 ing life-sentence for murder. What you are going to see is my life as I re-
member it. What you are going to hear is my version of the story.

SLUGGER *and* BANDIT *run on shouting.*

SLUGGER Rats.
BANDIT Chasin' rats.
10 SLUGGER Chasin' rats roon the backs.
BANDIT Chasin' rats roon the backs wae a wee dug...
SLUGGER Chasin' rats roon the backs wae a wee dug that wus rerr ut brekkin
their necks.
BANDIT It even goat a mention in the papers that wee dug, because it kilt
15 that many rats.
SLUGGER Hiya, Johnny.
BYRNE Hiya, Slugger. Hiya, Bandit. Back tae school again...*This line by way
of explanation to audience.*
SLUGGER School! School! Back tae school. Ah hate a Monday.
20 BANDIT Ah hate the fuckin' school. School's rubbish!
SLUGGER Aye, whit's it aw aboot anyway? Who wants to learn aw that shite they
teach yae?
BYRNE You're that stupit, yae couldnae learn anythin anyway, even if yae
wahntit tae.

5 SLUGGER Listen to who's talkin. The teacher says you're a dead cert fur truble.
      He's goat you marked doon fur the Borstal already.
   BYRNE Fuck 'im.
   BANDIT Fancy doggin' it?
   SLUGGER Aye. Fancy it? We could go doon the shoaps an' dae some knockin'.
0   Fancy it, Johnny?
   BYRNE Och, I don't know. We did that yesterday - and the day before. Ah
      think we're just wastin' oor time. Bars a chocolate an' boatles o scoosh.
      Ah wis aboot sick yesterday wae the amount ah ate.
   BANDIT Well, you were the wan that insistit oan goin' back tae the shoap an
5   daein' it agen.
   BYRNE That wis just because ah wus bored. There's no much fun tae it wance
      you've done it a few times. An' enyway, its no bars o choclate we need, its
      money!
   SLUGGER Back tae that agen.
0 BANDIT You bet your life its back tae that. Money. Lolly. Cash. It aw comes
      back tae that sooner or later, doesn't it?
   BYRNE Aye, well you know how we were talkin aboot daein a few shoaps at night?
   BOTH Aye.
   BYRNE An' we were tryin tae figure oot how we wid dae the loaks?
5 BOTH Aye.
   BYRNE Well, I've been thinking...
   BOTH Miracles!
   BYRNE During the day, when they close up the shop for a coupla hours tae go
      hame an' huv a bit tae eat an' a wee snooze, maybe a pint doon ut the boozers
0   ...they cannae be bothered pittin aw thae loaks oan...its no worth it fur
      the shoart time thair oot...and enyway, they know that thieves only wurk ut
      night...
   He smiles at them. They think about this.
      ...so...if we go during the day...
5 SLUGGER Goat ye.
   BANDIT Ya beauty.
   BYRNE So whit ur we waitin fur? Cumoan.

                              From Tom McGrath and Jimmy Boyle, *The
                              Hard Man*, (Edinburgh, Canongate Press,
                              1977), 8-10.

                              Notes

Notice non-standard spellings for standard word forms in *truble* (25), *agen* (35)
and *wurk* (51). The value of these spellings is probably to suggest a certain
degree of localisation to the actor or reader. *Miracles* (47) is a conversational cliché. Notice *how* (42) as a complementiser. The orthography combines
traditional apostrophe spellings with spellings influenced by other Glasgow
writers.

    A Radio Scotland production by Tom Kinnimont was broadcast on October 9,
1980. The adaptation included a number of minor changes, and the addition of
extra lines following *society* (4):

         Ah'm not really used to takin the air an broadcastin so if Ah
         get ma words mixed up youse'll have tae excuse me. The nearest
         Ah ever goat tae the BBC was nickin transistor radios oota record
         shoap windaes.

5.3.4 John McGrath, *The Game's a Bogey*

This play was written for the socialist theatre group, the 7:84 Company. (The figures are the statistics of capital ownership in the U.K. - seven per cent of the population own 84 per cent of the wealth). 7:84 productions combine songs and comic and serious sketches around a theme. *The Game's a Bogey* concerns the life and thinking of John MacLean, a Glasgow Communist who was a prominent figure in the First World War period. Sketches about modern Glasgow life show how his politics are still relevant today. 'The game's a bogey' is a children's formula for gaining respite or ending a game.

The first passage below introduces Ina, a working class girl who will be trapped by her domestic ambitions. The role of stand-up comedian which she plays here is unusual for a woman on the British stage. The one-liners and creative insults constitute the type of conversation known as 'patter'. The second passage introduces the character McChuckemup, a crooked businessman of a kind similar to Mason in T32, but here portrayed as comic. He is about to sack two workers who have just been heard discussing working life. The third passage is from a sketch involving two first generation immigrants to Glasgow, Ali Waddell Singh, a Pakistani Rangers supporter, and Giotto Stein, an Italian Celtic supporter. Willie Waddell and Jock Stein are former managers of the respective football teams. These two teams provide a focus for ethnic rivalry between Protestants (Rangers) and Catholics (Celtic) in Glasgow. The strength of this rivalry is here shown as subsuming the ethnic identity of immigrant groups in the city. The Pakistani speaker (not included here) and the Italian speaker are shown as using dialectal English in combination with their respective foreign accents.

TEXT 44

Ina: Oh, hello Willy, how are ye? See that's my cousin
                        Willy away back there... Oh hell, no it's no. Believe
                        me or believe me no, he's the spittin image o' oor
       cousin Willy. Course everybody thinks I look like Hayley Mills. I don't be-
5   lieve them really - when they tell me that I just say, pull the other one, it's
       got bells on. Oh, dear there's a hell of a smell around here - do you smell
       it, hen? Oh so help me, will you look what I've just stood on. God, my new
       shoes too. Do you like them? I got them for Sadie's wedding last Sat'day.
       Oh, it was a lovely wedding, fair enjoyed mysel - even when the fightin' started
10   it was great. Mind you, there was no need for the bridegroom's faither to tell
       everybody about Sadie's mother and the tally man. I mean everybody knows about
       it, he didna have to broadcast it like that, and 'specially at his own daugh-
       ter's wedding. Listen, do you know something - I'm the last o' oor gang that's
       no married yet - no that it's bothering me. Ah, don't get me wrong, I've had
15   ma chances. Trouble is, none of them came up to my expectations - in fact half
       o' them didna even come up to ma shoolder. Ach, take wee Freddie, TV mechanic,
       a right tube. Too used to his horizontal hold for my liking - know what I mean
       darlin'? And then there was Luigi, curly hair, Roman nose and hands to match -
       that's right, desert's disease, wandering palms. Aye! he thought he was magic,
20   so he was, he vanished one night wi' a poof. Uh, uh. Oh but listen, I must
       tell you this - I was nearly engaged once to Archie from the burroo - a right
       drip. Good character, good job, good prospects - good God - I'm no desperate.
       Och, who am I kidding, I am getting desperate. Do you know how old I am? --
       eighteen! Oh I'll be left on the shelf soon if I don't look out. Oh, I can
       just imagine ma man though - tall, dark, handsome - and working! No foreigners
       I dinna fancy foreigners. Mind you, Sacha Distel could have me if he played

his cards right - I'm a right case, aren't I? Listen, if that Sadie can get a
man, I can get a man. I used to call her Radar - every time she turned roond
she picked something up. And her make up - she calls it pan stick, I call it
30 polyfiller. Honest to God, everytime she brought oot her lipstick, it backed
doon the tube. Oh, it takes all sorts though doesn't it? Its all goin' to be
great when I find my Mr. Right. We're going to have a semi-detached, garden,
two weans and a budgie. Aye, that'll be the day - still, you never know your
luck do you?

From John McGrath, *The Game's a Bogey*
(Edinburgh: Edinburgh University Students
Publications Board, 1975), 7.

Notes

In *Sat'day* (8), the spelling is perhaps intended to show assimilation of [ɾ]
for /t/ with a following /r/ in the next syllable. *Aren't I* (27) is unidiomat-
ic: cf. *amn't I* or *int I*. In the Radio Scotland production (see below), *eh
hen* was substituted. *Pan stick* (29) is a cleansing product used by young girls
as a cheap lip gloss. *Polyfiller* (30) is a hyperdialectal form of *Polyfillah*,
a product used to fill cracks in plaster.

There are a number of puns here. *Tube* (17), an insulting term for a man,
puns on television tube. *Horizontal hold* (17), again with reference to a television set, puns on *hold* 'embrace'. *Roman* (18) is also *roamin'*. *Poof* (20) is
a conventional representation of a magician's sound effect, but also an insulting term for a male homosexual.

TEXT 45

Andy   Counter-inflatability. As I see it, counterinflatabil-
McChuckemup: ity is the only way to make a bob or two in the present
                            day and age. Know what I mean, eh? So to put you in
the picture - to let you to understand, as it were - I'll try to fill yous in
5   as to how this wee erconomic theory knocked it off for yours truly. Now I'd
just like to introduce meself to yous an' that the night - the name is Andy
McChuckemup here, now wi' the Cramemin Investments Ltd., Govan, formerlerly, before the noo, wi' the Shettleston Partly-Used Tin and Metal Dealers. Now, as
I was trying to explain to you, about wor counter-inflatability theory - now
10 I think I could best do this by giving you an example. Now if you take the
case of your two boys there - your two working class lads - now they're nice
enough lads in their way, but not to put too fine a point on it - they're as
thick as keech in the neck o' a bottle. So this is where me and my wee company steps in and applies wor counter-inflatability theory, by taking over this
15 wee run-doon knackered wee engineering shop here, down on the Clydeside, for a
price o' a few packets o' crisps, by the way - we were thinking of taking over
a wee secondhand newspaper business but that kinda fell through, you know -
Running it down until it is finito - that's a wee word I picked up in Yugoslavia
last year - until it's reduced to hee-haw, and then get rid o' your workers and
20 develop the site as the Phase 1, Partick Area, of the Clydeside Marina. You
see, to my mind, as I see it, the days o' your Clydeside as an industrial area
is oot the game. As your relicologists, - er, as your environment - as your
clever buggers have been pointing oot for some time, there is a definite drift
down the Clyde, past Rothesay, up the West Coast and into your Highlands and
25 Islands - that's where your work is goin', and that's where your working boys
is goin', and they're getting a wee bit o' fresh air, and they're getting away

frae all this union nonsense, wi' your Tommy MacLeans and your John Reids and
your Micky McGeeGees. And they're leaving the Clydeside for the likes o' mysel
to bustle in.   ibid, 33-4.

Notes

Secondhand newspaper business (17) is a topical reference to the closure of the
Glasgow works of the *Daily Express*. For *Tommy MacLeans* (27) read John MacLean;
for *John Reids* (27), Jimmy Reid; and for *Micky McGeeGees* (28), Mick McGahey,
a British trade unionist. *McChuckemup* is, of course, *McThrow/them/up*, and
Cramemin (7) is *Cram/them/in*.

   Counter-inflatability (1) is a malapropism for *counter-inflation*. The error
implies that it is not inflation, but the power to reflate the economy that is
being countered, i.e. that the activities of McChuckemup are inherently reces-
sionary. *Knackered* (15) 'exhausted' is a dead metaphor from the knacker's
yard. Notice the similarity between asset stripping and knackering horses.
The dead metaphor of *drift* (23) for a historical tendency is also brought to
life by McChuckemup's literal misunderstanding of it. The mispronunciations
erconomic (5) and *formerlerly* (7) show him as ignorant.

   Meself (6), as in HibE, is unusual - the expected Scots form is *maself*.
Wor (9) is usually an English dialect spelling - cf. Scots *wir* or *wur*. *Finito*
(18) 'finished' is an Italian stereotype. *Hee-haw* (19) 'nothing' is possibly
rhyming slang for *damn/fuck aw*.

TEXT 46

Giotto Stein   Now this guy, he's a deed, ye ken, and he's go up to heaven,
                  he's a knocka the door and Peter come out - He's a good guy
                  Peter, a bit of a brick, ken? So he says to Peter "Can I get
      in friend?" Peter says "No no, your name's no i' the book - you've beena the
5   bad boy, ye have to dae the punishment." So the guy says "What have I tae
      day?" So Peter says "There's a spoon. I want he tae go doon and empty the
      Clyde." So the guy's take the spoon, he's awa' doon he's empty the Clyde. Oh
      he says "Stuffa this for a monkey's uncle." So he's awa' back up to heaven.
      Anyways he says "Peter, ma friend, I'm no like your job, goin' ta give us some-
10   thin' easier, gunnae? Here's backa your spoon." So Peter am think for a mo-
      ment. He says "I tell you what ma friend, I tell you what. I want you to go
      doon and help Rangers catch up with the Celtic in the League." And the guy
      says 'Ah come on you cheeky bastard, gi' us back the spoon."   ibid, 47.

Notes

An extraneous *a*, introduced mainly after verbs, e.g. *he's a deed* (1) and *knocka*
(2), is a stereotype of Italian-accented English, as is the generalisation of
is as a marker of the past tense, e.g. *he's go* (1). But cf. *am* (10). *He* (6)
is apparently a misprint for *ye*. *Stuff this for a monkey's uncle* (8) is a
blend of two clichés: *(you can) stuff this (where the monkey stuffed his nuts)*
and *(if I do this) I'm a monkey's uncle*.

   The play was produced for Radio Scotland by Stewart Conn, and broadcast on
December 11, 1980. The scene in T46 was omitted, for reasons of length, and
because the football references are dated. Stewart Conn also felt that the
rapport created here with the studio audience when the play was recorded would
tend to exclude the radio audience (personal correspondence).

5.4   Poetry and song

The poet setting out to write in dialect is limited by the resources of dialect
vocabulary. The prevailing nostalgia in Scottish literature, mentioned in
Chapter 1, is particularly acute in dialect writing, as the writer is almost
driven into the past in search of subject matter for which an extensive dialect
vocabulary exists. Childhood and change are therefore common themes. Some
writers associate Glasgow dialect with popular forms, for instance the folk
song. The best compositions in this genre may pass into the folk repertoire.
On the other hand a bathetic little poem, "Black Friday", by James Copeland
(MacCaig and Scott, 1970: 67-8) which could not be included in the present
volume, begins:

> Oot behind a lorry,
> Peyin nae heed,
> Ablow a doubledecker,
> A poor wean deid.

This is the rhythm of the children's jingle given as T51 below. A form well
suited to the use of dialect is the dramatic monologue or dialogue, where clever linguistic choices invite inferences about the speaker and the situation.
However, few writers of stature confine themselves to dialect writing, and
many give it up after a period of experimentation with it.

5.4.1 Children's songs and jingles

No recent collection of Glasgow children's lore is available. However, the
British study of Opie and Opie (1959) includes some Glasgow material. Some
of the children's terms mentioned for Glasgow are: *bags* and *chops* for gaining
possession of an object; *keys* for gaining respite; *dumps* for the series of
blows, one for each year, which a child receives on a birthday. *Bing bang
skoosh* is the game of knocking doors and running away. *Chickie mellie* is also
given for this, as well as for more elaborate pranks. *Gloshins* is given for
the more usual *guisers*, children knocking on neighbours' doors for apples and
nuts at Hallowe'en. A tell-tale is a *clype* -cf. *grass* from MacLaren's pupils
(see 2.3.3 above). *Skinny malinky* and *bony moroney* are names for a thin person, and *cowardy custard* for a *coward*. *Dan* is a nickname for a Catholic (more
recently, *Tim*), and *Billy* for a Protestant (from William of Orange); cf. the
challenge 'A Billy or a Dan or an auld tin can?'

   The street songs below are from those collected by Opie and Opie (1959), or
are known to adults at the present time. Those quoted from Weir (1973) probably date from the period between the Wars, while the remaining two are known
to younger adults.

TEXT 47

'The barra broke at ten o'clock
An' ah loast ma hurl on the barra.
Aw the bonnie wee barra's mine,
It disnae belang tae O'Hara,
The fly wee bloke, stuck tae ma rock,
But ah'm gonny stick tae his barra.'

From Molly Weir, *Shoes were for Sunday*
(London: Pan Books, 1973; first published, 1970), 36

Notes

Weir writes (1973: 35-6) that this was one of the few street songs which she
consciously learned as a child, having thought that the first two lines were
the whole song. *Rock* (5) 'distaff' was probably not understood by children of
her generation.

TEXT 48

Ah'm no' comin' oot the noo, the noo,
Ah'm no' comin' oot the noo.
Ah'm very sorry Lizzie MacKay, for disappointin' you.
Ma mother's away wi' ma claes tae the pawn
To raise a bob or two.
An' ah've juist a fur aroon' ma neck,
So ah'm no' comin' oot the noo.   ibid, 37.

Notes

Weir writes (1973: 37) that this song was acted out by peeping out of a window.

TEXT 49

Born in a tenement at Gorbals Cross,
Of all the Teddy boys he was the boss,
Got him a slasher razor five feet wide,
Chopped up his mother and dumped her in the Clyde.
    Davy Crewcut, Davy Crewcut,
    King of the Teddy boy gang.

From Iona and Peter Opie, *The Lore and
Language of Schoolchildren* (Oxford:
Clarendon Press, 1959), 120.

Notes

The song is set to the theme tune of the Walt Disney film *Davy Crockett*, hence
the distortion *Davy Crewcut*. *Got him*(3) is an Americanism, and perhaps an influence from the original of the song. The Gorbals was one of the first districts of Glasgow to be cleared of slums and redeveloped, and the name is still
evocative of the worst stereotype of the city. The Teddy boys were a grouping
amongst British youth in the fifties, based on music and a macho image.

TEXT 50

What's your name?
Baldy Bain.
What's your ither?
Ask ma mither.   ibid, 157.

Notes

This is a ritual exchange between children. *Baldy Bain* (2) is a children's
taunt for a bald man.

TEXT 51

Skitter up a lamp post
Skitter up a tree,
If you see a Bobbie man
Skitter in his e'e.   ibid, 27.

TEXT 52

Skinny-malinky long-legs, big banana feet,
Went tae the pictures, an couldnae find a seat.
When the picture started, Skinny-malinky farted,
Skinny-malinky long-legs, big banana feet.

Notes

This is the usual version of the verse given in Opie and Opie (1959: 168)

TEXT 53

Ah went tae the pictures the morra,
Ah goat a front seat at the back,
A wumman she gied me some biscuits,
Ah ett them an gied her them back.
Ah fell fae the pit tae the balcony,
Ah broke ma front bone at the back,
An when Ah came oot i the pictures,
Ah nearly hauf killt a deid cat.

From "I dare say ye'll hae mind" with
Peter Mallan, Radio Clyde, 27 May 1979.

5.4.2 Edith Little, "The Barrows"

Edith Little writes recitations for performance in old folks' homes and similar
institutions. The verses which follow are from a poem about the Barrows, usually known as the Barras, a market near the old city centre. The orthography
is sometimes idiosyncratic, but otherwise the language is fairly dense literary Scots, without identifiable Glasgow features.

TEXT 54

```
       It's freezing and it's damp, but they'll be at their stall,
       Wrapped up in mufflers to keep oot the cauld,
       Vacuum flasks and cups, haundless and cracked,
       Gloves wi' half fingers to heal up the hacks,
5      Ankle boots and men's socks, who can be choosers,
       Wi' yon draught blawin' up the leg o' yer troosers?

       Dresses and coats, bundles o' bras,
       "Of course it's yer size, but if it's too sma',
       Gey it away to yer daughter-in-law."
10     "But I haven't got one", says I all uppy,
       "Well a' I can say is yer bluidy lucky."
```

From Edith Little, "The Barrows", 19-20
in *When Sixpence was a Fortune* (Milngavie
Heatherbank Press, 1978), 19.

Notes

In *cauld* (2) the /d/ is deleted to rhyme with *stall* (1). *Choosers* (5) normally
only occurs in the cliché *beggars can't be choosers*. *Uppy* (10) is usually
uppity.

5.4.3 Adam McNaughton, "Skyscraper Wean"

"Skyscraper wean", also known as "The jeely piece song", is part of the repertoire of many Scottish folksingers. It used to be that women could supervise
their children and toss things out to them, including packed lunches, from
tenement windows. This is, of course, impossible in high-rise flats. McNaughton
makes the missing sandwiches into a symbol of material and cultural deprivation,
all the more memorable for being humorous.

TEXT 55

I'm a skyscraper wean; I live on the nineteenth flair,
But I'm no gaun oot tae play ony mair,
'Cause since we moved tae Castlemilk, I'm wastin' away
'Cause I'm gettin' wan meal less every day:

Chorus: Oh ye cannae fling pieces oot a twenty storey flat,
          Seven hundred hungry weans'll testify to that.
          If it's butter, cheese or jeely, if the breid is plain or pan,
          The odds against it reaching earth are ninety-nine tae wan.

On the first day ma maw flung oot a daud o' Hovis broon;
It came skytin' oot the windae and went up insteid o' doon.
Noo every twenty-seven hoors it comes back intae sight
'Cause ma piece went intae orbit and became a satellite.

On the second day ma maw flung me a piece oot wance again.
It went and hut the pilot in a fast low-flying plane.
He scraped it aff his goggles, shouting through the intercom,
"The Clydeside Reds huv goat me wi' a breid-an-jeely bomb."

On the third day ma maw thought she would try another throw.
The Salvation Army band was staunin' doon below.
"Onward, Christian Soldiers" was the piece they should've played
But the oompah man was playing a piece an' marmalade.

We've wrote away to Oxfam to try an' get some aid,
An' a' the weans in Castlemilk have formed a "piece brigade."
We're gonnae march to George's Square demanding civil rights
Like, nae mair hooses ower piece-flinging height.

> From Norman Buchan and Peter Hall, eds.,
> *The Scottish Folksinger* (Glasgow and
> London: Collins, 1973), 23.

Notes

Castlemilk (3) is one of the largest of the peripheral housing schemes. George
Square (23) is the new city centre. *Piece brigade* (22) is a pun on *Peace
Brigade*.

5.4.4 Ian Hamilton Finlay, *Glasgow Beasts*

The dialect here is used for whimsy, by a writer who is not a native Scot. The first person of the poem sequence is reincarnated as different animals. The use of the dialect lends humour to the plight of the various beasts.

TEXT 56

```
     syne
     ah wis a midgie
     neist a stank
     foon that kin o
5    thankless
     didjye
     ever
     spen
     a
10   hail simmer
     stottin
     up
     an
     doon
```

> From Ian Hamilton Finlay, *Glasgow Beasts,*
> *an a Burd, an Inseks, an, aw, a Fush*
> (Edinburgh: The Alna Press, 1960), un-
> paginated.

Notes

Midgie (2) is the diminutive of *midge*. There is possibly a pun on *midgie* 'mid-den', given the collocation with *stank*. The vocabulary is literary. *Syne* (1) and *neist* (3) in particular, would be unlikely in Glasgow speech.

TEXT 57

```
     hooch
     a heilan coo
     wis mair liker
     it
5         the hiker
     s
     hoo hoos
     ferr feart
     o ma
10   herr-do
```
                              ibid.

Notes

Hooch (1), a vocal gesture uttered when dancing, is a Highland English stereo-type. The long-haired Highland cow is also stereotyped on postcards, and so on. Notice how the vowel /u/ is foregrounded by repitition and rhyme. *Hoo hoos* (7) seems to be an *ad hoc* variation on *ho ho*. The effect is onomatopoeic - cf. *moo*. The /z/ sound is also foregrounded. Notice the seperation of the plural morpheme from *hikers* (5, 6), and the addition of ⟨s⟩ to *hoo hoos*. This might suggest animal breathing.

TEXT 58

```
honess
pals
like
no been born
a cleg
s e bess
```
                    ibid.

Note

No been (4) is either 'know being' or 'not being'.

TEXT 59

```
   come back
   as a coal-horse
   ho the
          heavy
   an
5  hauf the day
   wi yir piece
   hauf-etten
   hung
   roon yir
10 ear
```
                    ibid.

Note

The initial /h/ which is prominent here could be made to suggest animal breathing, again.

5.4.5 Stephen Mulrine, "Nostalgie"

"Nostalgie" is something of a self-parody, regretting the loss of familiar scenes, but going to the opposite extreme in avoiding a rose-coloured view of them.

TEXT 60

```
     Well, the George Squerr stchumers've  pit the hems
     oan Toonheid's answer tae London's Thames;
     thuv peyed a squaad ooty Springburn broo
     tae kinfront the Kinawl wi its Watterloo,
 5   an dampt up Monklan's purlin stream
     fur some dampt bailie's petrol dream,
     some Tory nutter wi caurs oan the brain--
     jis shows ye, canny leave nuthin alane,
     the scunners.

10   Aye, thuv waistit Toonheid's claim tae fame,
     an minny's the terrs Ah hud as a wean,
     fishin fur roach aff the slevvery wa,
     an pullin in luckies, mibbe a baw,
     ur a bike, even, howked up ooty the glaur--
15   bit thuv timmed oot the watter, fur chuckies an taur,
     jis cowped the Kinawl fulla slag, ten a penny,
     an wheecht aw the luckies away tae the Clenny,
     in hunners.

     An thuv plankt the deid dugs aw swelt wi disease,
20   an pickt oot thur graves wi wee wizzent trees
     tae relieve the monotony, eight tae a mile--
     brek wan stick aff, thull gie ye the jile.
     Ach, thurs nuthin tae beat a gude pie in the sky,
     bit Ah've seen the Kinawl easy-oasyin by,
25   an it isnae the same Toonheid noo at aw,
     an therrs even the rats is shootin the craw--
     nae wunners.

     Fur thuv drapped an Emm Wan oan the aul Toonheid,
     an thurs nae merr dugs gonny float by deid--
30   jis caurs, jis breezin alang in the breeze,
     terrin the leafs aff the hauf-bilet trees,
     hell-bent fur the East, (aye, yir no faur wrang)
     wi thur taur an thur chuckies tae see thum alang--
     ach, nivver mind, son, they kin aw go tae hell,
35   an we'll jis stick like the Monklan itsel--
     non-runners.
```

From Stephen Mulrine, *Poems* (Preston: Akros, 1971), unpaginated.

Notes

Finite clauses can appear in the complement of existential sentences in ScE, as in 26. *Shoot the crow*, Scots *craw*, is rhyming slang for *go*.

5.4.6 Stephen Mulrine, "the weeber bird"

The language of this poem lies towards the standard pole of the ScE continuum.
However, there are many non-standard spellings. This draws attention to sound,
and suggests a speaking voice. There are actually two voices in the poem, the
latter having the last three lines. The subject of their conversation, 'the
weeber bird' appears to be present. There are several stylistic features which
are appropriate to talking about a child in its presence: the repetition of
phrases (once to the adult, again more slowly and on a higher pitch to the
child), the use of diminutives in reference to objects associated with the
child (the adjective *wee*), and the general lack of sensitivity to the child's
dignity, which provokes a dismissive reaction from the second voice. There is
thus a tension in the poem between a sympathy which is patronising, and an em-
barassed and repressed reaction to this.

There is also a tension between different ideas of the supernatural. The
modern mind has prettified the fairy world, which in older tales is primordial
and menacing. The evidence of hard work on 'the weeber bird's' thumbs, whether
or not it is only dye from the leather, relates to older ideas of the fairy
people labouring in a mirror world underground, while the ludicrous image of
little animals wielding gold and silver tools belongs to tales of Santa Claus.

TEXT 61

```
        the weeber bird wurks
        in the fairyboot wurks-
        hop down on prospect-
        hill road dont ye
        wee sun
        makin fairyboots
        makin fairyboots
        wi his wee
        silver hammer
        an his wee
        golden nails
        dont ye
        wee sun
        youve got that weeber
        destroyed so you have
        look at his thumbs
        look at his thumbs
        ach its only green
        dye aff the lea-
        thur
```

From Stephen Mulrine, *Poems* (Preston:
Akros, 1971), unpaginated.

Notes

Weeber is a nonce word suggestive of *weaver*, *weeper*, *wee berr* and a *weeb* noise.
The redivision of *workshop* (2, 3) gives *works*, a synonym, and *hop*, associated
with *bird*. *Sun*(5) is a visual pun. The endearment *wee son* is a masculine one,
women preferring more explicit expressions of affection. *Youve got that weeber
destroyed* (14, 15) is a weaker accusation than, e.g. *you have destroyed that
weeber*.

5.4.7 Tom Leonard, "Unrelated Incidents (2)"

Here Leonard attacks those who mistakenly say that people should speak as they
write. He uses a more phonologically accurate spelling system (for his own
accent), thus drawing attention to the vagaries of St E spelling. The consequent imposition of a Glasgow accent on the Deity in the quoted speech is no
more absurd than any other accent or variety. In any case, it is the 'content'
which matters.

TEXT 62

```
         ifyi stull
         huvny
         wurkt oot
         thi diff-
5        rince tween
         yir eyes
         n
         yir ears;
         - geez peace,
1o       pal!

         fyi stull
         huvny
         thoata lang-
         wij izza
15       sound-system;
         fyi huvny
         hudda thingk
         aboot thi dif-
         frince tween
20       sound
         n object n
         symbol;  well,
         ma innocent
         wee
25       friend - iz
         god said ti
         adam:

         a doant kerr
         fyi caw it
30       an apple
         ur
         an aippl -
         jist leeit
         alane!
```

From Alex Hamilton, James Kelman and Tom
Leonard, *Three Glasgow Writers* (Glasgow:
Molendinar Press, 1976), 35.

Notes

Leonard's orthography here and in numerous other Glasgow poems is a compromise between St E, which conceals the reality of regional and social variation, and a too precise transcription:

> It's trying to get this appearance of naturalness that seems to me the important thing – there's a point which the pursuit of exactitude would reach, where the reader would feel his attention being drawn more to the exactitude of transcription (with or without IPA) than to the actual "voice" being created. (Tom Leonard, personal correspondence).

He mentions also the risk of creating a superior or ironic attitude towards the voice. Compare the effect created by 'eye dialect', or using deliberate mis-spellings as a way of suggesting a lower class speaker.

5.4.8 Tom Leonard, "The Dropout"

Here Leonard presents a collage of the clichéd accusations of a domestic argument between mother and grown-up child. The dialogue is very well observed, especially its telegraphic quality – the syntax is highly asyndetic – which suggests that the same ground has been covered many times before.

TEXT 63

```
scrimpt nscraipt furryi
urryi grateful
no wan bit

speylt useless yi urr
twistid izza coarkscrew
cawz rowz inan empty hooss

yir fathir nivirid yoor chance
pick n choozyir joab
a steady pey

well jiss take a lookit yirsell
naithur wurk nur wahnt
aw aye

yir clivir
damm clivir
but yi huvny a clue whutyir dayn
```

From Tom Leonard, *Bunnit Husslin* (Glasgow: The Pluralist Press, 1975), unpaginated.

Notes

Naithur wurk nur wahnt (11), i.e. 'won't work but is unwilling to lack anything', is a cliché.

5.4.9 Edwin Morgan, "Stobhill"

"Stobhill" is a series of monologues, some in dialect, put into the mouths of
the people involved in an incident at Stobhill Hospital where a foetus alledg-
edly survived an abortion. The text below is the statement of the porter who
took the foetus to be incinerated.

TEXT 64, "The Porter"

```
        Ah know ah tellt them lies at the enquiry.
        Ah sayed ah thought the wean wis dead
        when ah took it tae the incinerator.
        Ah didny think the wean wis dead,
5       but ah didny ken fur shair, did ah?
        It's no fur me tae question the doctors.
        Ah get a bag fae the sister, right?
        She says take that an burn it.  She's only
        passin on the doctor's instructions,
10      but she seen the wean, she thought it wis dead,
        so ye canny blame her.  And the doctor says
        ye canny blame him.  Everybody wants
        tae come doon on me like a tonna bricks.
        Ah canny go aboot openin disposal bags -
15      if ah did ah'd be a nervous wreck.
        Ah passed two electricians in the corridor
        and ah tellt them the wean wis alive
        but they thought ah wis jokin.  Efter that
        ah jist shut up, an left it tae the boilerman
20      tae fin oot fur hissel - he couldny miss it
        could he?  The puir wee thing wis squeelin
        through the bag wis it no?  Ah canny see
        ah had tae tell him whit wis evident.
        - Ah know ah'm goin on aboot this.
25      But suppose the kiddy could've been saved -
        or suppose the boilerman hadny noticed it -
        mah wee lassie's gote a hamster, ye ken? -
        and ah fixed up a treadmill fur it
        and it goes roon an roon an roon -
30      it's jist like that.  Well ah'm no in court noo.
        Don't answer nothin incriminatin, says the sheriff.
        And that's good enough fur yours truly.
        And neither ah did, neither ah did,
        neither ah did, neither ah did.
```

From Edwin Morgan, "Stobhill", 87-91 in
From Glasgow to Saturn (Cheshire:
Carcanet Press, 1973), 91.

Notes

Kiddy (25) is an unusual choice of words. The affectionate diminutive suggests
embarassment, and highlights the problem of how to regard the unborn child.
The other words used are *wean* (four times) and *puir wee thing* (21). (Adjective
- *wee thing*) is often applied to babies, but here *thing* takes on sinister over-
tones. The *non sequitur* in 27 is disconcerting. *Yours truly* (32) is a cynical

way of referring to oneself, here indicating a pretended toughness. The repitions of *neither ah did* (33, 34) can be read as alternately main clauses and sentence tag, with stress alternately on *neither* and *did*. The repitition suggests that the words take on further meanings in the act of utterance, and this clearly relates to the porter's failure to intervene.

Notice *shair* (5) rather than a spelling suggesting /εr/, and *puir* (21) rather than *perr*.

5.4.10 Alex Hamilton, "Poor Tom"

The style of this poem is an interesting reflection of attitudes towards St E. The tone is circumspect and verbose up to the code-switch in the last line, indeed the last word, where we get down to facts.

TEXT 65

My cat has a well-developed
bourgeois
sense of property.
That is
each cardboard novelty he finds
is taken.

For his own.

That is
my cat.

I have

that is my cat's master has

a well-developed
feline
sense of smell.

That is
the gonads
offended.

And were took.

From *Words* 5 (1978), 29.

5.5 Journalism and reminiscence

To a large extent, Scotland has its own newspapers. The English tabloids are replaced by the *Daily Record* and the *Sunday Mail*. The quality English papers are largely replaced by the *Scotsman* and the *Glasgow Herald*, and there is a new Sunday paper, the *Sunday Standard*. There are also numerous local and evening papers. The Scottish press regularly admits dialect in certain specialised areas, particularly cartoons and anecdotes with dialogue. Feature and sports writers also often flatter their readers by using dialectal items for key terms. The same practise is found in reminiscence, where it lends verisimilitude. These dialectal items are sometimes put between quotation marks, sometimes not.

5.5.1 'Shadow', *Midnight Scenes and Social Photographs*

Alexander Brown, who wrote under the pen-name of 'Shadow' was a printer in
Glasgow. His 'social photographs' are the record of his expeditions into the
dreadful slums of 19th century Glasgow, and an attempt to bring living conditions there to public attention. Some of the items published in *Midnight
Scenes* appeared originally in the *Glasgow Argus* in 1857. Brown makes liberal
use of quoted speech, as in the conversation below, but tends to modify the
dialect in the direction of literary Scots. In particular he prefers standard
syntax, as in literary Scots, and for similar reasons. Brown wishes to create
a positive attitude towards the speakers, and therefore portrays their language
as colourful (non-standard lexis and lexical incidence), but not slovenly (non-
standard grammar).

TEXT 66

"What a rare story that was," says this poor unfortunate, after a long pause
in the conversation, "about auld Johnny Clerk (afterwards Lord Eldin) when
comin' hame ae mornin' fou', just twa hours afore the Coort o' Session met, an'
meetin' wi' a gentleman in Picardy Place, said, 'Can ye tell me, man, whaur
5   Johnny Clerk lives?' 'You're Johnny Clerk yoursel',' replied the stranger.
'D--n you, sir, I didna want to ken wha he was, but whaur he lives.'" For the
recital of this rather stale joke, a little good-humoured laughter, of course,
follows by way of approbation. Desirous of giving a turn to the conversation,
our friend with the spectacles inquires if any of the company has heard Dr.
10   Cumming during the day? "Dr. Cumming!" says a shrewd little well-dressed man
in the corner, "I wudna gang the length o' my tae to hear him. He's everlast-
ingly foretellin' the end o' the world in twa-three years, but he aye tak's
gude care to secure the copyricht o' his books, an' hae a lang lease o' his
hoose, in case he shouldna' tell richt."

> From 'Shadow', *Midnight Scenes and Social
> Photographs* (1858), reproduced, with an
> Introduction by John McCaffrey, as
> *Glasgow 1958* (Glasgow: Glasgow U. P.,
> 1976), 26-7.

Notes

Rare (1) or *rerr* is still a popular superlative. *Ae* (3) 'one' is now pronounced
/je/ in Southern and Central Scotland. There was formerly a distinction between *ae*, determiner, and *ane* or *yin*, pronoun. *Yin* is now usual in both func-
tions, alongside *wan*. *The length of myself* is the current idiom, rather than
the length o' my tae (11).

5.5.2 Alex Mitchell, "Little stories from the police courts"

Mitchell's "Little stories from the police courts" have appeared since the late
1920s in the *Weekly News*, a tabloid paper. At first they were based on actual
incidents, but quickly became fictional exercises. Mitchell is a very good
observer of the dialect, but tends to conflate the speech of several generations.

TEXT 67

Whack from Rita for disco champ

THE Okeydokey Club was packed. It was the occasion of the Grand Yuletide Ball and the Okeydokey Disco-dancing Championship Finals.

A cheer went up from the excited throng when, after a stirring fanfare from Fred and his Band of Boogie Woogie Bachles, the picturesque figure of Santa Claus appeared.

From the depths of his luxuriant white beard came the distinctive voice of Wee Andy, M.C.

"Permit me for to extend festive greetings to youse all!" he called heartily.

"Without no more delay, we shall commence the festive proceedings with our exciting contest," he announced. "This will bestow on the winner the title of Okeydokey Disco-dancing Champion."

This was the cue for the band to strike up disco music.

A succession of young ladies and gents went through their dance routines. Amongst the competitors was Rita the Critic.

Spiky hair

As she danced she had some advice to offer the band. "Keep up ra beat therr!" she urged. "Huz the drummer goat bevvied an' fell asleep?"

She was followed by Di, an extremely thin maiden with multi-coloured, spiky hair, who wore a diamante-studded leotard. Her energetic gyrations impressed the crowd.

They also impressed the sole judge, Wee Andy, who declared her to be the winner.

"Never have I saw such expertiseness as we seen from this young lady," he enthused as he presented the delighted Di with a bottle of champagne and an inscribed plastic plaque.

"She can dance nane,"

LITTLE STORIES FROM THE POLICE COURTS

was Rita's verdict. "It's a blinkin' carve-up."

Wee Andy was shocked. "Never has a more scurrulous accusation been made against me!" he cried.

"Don't boather aboot hur!" shrilled Di. "She's no' pleased because she didny get a prize fur hur impersonation o' an elephant hoppin' aboot oan rid-hoat bricks."

"Ya ugly skelington!" yelled Rita, advancing on the disco - dancing champion. "Ah'll brek ye in two!"

"Ladies! Ladies!" Wee Andy pleaded. "I besiege you not to spoil the season of goodwill!"

Low whistle

His plea was in vain. As Rita's hand shot out he barely had time to step back.

His low, emergency whistle was almost drowned by Di's screech as she received a hefty whack on the face.

Nevertheless, Wee Andy's henchmen were quickly on the scene and Rita was escorted from the premises.

In court for assault, she was unrepentant. "That skinny dame wiz lucky tae escape wi' only the wan thump," she said when paying her £10 fine.

From *The Weekly News*, December 27, 1980.

Notes

Mitchell's practice with regard to non-standard grammar is quite the opposite
of 'Shadow's'. He uses as many items as possible and combines them with mispronunciations like *expertiseness* (column 1, 52) and malapropisms like *besiege*
(column 2, 77) = *beseech* for comic effect. *Skelington* (column 2, 72), a joking
mispronunciation of *skeleton*, is a current idiom. *Okeydokey* (3) is a redupli-
cative form of *okay*. *Nane* (column 1, 58) 'not at all' was formerly an emphatic
alternative to *no* 'not', at least in Southern Scotland. It is now restricted
to clause final position, often in collocation with *can*, as here. Notice *the
wan* (column 2, 96) - cardinal numerals can take the definite article in ScE.

5.5.3 Albert Mackie, *Talking Glasgow*

Albert Mackie's *Talking Glasgow* may be included in this section, as Mackie is
primarily a journalist, and the style of the book is journalistic. Mackie is
not a native of Glasgow, and does not make clear what his sources are, but on
the whole his observations appear to be accurate, although, like Mitchell's,
they extend over a long period of time. His examples of Glasgow speech, as in
the passage below, are a little too rich in traditional Scots lexis.

TEXT 68

'But see thae Embruh folk? Ye'd need a innerduction, so ye wid. They nivver
open their mooths till they've kent ye aboot a week. No that ye could unnerstaun them if they ivver dae speak, wi their Panloaf Moarnside paa'er.
   'Ass thum the road tirra Waverley an they'll luck at ye as if ye wiz a Dalek
5 or sumpn. They hink y're sayin: "Tak me tae yer leader!" so they div.'
   'Moarnside' (Morningside) is the district in Edinburgh which corresponds in
legend to Kelvinside in Glasgow. Its inhabitants are popularly supposed to
speak an even more intensive Panloaf than the rest of the Edinburgh citizens.
   In fact there is a lot of broad Scots spoken in Morningside, and in Edinburgh
10 generally, but the inhabitants of the capital always put on their best English
when talking to strangers, including 'gents' from Glasgow.
   'Noo we Glesca folk are different awragirra. Come intae Glesca an' we spoat
right away ye're a stranger an' right away we're oot tae gie ye a helpin haun.
We'll say "Tak wan o thae green an yella wans" - ra busses, ken? - an' "Murra-
15 well - at's a rid wan doon at ra Croass. Embruh's a green wan. Mulguy's a
blue wan fae Buchanan Street. Try ra Subway, but: ra Unnerground, like! It's
ra bess urra loat (the best of the lot), so it is. Yiz kin get jissaboot ony-
whaur on them Blue Trains, but." At's *us* - information while yiz wait.'
   This is a boast one must acknowledge to be justified. Glaswegians *are* very
20 friendly to strangers, and very willing to tell you about their city, of which
they are extremely proud.

From Albert Mackie, *Talking Glasgow*
(Belfast: Blackstaff Press, 1978), 48.

Notes

A *Dalek* (4), from a children's television programme, is a villainous extra-
terrestrial. *Innerduction* (1) is possibly to be read as [ɪnˀrɪdʌkʃɪn] but is
probably intended as a mispronunciation. Mackie makes use of ⟨r⟩ for /ð/ merged
with /r/, which is usually found only in comic texts, and ⟨'⟩ for [ʔ] in *paa'er*
(3). He shows another phonological item which usually goes unrecorded in spelling: /h/ for /θ/ in *hink* (5) and in *sumpn* (5), where the ⟨p⟩ probably represents voiceless [m̥]. The effect of showing phonetic assimilation in *Moarnside*
(3) and *ass thum* (4) is to suggest an uneducated speaker. *Jiss* (17) for *jist*
'just' is also used by other writers. In the body of the book, Mackie makes
sparing use of the device of running words together, but this is the basis of
a number of jokes in the 'glossary'.

Translation (1-5 and 12-18)

But those Edinburgh people, you know? You'd need an introduction, you really
would. They never open their mouths until they've known you for about a week.
Not that you could understand them if they ever do speak, with their Panloaf
Morningside language. Ask them the way to Waverley Station and they'll look
at you as if you were a Dalek or something. They think you're saying, 'Take
me to your leader!' they really do.

   Now, we Glasgow people are different altogether. Come into Glasgow and we
spot right away that you're a stranger, and right away we're trying to give you
a helping hand. We'll say, 'Take one of those green and yellow ones' - the
buses, you know? - and 'Motherwell - that's a red one down at the Cross.
Edinburgh's a green one. Milngavie's a blue one from Buchanan Street Station.
Try the subway, though: the Underground, as it were! It's the best of the lot,
it really is. You can get just about anywhere on those Blue Trains, though.'
That's *us* - information while you wait.

5.5.4 Andy Cameron, "Please yersel"

Andy Cameron is a disc jockey with Radio Clyde. His journalistic style in his
"Please yersel" column is similar to the variably localised speech of many
Radio Clyde presenters (cf. 3.9 above).

TEXT 69

WELL, it's all over. London is drowned in discarded kerry-oot bags and the polis are sighing great 5 **sighs of relief . . .**

This is when I can sit back and thank the great fitba' boss in the sky that I wasn't part of the Wembly Woe.

10   Mind you, the missus is not talking to me since I flung my can of Irn Bru at the telly.

And talking of tellies . . . what about this game at Hampden tonight. 15 We're getting more repeats from this lot than we get on BBC.

FORGOTTEN

How different it all was from my first visit to Wembley in 20 1967, a vintage year if you remember, when a skinny fella from Fife called Baxter teasted, tormented, and gave

I'VE GOT MY MAGIC WEMBLEY MEMORIES

lessons on how the game should be played, much to the annoyance of the English football team especially a little redheaded nyaff called Ball.

The result of 3-2 wasn't as important as the way it was achieved and the immediate chant from the 50,000 Scots was Sir Alf is on the dole, Sir Alf is on the dole. Sir Alf Ramsay of course had just 10 months earlier "acquired" the World Cup by playing every game in front of a Wembley full of Englishmen.

The first Wembley visit is always the best. The result is soon forgotten as the euphoria of a trip to the big smoke takes over.

memories of 1967 are mostly of the apres football events such as the West Indian Railwaymen on the train back to London singing "If ye hate the English Polis clap yer hands" or my pal George, looking decidedly "green" discovering that the chewing gum he had spat out during the game had landed between his shirt and sweater and was now spread all over his clothes or the wee Glasgow punter who on hearing my old man's accent when he jumped into his taxi said "Ah didnae know they had Glesga taxis doon there."

Of course no Wembley trip would be complete without a visit to Soho. My

What a let down. The strippers we saw wouldn't have been allowed to take their coats off in Glasgow never mind anything else and talk about being conned.

We were all patting each other on the back because we had discovered a club where we got in for nothing only to discover that they charged £3.50 tae get oot!

As I said it's all over for this year but I'll lay London to an orange that this week in clubs and pubs all over Scotland the following notice will appear on the wall: Join the Wembley club for 1981.

See big Wullie for details.

Have you heard...

● Wee Glasgow wummun who says to the butcher "Gies a haggis. Ah want tae spend a night wi Rabbie Burns. The butcher says: "Nae haggis hen. Here's a black puddin. Spend it wi Sammy Davis Jnr."

● The Rangers supporter who is so bitter, when his watch stops he won't even phone the talking clock because it's a T.I.M.

Beating the blues!

LAST WEEK while alone at home and feeling a bit down (I had just witnessed a team of 10 men take apart a team of 11 units by 4 goals to 2) I picked up one of my wife's many magazines and boy did that cheer me up.

I thought I suffered watching Rangers every week but my wife actually has to read these things just to find out what is happening in the romance stories.

They really are something else. How do women control their passions reading such provocative lines . . . "My heart leapt as he touched me under the tabl ewith his Wellington boots." . . . "She unzipped her anorak to reveal her thermal vest, the very one he had given her as a surprise 1st anniversary present." The parts I like best are the adverts.

If you want the perfect face, it's lotions and potions by the barraload. First you put on cleansing stuff to get your face ready for more cream. It could be protein, herbal, or plain cucumber.

Once that lot's on there are toners, blushers, and rouges. It's like goin oot wi the Multi Coloured Swap Shop!

And after your big night out you've to go through it all again. The cream to take it off, a lotion to clean the pores and another belt of toner!

What next? Slop on some night cream before goin to yer kip. Crazyl

The problem page in these periodicals had me roaring.

Dear Mary: "I've been seeing a man for 18 years and have discovered recently that he has a wooden leg—should I break it off."—Anxious, Blairdardie.

Dear Anxious: Yes break it off immediately and tell him to hop it.—Mary.

Dear Lydia: "I am really worried about my husband. He imagines he's a pair of curtains. What can I do?"—Eunice, Edinburgh.

Dear Eunice: You must help him to pull himself together.—Lydia.

From Andy Cameron, "Please yersel", *Evening Times*, May 28, 1979.

Notes

Teasted (22) is a misprint for *teased*. *Irn bru* (11, 12) 'iron brew' is a soft drink, advertised in Scotland as 'your other national drink - made in Scotland from girders.'

Have you heard ...: *Tim* is a derogatory term for a Catholic.

5.5.5 Molly Weir, *Shoes were for Sunday*

Molly Weir, in a series of autobiographical writings, gives a nostalgic account of respectable poverty in Glasgow during her childhood, in the inter-war years.

TEXT 70

What a choice of goods we had for our farthing! There were tiny sugarally pipes, with little scarlet dots inside the bowl, pretending they were burning tobacco. There were sweetie cigarettes at five for a penny, so naturally a farthing bought one, although it was a bitter disappointment to me that Jeannie
5 wouldn't break the odd one into bits to give me exact justice for my farthing. I wasn't really convinced when she told me, 'Ye aye loss a wee bit, hen, when ye don't buy in bulk,' and I dreamed of the day when I would spend a whole penny and buy *five* cigarettes at once, ration myself carefully over a few days, and gain an extra sweet smoke.
10 Sweeties had been very expensive after war No 1, and tumbling prices came along in the nick of time for me to enjoy them. Never will I forget the day when the number of aniseed balls went up to forty a penny. There were queues at the wee shop that day, and it was indeed a land of plenty to be given ten balls, hard as iron, for a farthing. I nearly sucked my tongue raw until, with
15 dawning disbelief, I realized I'd have to leave some over for next day. For sweeties to last more than a few minutes was outside my experience until that moment, and it was a marvellous feeling to tuck that wee poke with the three remaining anisseed balls behind Grannie's hankies in the bottom of the chest of drawers, where my brothers couldn't make a raid without either Grannie or
20 me spotting them.

From Molly Weir, *Shoes were for Sunday*
(London: Pan Books, 1973; first published 1970), 33.

Notes

Notice the use of localised lexis and colloquial diminutives for certain key words.

5.5.6 Clifford Hanley, *Dancing in the Streets*

Clifford Hanley is a Glasgow journalist and novelist. His witty autobiography
includes reminiscences of Glasgow music halls and newspapers. Like Weir, he
uses dialect words for events and things associated with childhood or with
areas of life where dialect is spoken. The word *nyuck* is attested only from
this book.

TEXT 71

A TERRIBLE thing the drink, and no defence for us against it except the Band
of Hope chant..."honour my father and my mother and refrain from strong drink
as a beverage...." But it wasn't the drink that led us into crime. We couldn't
afford any kind of steady drinking on a halfpenny a week pocket money. We just
turned naturally to law-breaking out of the badness of our hearts. Even I,
essentially a sensitive, pure-minded keelie, was a hog for bad company. Something, I don't know, some original flaw in my character hurled me into the arms
of any fast set who were up to something no good if it looked easy enough.

So maybe it's just as well we flitted. That old Hanley wanderlust was
stirring in the family, and shortly after my fifth birthday I found myself in
the middle of the delirious excitement of a flitting.

Everybody else seemed to be busy hauling chairs and ornaments about, but
in the middle of this Mary found time to wash my face. A few minutes later
Johanne noticed me under somebody's feet and for want of anything better to
do with me she washed my face too - 'You want to look nice for the new house',
she said. That was all right with me. When nobody bothered with me for ten
minutes or so I went back to the jawbox and ran the tap over my head. I wanted
to make a proper job of the thing while I was at it. The flitting was abandoned
while half the team pulled me out from under the tap and dried me off, but nobody was much upset. One more little thing couldn't make any difference at a
Hanley flitting. Soon afterwards I was hurried, wrapped like a mummy to keep
the pneumonia out, downstairs, across Gallowgate and upstairs again. We had
moved from the second floor flat on the south side to the second floor flat
directly facing on the north side. We had begun to carve our way up through
the amorphous social strata of the city, for there's no doubt that from the
new windows, the old building was patently on the wrong side of the tracks.

> From Clifford Hanley, *Dancing in the
> Streets* (London: White Lion Publishers,
> 1979; first published, 1958), 31-2.

Notes

Names of institutions and afflictions take the definite article in ScE. I am
not sure which category *the drink* (1) falls into. Cf. *the pneumonia* (22).

5.5.7   Bud Neill, "Lobey Dosser"

Bud Neill's popular "Lobey Dosser" cartoons appeared in the Glasgow *Evening Times* in the 1940s and 1950s.   Lobey Dosser is a Wild West sheriff, and occasionally characters in the strip use stereotyped AmE, but on the whole, sympathetic characters speak in localised Glasgow English, while the villain, Bajin, i.e. Bad Yin, largely speaks in formal St E.

Figure 9, "Lobey Dosser"

From *The Evening Times*, January 10, 1950.

Notes

Lobey dosser is literally someone who sleeps in lobbies. See Glossary under DOSSER. *My man* and *I do declare* are stereotypes of upper class speech. On the other hand, *jookery pokery*, which Bajin also uses, is ScE. *Wish* (frame 2) is considered 'proper' in ScE, and is even used as a transitive verb, e.g. 'do you wish salad cream?'. Contrast *want* in frame 3.

5.5.8 *The Dampness Monster*

The subject of this political cartoon is the unsympathetic and obstructive attitude of some housing officials towards the problem of dampness in corporation housing. Some dampness is caused by a novel method of construction with prefabricated concrete, and aggravated by any activity which tends to produce moisture in the air. Such activities are listed and banned in frames 4-10 of the cartoon below. Officialdom is symbolically defeated, firstly by the patent absurdity of the bans; secondly by spelling mistakes; thirdly by the use of dialect in certain of the 'official' notices. To use the tenants' own vocabulary in reference to them is to acknowledge their right to self-definition.

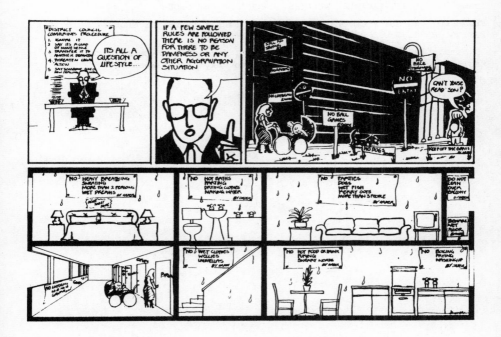

Figure 10

From Richard Bryant, *The Dampness Monster: A report of the Gorbals Anti-dampness Campaign* (Edinburgh: Scottish Council of Social Service, 1979), 15.

Notes

The notices on the walls, which may be unclear in the reproduction, read as follows:

Frame 1: DISTRICT COUNCIL COMPLAINTS PROCEDURE 1 IGNORE IT 2 SAY ITS A LOAD OF NONESENCE 3 TRANSFER IT TO ANOTHER DEPARTM... 4 THREATEN LEGAL ACTION 5 SAY SOMEONE ELSE IS NOW DEALING WITH I...

Frame 3: (clockwise from bottom left) NO LOITERING BY ORDER; NO SPITTING; STILL NO SPITTING; NO PIECE THROWING; NO ENTRY; KEEP OFF THE GRASS; NO DOGS; NO BALL GAMES

Frame 4: NO HEAVY BREATHING SWEATING MORE THAN 2 PERSONS WET DREAMS BY ORDER; HOME SWEET HOME

Frame 5: NO HOT BATHS FARTING DRYING CLOTHES MAKING WATER BY ORDER

Frame 6: NO PARTIES DOGS WET FISH KERRY OOTS MORE THAN 3 PEOPLE BY ORDER

Frame 7: DO NOT LEAN OVER BALCONY; BEWARE WET FLOOR BY ORDER

Frame 8: NO LOITERING LOUD NOISE GRAFFITI (The graffiti includes TONGS, a gang name, and CELTIC, a football team).

Frame 9: NO WET CLOTHES WELLIES UMBRELLAS BY ORDER

Frame 10: NO HOT FOOD OR DRINK PUKING SWEARY WORDS BY ORDER; NO BOILING FRYING WASHING UP BY ORDER.

Situation, as in *aggravation situation*, is a stereotype of bureaucratic English. *Piece throwing* is an allusion to "Skyscraper Wean" (see T55).

CONCLUSIONS

Localised Glasgow English is as divergent from RP-accented St BrE as any British dialect. However, it is placed under the double stigma of being divergent from the standard and also from culturally prestigious varieties of Scots. Perhaps for this reason, it has attracted less attention from linguists and critics than the size of the city and the extent and quality of the local dialect literature would lead one to expect.

I would like to conclude by focusing on some areas which have been dealt with only superficially in this volume. First of all, in phonology, there are a number of variants whose sociolinguistic distribution has not been studied in Glasgow, but which promise to show interesting patterns of sound change in progress. Are the deletion of /ð/ and its lenition and merger with /r/ related developments? If so, is the sequence the same in Belfast and in Edinburgh? Is Glasgow a centre of innovation for this variable? Do women in Glasgow have much /r/ for /ð/? Glottal realisations of voiceless plosives other than /t/ are also interesting. Is there an implicational scale from /t/ to /k/ and /p/? There may be a HibE influence in /d/ for initial /ð/. Would the distribution by age indicate that this was stable, increasing, or decreasing in frequency? Cacuminal /s, z/ is a problem. Occasional spellings in Scottish literature suggest a merger of /s/ with /ʃ/. Is there any meaningful distribution of this variant? Is it sporadic and idiolectal, or even a speech defect?

There are many marked intonation contours other than the high rising terminal associated with 'open' meanings, and the boosted initial peak of contours which introduce topics. There are tunes associated with mockery, sarcasm, irony, and unwillingness to commit oneself, as well as the upward and downward keyshifts mentioned by G. Brown *et al.* (1980). The problem of eliciting these under controlled circumstances is daunting, as the production of many of these tunes may depend on animated or even heated exchanges.

With regard to attitudes towards Glasgow speech, it may not be impossible to observe the process of formation of stereotypes and ideologies. Attention is usually focussed on formal education, but the mass media and the more popular types of dialect literature, for instance in journalism, may be as, or even more important.

Dialect literature, when it is as copious and as realistic as much of that sampled in this volume, provides a tantalising corpus of non-standard items in fictive contexts which one often feels are closely modelled on real speech events. And there can be no doubt that many writers, in producing dialect texts, are generalising from a wealth of careful observation. But how can this material be put to systematic use? A basic problem is the reliability of informants', including writers', judgements about the acceptability and currency of items, and the tendency of some informants to collapse observations of their own and their acquaintances' speech over several generations.

My experience in compiling this volume has been that many linguistic features which first came to my attention through the dialect literature have been confirmed to exist by the speech sampled on the tape. The discussion of code-switching in 1.8.3 is based mainly on Glasgow dialect literature. This type of writing has proved to be valuable not only in illustrating known facts about the speech variety, but also in generating hypotheses to be tested against speech.

BIBLIOGRAPHY

Abercrombie, David (1979), "The accents of Standard English in Scotland", in Aitken and McArthur (1979), 68-84.

Adams, G. B. (1948), "An introduction to the study of Ulster dialects", *Proceedings of the Royal Irish Academy*, 52:C:1 (1948), 1-26.

Adams, G. B. (forthcoming), *English in the North of Ireland* (Varieties of English Around the World, Heidelberg).

Agutter, A. J. L. (1979), "The linguistic significance of current British slang" (Edinburgh PhD thesis, unpublished).

Agutter, A. J. L. and L. N. Cowan (1981), "Changes in the vocabulary of Lowland Scots dialects", *Scottish Literary Journal*, Supplement 14 (1981), 49-62.

Aitken, A. J. (1976), "The Scots language and the teacher of English" in *Scottish Literature in the Secondary School*, 48-55.

Aitken, A. J. (1977), "How to pronounce Older Scots" in Aitken *et al.* (1977), 1-21.

Aitken, A. J. (1979), "Scottish speech: a historical view with special refer-ence to the Standard English of Scotland" in Aitken and McArthur (1979), 85-118.

Aitken, A. J. (1981), "The Scottish vowel-length rule" in Benskin and Samuels (1981), 131-57.

Aitken, A. J. *et al.*, eds. (1977), *Bards and Makars* (Glasgow).

Aitken, A. J. and Tom McArthur, eds. (1979), *Languages of Scotland* (Edinburgh).

Armstrong, Gail and Mary Wilson (1973), "Delinquency and some aspects of housing", in Ward (1973), 68-84.

Atlas of Glasgow and the West Region of Scotland (1973), Department of Geography, University of Strathclyde (Edinburgh).

Bell, J. J. (1933), *Wee Macgreegor* (London).

Benskin, Michael and M. L. Samuels, eds. (1981), *So Meny People Longages and Tonges: Philological Essays in Scots and Mediaeval English Presented to Angus McIntosh* (Edinburgh).

Berdan, Robert (1978), "Multidimensional analysis of vowel variation" in Sankoff (1978), 149-60.

Blake, George (1935), *The Shipbuilders* (London).

Boyle, Jimmy (1977), *A Sense of Freedom* (London).

Brittain, J. A. (1977), *The Inheritance of Economic Status* (Washington).

Brown, Keith (unpublished), "Relative clauses in a corpus of Scots speech".

Brown, Keith and Martin Millar (1980), "Auxiliary verbs in Edinburgh speech", *Transactions of the Philological Society* (1980), 81-133.

Brown, Keith and Jim Miller (1975), "Modal verbs in Scottish English", *Work in Progress* (Department of Linguistics, University of Edinburgh), 10 (1975), 99-114.

Brown, Kenneth (1981), "Small group discussion of poetry", *Teaching English*, 14: 2 (1981), 29-34.

Brown, Gillian *et al.* (1980), *Questions of Intonation* (London).

Brown, Penelope and Stephen Levinson (1978), "Universals in language usage: politeness phenomena" in Goody (1978), 56-289.

Bryant, Richard (1979), *The Dampness Monster: A Report of the Gorbals Anti-Dampness Campaign* (Edinburgh).

Bryden, Bill (1975), *Benny Lynch* (Edinburgh).

Burgess, Moira (1972), *The Glasgow Novel 1870-1970: A Bibliography* (Glasgow).

Campbell, James (1979), "The Scottish lie nailed", *New Society*, 23 August 1979, 410-11.

Catford, J. C. (1957a), "The Linguistic Survey of Scotland", *Orbis* 6 (1957), 105-21.

Catford, J. C. (1957b), "Vowel systems of Scots dialects", *Transactions of the Philological Society* (1957), 107-17.

Chambers, J. K. and Peter Trudgill (1980), *Dialectology* (Cambridge).

Chambers Twentieth Century Dictionary (1972, 1978), ed. A. M. Macdonald (Edinburgh).

Checkland, S. G. (1977), *The Upas Tree: Glasgow 1875-1975* (Glasgow).

Cruttenden, Alan (1981), "Falls and rises: meanings and universals", *Journal of Linguistics* 17: 1 (1981), 77-92.

Currie, Karen (1979), "Intonation systems of Scottish English" (Edinburgh PhD thesis, unpublished).

Davies, Alan, ed. (1975), *Problems in Language and Learning* (London).

Dowie, Alan (1979), "Persepshuns", *Drumlin* (The Magazine of Glasgow University Geographical Society), 24 (1978-9), 58-62.

Esling, John (1978), "Voice quality in Edinburgh: A sociolinguistic and phonetic study" (Edinburgh PhD thesis, unpublished).

Glen, Duncan (1974), *A Bibiography of Scottish Poets from Stevenson to 1974* (Preston).

Goody, Esther N., ed. (1978)), *Questions and Politeness: Strategies in Social Interaction* (Cambridge).

Gregg, Robert J. (1972), "The Scotch-Irish dialect boundaries in Ulster", in Wakelin (1972), 109-39.

Hamilton, Alex (1976a), "Gallus, did you say" in Hamilton *et al.* (1976), 2-14.

Hamilton, Alex (1976b), "Our Merry" in Hamilton *et al.* (1976), 15-28.

Hamilton, Alex *et al.* (1976), *Three Glasgow Writers* (Glasgow).

Hanley, Clifford (1958, 1979), *Dancing in the Streets* (London).

Hannington, Val (1936, 1979), *Unemployed Struggles 1919-1936: My Life and Struggles Amongst the Unemployed* (London).

Hechter, Michael (1975), *Internal Colonialism: The Celtic Fringe in British National Development, 1536-1966* (London).

Hughes, Arthur and Peter Trudgill (1979), *English Accents and Dialects* (Great Britain).

Jacobs, Jane (1965), *The Death and Life of Great American Cities: The Failure of Town Planning* (Middlesex).

Johnston, James B. (1934), *Place-Names of Scotland* (London).

Johnston, Paul (1979), "A synchronic and historical view of Border area bimoric vowel systems" (Edinburgh PhD thesis, unpublished).

Johnston, Paul (forthcoming), "A sociolinguistic investigation of the Standard Scottish English of Morningside". ⤳ *in Edinburgh,*

Kelman, James (1973), "Nice tae be nice", *The Glasgow Review* IV: 3 (1973), 42-7.

Labov, William (1972, 1978), *Sociolinguistic Patterns* (Oxford).

Lander, Steve and Ken Reah, eds. (1981), *Aspects of Linguistic Variation: Proceedings of the Conference on Language Varieties, July 1980* (The Centre for English Cultural Tradition and Language, University of Sheffield, Conference Papers Series, 1). .

Leonard, Tom (1975, 1978), *Bunnit Husslin* (Glasgow).

Leonard, Tom (1976), "Unrelated incidents" in Hamilton *et al.* (1976), 34-44.

Macafee, Caroline (1981), "Nationalism and the Scots Renaissance now", *English World-Wide* 2: 1 (1981), 29-38.

McAllister, Anne (1938), *A Year's Course in Speech Training* (London).

McArthur, Alexander and H. Kingsley Long (1935, 1978), *No Mean City* (London).

Macaulay, R. K. S. (1975), "Linguistic insecurity", in McClure (1975), 35-43.

Macaulay, R. K. S. (1977), *Language, Social Class, and Education: A Glasgow Study* (Edinburgh).

Macaulay, R. K. S. (1978), "Variation and consistency in Glaswegian English" in Trudgill (1978), 132-43.

Macaulay, R. K. S. and Gavin D. Trevelyan (1973), "Language, education and employment in Glasgow: A report to the Social Science Research Council", 2 vols. (unpublished).

MacCaig, Norman and Alexander Scott, eds. (1970), *Contemporary Scottish Verse 1959-1969* (London).

McClure, J. Derrick (1972), "Dialect in *The House with the Green Shutters*", *Studies in Scottish Literature* IX: 2-3 (1971-72), 148-63.

McClure, J. Derrick, ed. (1975), *The Scots Language in Education* (Association for Scottish Literary Studies, Occasional Papers 3).

McClure, J. Derrick (1980), "Western Scottish intonation: a preliminary study" in Waugh and van Schooneveld (1980), 201-17.

McClure, J. Derrick. ed. (1981), "Urban Scots", *Teaching English* 15: 1 (1981), 35-40.

McCormick, Malcolm (1977), *Bring on the Big Yin* (Glasgow and London).

McGinn, Matt (1976), *The Big Effen Bee: Popular Songs and Stories* (Glasgow).

McGrath, Tom and Jimmy Boyle (1977), *The Hard Man* (Edinburgh).

Mackie, Albert (1978), *Talking Glasgow* (Belfast).

McQuaid, John (1968), "An inquiry into the personality structure of the Scot", *British Medical Students' Journal* 23 (1968), 43-5.

Mather, James and H. H. Speitel (1975, 1977), *The Linguistic Atlas of Scotland*, vols. I and II (London).

Millar, Martin and Keith Brown (1979), "Tag questions in Edinburgh speech", *Linguistische Berichte* 60 (1979), 24-45.

Milroy, James and Lesley (1978), "Belfast: change and variation in an urban vernacular" in Trudgill (1978), 19-36.

Milroy, Lesley (1980), *Language and Social Networks* (Oxford).

Nicolaisen, W. F. H. (1976), *Scottish Place-Names, Their Study and Significance* (London).

Opie, Iona and Peter (1959), *The Lore and Language of Schoolchildren* (Oxford).

The Oxford English Dictionary and Supplements, eds. James A. H. Murray *et al.* (Oxford, 1889-).

Partridge, Eric (1937, 1966, 1970), *A Dictionary of Slang and Unconventional English*, 2 vols. (London).

Partridge, Eric (1949, 1968), *A Dictionary of the Underworld, British and American* (London).

Patrick, James (pseud.), (1973), *A Glasgow Gang Observed* (London).

Petyt, Malcolm (1978), "Secondary contractions in West Yorkshire negatives" in Trudgill (1978), 91-100.

Petyt, Malcolm (1980), *The Study of Dialect* (London).

Pryde, Helen W. (1947), *The First Book of the McFlannels* (London).

Reid, Jimmy (1976a), "Reid interview", *Masque*, April 1976, 11-15.

Reid, Jimmy (1976b), *Reflections of a Clyde-built Man* (London).

Research Committee of Glasgow Local Association, Educational Institute of Scotland (1935), "Glasgow speech: Common errors in language usage", Supplement to *The Scottish Educational Journal*, 8 March 1935, i-viii.

Romaine, Suzanne (1978), "Postvocalic /r/ in Scottish English: sound change in progress?" in Trudgill (1978), 144-57.

Romaine, Suzanne (1980), "A critical overview of the methodology of urban British sociolinguistics", *English World-Wide* 1: 2 (1980), 163-98.

Sankoff, David (1978), *Linguistic Variation: Models and Methods* (New York).

The Scots Style Sheet (1947, 1974), *Lallans* 2 (1974), 4-5.

Scottish Literature in the Secondary School (1976), (Report of a sub-committee on the study of Scottish literature in schools, Scottish Education Department, Scottish Central Committee on English; Edinburgh).

The Scottish National Dictionary, eds. William Grant and David Murison, (Edinburgh, 1931-1975).

Shuken, Cynthia (1979), "Gaelic influence on the English of Lewis and Skye", (Paper presented to the Universities' Forum for Research on the Languages of Scotland, 5 November 1979; unpublished).

Slaven, Anthony (1975), *The Development of the West of Scotland: 1750-1960* (London).

Speitel, H. H. (1969), "Some studies in the dialect of Midlothian", 2 vols. (Edinburgh PhD thesis, unpublished).

Speitel, H. H. (1975), "Dialect" in Davies (1975), 34-59.

Speitel, H. H. (1981), "The geographical position of the Scots dialect in relation to the Highlands of Scotland" in Benskin and Samuels (1981), 107-129.

Spence, Alan (1977), *Its Colours they are Fine* (London).

Strathclyde Regional Council (1976), *Strategic Issues for Strathclyde: Survey Report, 1976* (Glasgow).

Tait, Bill (1942), "Smile with Tait", *The Evening Citizen*, 25 February 1942.

Thakerar, Jitendra N. (1981), "Towards an understanding of stylistic variation in language behaviour" in Lander and Reah (1981), 27-38.

Thomson, Bill (1976), "Me an' ma urban kailyard tae: An appreciation of Billy Connolly", *Masque*, April 1976, 1-3.

Thomson, Geddes, ed. (1981), *Identities: An Anthology of West of Scotland Poetry, Prose and Drama* (London).

Trotter, R. de B.(1901), "The Scottish Language", *The Gallovidian* (1901), 22-29.

Trudgill, Peter, ed. (1978), *Sociolinguistic Patterns in British English* (London). — Er Macauley.

Wakelin, Martyn F. (1972), *Patterns in the Folk Speech of the British Isles* (London).

Ward, Colin, ed. (1973), *Vandalism* (London).

Waugh, Linda R. and C. H. van Schooneveld, eds. (1980), *The Melody of Language* (Baltimore).

Wentworth, Harold and Stuart Berg Flexner, eds. (1975), *Dictionary of American Slang* (New York), 2nd. ed.

Williams, Glyn (1982),"Bilingualism, class variety and social reproduction", (Paper presented to the Sociolinguistics Symposium, Sheffield, 29 March - 1 April, 1982; unpublished).

Wishart, Ruth (1976), "An introduction to the UCS crisis 1971-72" in Reid (1976b), 77-83.

Wells, J. C. (1982), *Accents of English*, 3 vols. (Cambridge).

Worsdall, Frank (1979), *The Tenement, a Way of Life: A Social, Historical and Architectural Study of Housing in Glasgow* (Great Britain).

Wright, Joseph, ed. (1898-1905), *The English Dialect Dictionary*, 6 vols. (London).

Wright, Joseph, (1905), *The English Dialect Grammar* (Oxford).

GLOSSARY

This glossary lists non-standard lexical items occurring in the texts or mentioned in the book. Items with recognisable StE cognates. such as *hame* 'home' and *goat* 'got' are not listed. It is hoped that the discussion in Chapter 2 will enable readers to identify such items. Unless otherwise stated, information on Scots items is adapted from the SND. Many of these are also found outside Scotland, especially in the North of England and Northern Ireland. For items labelled 'slang', information is adapted from Partridge (1966), unless otherwise stated. The present writer's comments and speculations are in brackets.

ARGLE-BARGLE, n. and v. Dispute. Blend of *argue, bargain, haggle*. Scots.
AY, adv. Always. Scots.
BACHLE, n. See BAUCHLE.
BAG, n. Pejorative term for an older woman. Br slang.
BAGGIE, n. The fry of the minnow, literally 'big-bellied'. Scots.
BAGS, interj. Children's call for gaining possession of an object. Br slang.
BAHOOKIE, n. Arse. Children's term. Scots.
BAIRN, v. Impregnate. (Solecism in T30: give birth). Scots.
BALLOON, n. (Fool, because full of hot air).
BAMPOT, n. (A gullible person. Possibly related to Br slang *bam*, n. and v., joke, trick. Glasgow and Central Scotland).
BAMSTICK (Variant of BAMPOT).
BANNOCK, n. Oatcake. Scots.
BARK, n. Irish person. 19th c Br slang.
BARNFY, n. Fight, possibly related to *Barney*, an Irish male name. Br slang.
BATTER, n. Alcohol (Mackie, 1978: 87). *On the batter*, engaged in prostitution or given to debauchery, from French *battre le pavé*. Br slang.
BAUCHLE, n. Old shoe, hence a badly dressed man. Scots; obscure etymology.
BAWBEE, n. Halfpenny in old Br currency, originally 6d Scots. Scots.
BAWR, n. Practical joke. Also *bar*. Scots.
BEDDIE-BAW, n. Bed. Baby-talk. Diminutive of *bed* + *ba'*, lull to sleep. Scots
BEFLUM, v. Cajole. Scots; obscure etymology.
BEGOB, interj. Disguised oath, *by God*. HibE (stereotype) (EDD).
BELDYHEIDIT, adj. Reckless (Mackie, 1978: 88). Bald-headed. Scots.
BENDER, n. Drinking spree. Br slang *ex* U. S. A.
BEVIED, adj. Drunk. See BEVVY.
BEVVY, v. Drink. n. Alcohol. From Parlyaree, or reduced from *alcoholic beverage*. Br slang.
BIFF, n. The tawse. (Cf. *biffs*, a caning; Australian schoolboys' slang).
BING BANG SKOOSH, n. phrase. Ring the doorbell and run away; a children's prank. Usually *ring, bang, scoosh*. (Cf. *bing* go, run, spring up; Scots tinkers' cant). Edinburgh and Glasgow.
BINT, n. Pejorative term for a girl; girlfriend. Br slang *ex* Arabic.
BLETHER, v. and n. Drivel. Scots.
BLIN' FU', adj. Drunk, literally 'blind full'. Scots.
BLOOTERED, adj. Drunk, literally 'covered in mud', or indirectly through a sense of 'knocked over'. (Cf. Scots *bluiter*, cover in mud).
BOAK, v. and n. Vomit. Scots.
BOB, n. Shilling in old Br currency. Br slang.
BOBBY, n. Policeman. Br slang (or colloquial).
BODIE, n. Indefinite term for a person, used familiarly. Scots.
BOGEY - *the game's a bogey*, children's call to cancel a game. Central Scotland.
BOGGING, adj. Smelly. (Cf. Br slang *bog* v. shit; and *bog-house* toilet, reduced to *bog*). Glasgow (Agutter and Cowan, 1981).

BOMBED OUT, adj. Not wanted (MacLaren). (Forced out).

BOOKIE, n. Bookmaker. Br slang.

BOOT, n. Pejorative term for a girl. Edinburgh and Glasgow. (Agutter, 1979).

BOOZE UP, n. phrase. Drinking bout. Br slang.

BOOZERS, n. pl. Pub. (Cf. *boozer* , pub; Br slang).

BOTHAN, n. Unlicensed pub. Lewis and Glasgow *ex* Gaelic.

BOUFING, adj. Smelly. (Cf. Scots *bouf* v. bark. Also cf. *humming* and *honking*, likewise transferred from the sense of hearing. Glasgow and Central Scotland).

BRAMAH, n. Complimentary term for a girl. Br slang *ex* Hindi-Urdu.

BRAMMER, n. See BRAMAH.

BRASSIE, n. A red face (MacLaren). (Cf. Br slang *to have a brass neck*, to be impudent. Confused with local *to have a red neck*, to be ashamed).

BRAW, adj. Handsome, general term of commendation. Scots (stereotype).

BRAXY, n. A disease of sheep. Scots.

BREADSNAPPER, n. Joking term for a child, suggested by *bread-winner*. Glasgow. (SND and Partridge, 1966).

BREEKS, n. pl. Trousers. Scots.

BRISTOLS, n. pl. Breasts. Br rhyming slang: *Bristol City* (a football club) = *tittie*.

BROO, n. Labour Exchange, literally 'bureau'. *On the broo*, receiving Unemployment Benefit. Scots.

BUCKET, n. Usual ScE term for a wastepaper basket.

BUNG FOO, adj. Drunk, literally 'full to the bung'. Scots.

BUROO, n. See BROO.

BUSIES, n. pl. Police. (Cf. Br slang 'detectives').

BUT-AN'-BEN, n. Two-roomed cottage, literally 'outer and inner'. Scots (stereotype).

CADIE, n. Cloth cap (Mitchell). (Cf. Br slang 'hat').

CALLY DOSH, n. Money. Br slang *ex* Australia.

CAMSTAIRY, adj. Perverse. Scots.

CANNED, adj. Drunk. Br slang.

CAST OOT, v. phrase. Quarrel. Scots.

CHANCER, n. Con-man. Br slang.

CHANTY, n. Reduced from *chamber (pot)*. Scots. Also *chanty-wrassler*, a suspicious character, literally 'potty wrestler'. Central Scotland.

CHAVVER, n. Prostitute, pejorative term for a woman. Br slang *ex* Romany.

CHIB, n. and v. Knife, weapon. Variant of *chive*, knife. Br slang *ex* Romany. (SND and Partridge, 1949).

CHICKIE MELLIE, n. Boys' prank. Scots.

CHIEL, n. Fellow, young man. Scots form of *child*.

CHIN, v. Hit someone, originally on the chin. Br slang *ex* Glasgow.

CHINA, n. Pal. Br rhyming slang: *china plate* = *mate*.

CHINEX, n. Chewing gum (MacLaren). (Cf. Br slang *chinny*, sugar, *ex* Hindi-Urdu).

CHOPS, n. pl. Children's call to claim an object. Scots.

CHUCKIE, n. Pebble used in children's games. Reduced from *chuckie stane*; *chuck* v., throw. Scots.

CLABBER, n. Mud. West of Scotland and Northern Ireland *ex* Gaelic. Also *clabber jigging*, street dancing, only in McArthur and Long (1935).

CLARTY, adj. Dirty. Scots: obscure etymology.

CLEG, n. Horse-fly. Scots.

CLICK, n. and v. Date (a member of the opposite sex). Br slang *ex* Scots.

CLINK, n. Prison. Br slang.

CLINGING, adj. Smelly. (Cf. Scots *cling*, diarrhoea in sheep. Cf. also

MINGING).

CLISHMACLAVERS, n. pl. Gossip. Scots: coined on phonesthetic principles.

CLOCK, v. Watch. Br slang.

CLOSE, n. Narrow passage between houses. Edinburgh and Scots. Also, entrance to a tenement. Glasgow and Scots.

CLUDGIE, n. Reduced from *(water) closet*. Central Scotland.

CLYPE, v. and n. Tell tales, one who tells tales. Scots.

COLLIESHANGIE, n. Uproar. Scots; obscure etymology.

COP, v. Receive, catch on to. Br slang.

CORRIE (FISTED), adj. Left (handed). Also *car*, *kerr*. Scots.

COUTHIE, adj. Sociable. Scots (stereotype).

COW, n. Pejorative term for a woman. Br slang.

COWBOY, n. (Reckless and unreliable character, shady businessman. Cf. Br slang 'a gunman who is fond of displaying his weapons' *ex* U. S. A. (Partridge, 1949)).

CRAPPY, adj. Afraid. From Br slang *crap*, v. shit. Glasgow. (SND and Partridge, 1966).

CRASH, v. Kill. Obsolete Br slang. (Partridge, 1949).

CRAWBAG, n. Coward. (Cf. *crap-bag* (Patrick, 1973), and *crawfish*, v. back out, Br slang *ex* U. S. A. (Partridge, 1949)).

DAFT, adj. Foolish. Scots or colloquial.

DAN, n. Nickname for a Roman Catholic. Reduced from the name *Daniel*, popular amongst Catholic Irishmen. Glasgow.

DANDER, n. Ruffled temper, as in *to get one's dander up*. Br dialectal and AmE colloquial. (OED).

DAUD, n. Large lump. Scots.

DING, v. Knock, beat. Scots.

DEOCHANDORUS, n. Parting drink. Scots.

DESTRUCT, v. Destroy. Mainly AmE. (OED).

DICK, n. Detective. Br slang *ex* Hindi-Urdu.

DINGY, n. Lie. (Cf. *dinge*, v. slander, and *dingy*, adj. slandered. Br slang *ex* U. S. A.).

DOD, iterj. Exclamation of surprise or for emphasis. Disguised form of *God*. Scots.

DOG, v. Play truant. Glasgow (SND) and neighbourhood. (LAS).

DOSSER, n. Frequenter of doss-houses. Br slang. *Lobey dosser* (cf. Br slang *(h)appy dosser*, homeless vagrant sleeping in lobbies and cellars).

DOOT, v. Suspect, with implication of probability, rather than uncertainty as with St E *doubt*.

DOUR, adj. Sullen, stern. Scots.

DOWT, n. Cigarette end. West of Scotland *ex* dialects of England.

DROOKIT, adj. Soaked. Scots.

DRUCKEN, adj. Drunk. Scots form.

DUDYEN, n. Pipe. HibE (but see SND and EDD *dudgeon*).

DUMPS, n. pl. Thumps on the back given by children to a child whose birthday it is, one for each year. Scots.

DUNNY, n. Tenement cellar. Reduced form of *dungeon*. Scots, now mainly Glasgow.

EASY-OASY, v. (Cf. Scots adj. Reduplicated form of *easy*).

FERRY, n. Local form of *fairy*. Pejorative term for a homosexual man. Br slang *ex* U. S. A.

FIKE, n. A fussy person, a fidget. Central and Southern Scotland.

FIRLOT, n. Measure of grain, a large quantity. Obsolescent Scots.

FLAFF, v. Flap. Scots, imitative in origin.

FLEEIN', adj. Drunk, excited. Scots.

FLICHTER, v. Flutter. Scots, imitative in origin.

FLIT, v. Move house. Scots.

FLITTING, n. Removal. Scots.

FLOOMPY, adj. (Nonce word, suggesting loose and awkward clothing).

FLYTE, v. and n. Scold, a scolding. (Solecism in T24a: scolding as an abstract noun).

FOO, adj. See FU.

FORPIT, n. A measure of dry goods. Scots.

FOU', adj. See FU.

FOZY, adj. Out of condition, soft-headed. Scots.

FLY, adj. Shrewd. Br slang *ex* Scots.

FU, adj. Drunk, literally 'full'. Scots.

FU AS A PUGGIE, adj. phrase. Drunk, literally 'full as a monkey'. Scots.

FU AS A WULK, adj. phrase. Drunk, literally 'full as a whelk'. Scots.

FUFF, v. Puff. Scots, imitative in origin.

FUNKY, adj. Strong smelling, sweaty, hence applied to music. Br slang *ex* U. S. A. (OED).

FUZZ, n. The police. Br slang *ex* Canada.

GABERLUNZIE, n. Beggar. Archaic and literary Scots.

GALLUS, adj. Form of *gallows*, hence reckless, unreliable. Scots. In ameliorative sense, anything good of its kind. Glasgow and Central Scotland.

GANDER, n. A peek. Br slang *ex* U. S. A.

GARNSEY, n. Pullover. From the place-name *Guernsey*. Usually *gansey*, even in Scots. (/r/ restored as a hyper-dialectalism).

GEMMIE, n. One who is *game*. (Glasgow and Central Scotland).

GENUINE, interj. (Used to emphasize the truth of a statement. Cf. *honest*).

GET, v. To be allowed (generally to go somewhere). Scots.

GET KNOTTED, imperative. Go away, literally '(go and) have sex', but not so understood in general use. Br slang.

GEY, adj. Very, rather. Scots form of *gay*.

GILPY, n. Mischievous young person. Obsolescent Scots.

GINGING, adj. Smelly. (Cf. MINGING).

GLAIKIT, adj. Stupid. Scots.

GLAUR, n. Mud. Scots; obscure etymology.

GLOAMING, n. Twilight. Literary St E *ex* Scots.

GLOSHINS, n. pl. Children going from door to door in fancy dress at Hallowe'en. (Cf. obsolete Scots *glossins*, blushes).

GRAITH, n. Equipment, hence soapsuds Scots. East of Scotland (LAS), in latter sense.

GRAND, adj. and adv. Splendid. (Old fashioned superlative).

GRASS, v. Inform, tell tales. Br slang.

GROG, v. Spit. (Glasgow).

GROSER, n. Gooseberry. Scots.

GUISERS, n. pl. Children going from door to door in fancy dress at Hallowe'en. Scots.

GUMPLE-FOISTED, adj. Sulky, bad-tempered. Scots; coined on phonesthetic principles.

HAIRY, n. Hatless young woman, girl. Glasgow. (SND and Agutter and Cowan, 1981).

HALF-ARSED, adj. Ineffective. Br slang *ex* Canada.

HEIDBANGER, n. Lunatic, literally 'head banger', i.e. one who bangs his head off the wall. Glasgow and more widely (Agutter and Cowan, 1981).

HEIDCASE, n. Lunatic, literally 'mental patient'. (Glasgow and more widely).

HEN, vocative. Term of familiar address to a woman or girl. Scots.

HING AFF, imperative. See HING-ON.

HING-ON, n. An arm-in-arm walk. Glasgow. Hence *hing aff*, imperative, let go. (Partridge, 1966).

HINGOOT, n. Pejorative term for a girl. Glasgow. (Agutter and Cowan, 1981). (Cf. Br slang *hang out of*, penetrate sexually).

HODDENDOON, adj. phrase. Oppressed, literally 'held down'. Scots.

HOG, n. Pejorative term for a girl. (Cf. Br slang *hog*, v. to have sex).

HOOCH, interj. Exclamation of exhiliration when dancing, especially Highland dancing. Scots. (Conventional representation of a vocal gesture).

HOOF IT, v. phrase. Go on foot. Br slang.

HOWK, v. Dig. Scots.

HUCKLE, v. Arrest. Glasgow. (Agutter and Cowan, 1981)

HUMDUDGEON, n. Fuss, needless complaint. Obsolete Scots.

HUMGRUFFIANLY, adj. Nonce formation on *humgruffian*, variant of *humgriffin*, a terrible person (itself phonesthetic). (*Chambers Twentieth Century Dictionary*).

HUMMING, adj. Smelly. Br slang *ex* Scots and Northern dialect.

JAM, n. Good luck. Br slang.

JANE, n. Girl. Br slang *ex* Australia. Also with ameliorative sense, sweetheart. Glasgow. (Partridge, 1966).

JAW BOX, n. Sink, in kitchen or on common stair of tenement. Central Scotland and Ulster. From Scots *jaw*, v. slop out.

JEELY, n.₁ Jam, literally 'jelly'. Scots.

JEELY, n.₂ Gelignite. (Cf. Br slang *jelly*, *ex* Australia).

JOOKERY POKERY, n. Trickery, double dealing. Scots.

JORRIE, n. Girl. Only in McArthur and Long (1935).

JUDY, n. Pejorative term for a girl. Br slang.

KEECH, n. Shit. Scots.

KEELIE, n. Pejorative term for a male working class Glaswegian, formerly also Edinburgh. "The lumpen proletariat as regarded by the proletariat" (Mackie, 1978: 94-5). Scots *ex* Gaelic.

KEN, v. Know. Scots.

KERRY-OOT, n. Local form of *carry-out*, the usual ScE term for take-away food and drink.

KEYS, n. pl. Call for a state of truce in children's games. Central and Southern Scotland.

KIPPAGE, n. Disorder, fuss. Scots.

KNOCK, v. (Steal. Reduced from Br slang KNOCK OFF).

KNOCK OFF, v. phrase. Complete easily, steal. Br slang.

LOLLY, n. Money. Cockney slang.

LOUNDER, v. Walk noisily, skulk. Scots.

LUCKY, n. (Reduced from West of Scotland *lucky thing*, an unexpected find).

LUMBER, n. A member of the opposite sex picked up at a dance, etc. (Cf. Br slang *lumber*, v. to court a girl). Hence, a girl (Agutter, 1979). Glasgow (Agutter and Cowan, 1981).

MAGIC, adj. (Current superlative. Glasgow and Central Scotland).

MALKY, n. Weapon. Glasgow.

MAP, n. Face. Br slang.

MARKS - *I have your marks*. (Possibly, 'I have information in writing about you'. Cf. Scots *mark (down)*, note down).

MAUN, aux. v. Must. Scots.

MEALIE-PUDDIN, n. Oatmeal sausage. Scots.

MELT, v. Defeat, beat; originally by a stroke to the *melt*, spleen. Br slang *ex* Scots.

MENTAL, adj. Mentally disordered. Colloquial BrE. (OED).

MESSAGES, n. pl. Shopping. *To go the messages*, to do the shopping. Scots.

MICKEY, n. Chamber pot, toilet. Reduced from *micturating pot*. Central Scotland.

MIDGIE, n.$_1$ Reduced form of *midden*. Glasgow.

MIDGIE, n.$_2$ Diminutive of *midge*.

MINGING, adj. Smelly, bad of its kind. Scots. (Cf. also Scots *ming*, n. shit).

MIROCLOUS, adj. Drunk. Scots form of *miraculous*. Hence Br slang *miraculous*.

MIXTER-MAXTER, n. A jumble. Reduplicated form of *mixter*, mixture. Scots.

MUCKLE, adj. Big. Scots.

MUG, n. Fool, i.e. something into which one can pour anything. Br slang.

MURGEON, v. Grimace. Scots.

MUTCHKIN, n. Measure of liquids or powders. Scots.

NAIN, adj. Variant of *ain*, own. From redivision of *mine ain*, my own. Scots.

NEIST, adj. Next, nearest. Scots.

NETTERIE, n. Spider. (Reduced form of *nettercap*, itself from redivision of *an ettercap*. Scots). Forms of *ettercap* now have a quite limited distribution in the East of Scotland north of the Forth (LAS).

NICK, n. Policeman (Bell, 1933). Police station. Br slang.

NIRL, v. Shrivel. Scots.

NIT, v. Leave alone. Only in McArthur and Long (1935). (Cf. *keep nit*, keep watch, variant of *keep nix*, Br slang *ex* Romany).

NOOP, n. Knob, protruberance. Scots.

NYAFF, n. Anything or anybody dwarfish. Originally imitative of a small, yappy dog. Scots.

NYUCK, n. Contemptuous term for a person. Only in Hanley (1958). (Cf. NYAFF).

OCHONEE, interj. Exclamation of sorrow, now mostly weariness or exasperation. Scots. (Conventional representation of a vocal gesture).

ON ONE'S TOD, prep. phrase. Alone. Br rhyming slang: *on one's Tod Sloan* (a famous boxer of the 1890s) = *on one's own*.

ON THE SLATE, prep. phrase. On credit, literally 'chalked up on a slate'. Br slang.

PAA'ER, n. See PATTER.

PAP, v. Smash, throw. Scots form of *pop*.

PANLOAF, n. An affected posh accent, since *panloaf* was formerly more expensive than *plain*. Scots.

PATTER, n. Cheapjack's oratory, hence witty or glib conversation. Br slang.

PEERY-HEIDIT, adj. In a state of confusion, literally 'spinning-top headed'. Central and Southern Scotland and Ulster. *To become peery-heidit*, to lose one's head (Bell, 1933).

PICKLE, n. A small amount, an indefinite amount. Scots.

PIE-EYED, adj. Drunk. Br slang. *ex* U. S. A.

PIECE, n. Piece of bread, packed lunch. Scots.

PIGGIES, n. pl. Pieces of broken china used in children's games. Scots. East of Scotland (LAS).

PIT ABOOT, adj. phrase. Upset, literally 'put about'. Scots.

PIT THE HEMS ON, v. phrase. Curtail, literally 'put the horse collar on'. Also *haims*. Scots.

PLACK, n. Coin of the smallest denomination. Scots.

PLANK, v. Set down, stow away. Scots.

PLONK, n. Cheap wine. Br rhyming slang: *plink plonk* = *vin blanc*.

PLUNK, v. Play truant. West of Scotland (LAS).

POKE, n. Paper bag. Scots.

POLIS, n. Scots form of *police* with stress on the first syllable.

POOF, n. Pejorative term for a homosexual man. Br slang.

PREEN, n. Pin. Scots.
PRESS, n. Large cupboard. Scots.
PRIG, n. Thief. Br slang.
PSYCHIE, adj. (Lunatic. Reduced form of *psychiatric*).
PUGGLED, adj. Drunk. Cf. *puggle*, n. idiot; Br slang *ex* Hindi-Urdu. (Cf. also
  FU AS A PUGGIE). Br slang.
PUNTER, n. Client, victim, hence ordinary man. Br slang.
RAMFEEZLE, v. Muddle. Scots; coined on phonesthetic principles.
RARE, adj. General term of commendation. Colloquial (Partridge, 1966).
RERR, adj. Local form of RARE.
RICKLE, n. Loose pile of objects. Scots.
RIDDIE, n. (Reduced form of *red neck* as in *to have a red neck*, be ashamed;
  Scots. Glasgow).
RINTHEREOUT, n. Vagrant, literally 'run outside'. Obsolescent Scots.
ROCK, n. Distaff. Scots.
ROOKIES, n. pl. Police (MacLaren). Raw recruits. Br slang.
SANNY, n. Reduced form of *sandshoe*. West of Scotland.
SAPPLES, n. pl. Soapsuds. West of Scotland.
SASSANACH, n. Joking term for an English person. Originally a Highland English
  term for a Lowlander, or English monolingual. Scots.
SCOOSH, n. Lemonade. v. Gush. Scots; imitative in origin.
SCREWS, n. pl. Police. Obsolescent Br slang, *ex* U. S. A. (Partridge, 1949).
  Prison warders. Br slang.
SCRIMLE, v. (Form of *scrammle*, Scots form of *scramble*, altered on phonesthetic
  principles. Nonce word).
SCUNNER, v. and n. Feel disgust, nausea, anything disgusting. Scots.
SHAG, n. Tobacco. St E (OED).
SHAKRIN, n. (Cf. Northern English *shaffling*, bungler, idle person (EDD), and
  Scots and Northern English *shake-rag*, beggar (EDD)).
SHERICKING, n. Public row. West of Scotland.
SHITEY, adj. Shitty. *Shite*, n. + *-ie*.
SHOOT THE CRAW, v. phrase. Go (without paying). Br rhyming slang: *shoot the
  crow = go. Craw*, Scots form of *crow*.
SIMMIT, n. Man's undervest. Mainly West of Scotland and Northern Ireland
  (LAS). (SND suggests an etymology from *samite*, fine silk cloth. If so,
  probably originally a joking term).
SKALIE, n. Slate pencil. Obsolescent Scots. Forms related to *skalie* are
  mainly Eastern (LAS).
SKELINGTON, n. (Joking mispronunciation of *skeleton*. West of Scotland).
SKIRL, v. Shriek. Scots.
SKITTER, v. Excrete liquid excrement. Scots.
SKITTERY, adj. *skitter* + *-ie*.
SKY, v. Leave hurriedly. Br slang (Partridge, 1949).
SKYTE, v. Slip, shoot off at an angle. Scots.
SLAG, v. Tease (MacLaren). (Cf. Br slang n., someone who is too timid to
  take offence).
SLASHER, n. Slashing weapon. ScE (OED).
SLEVVERY, adj. (Scots form of *slaver*, saliva + *-ie*).
SMASHED, adj. Drunk. (Cf. Br slang *smash*, drink (something), *ex* U. S. A.).
SMASHER, n. Anything excellent, a term of commendation for a girl. Br slang.
SMOWTS, n. pl. A game played with marbles. *Up for smowts*, the final move in
  a game played with marbles. Possibly reduced from *that's me out*. Glasgow.
SMUGGED, adj. Drunk. (Cf. Br slang *smug*, v. arrest).
SNAPPER, n. Dockworker employed by the day, and selected by the foreman snap-
  ping his fingers at him. (Joking term). Glasgow.

163

SNOOKS - *up for snooks*, the final move in a game of marbles. Cf. *snookered*. Glasgow.
SNUG, n. Small private room in a pub. Mainly dialects of England. (SND).
STAIKIE, n. (Weapon. Cf. Br slang *stake*, anything valuable. Glasgow),
STANK, n. Ditch, pond. Scots. Grating over a drain-opening. Glasgow and nearby (LAS).
STCHUMER, n. See STUMOR.
STEAMING, adj. Drunk. Scots.
STEWED, adj. Drunk. Br slang.
STICK TO, v. phrase. Keep close to. Scots. (In T47, possibly 'steal').
STOATIN, adj. Drunk, literally 'bouncing'. Scots.
STOATIR, n. Heavy blow. Br slang. Anything good of its kind. Glasgow. (The slang use is apparently from the slang v. *stoter*, deal a heavy blow; and the Glasgow use from *stote*, v. bounce, in the extended sense 'hit', perhaps influenced by the Br slang use).
STOCIOUS, adj. Drunk. Br slang.
STOT, v. Bounce. Scots.
STRUT - *strut your stuff*, dance, hence do your thing. Am slang (Wentworth and Flexner, 1975).
STUMOR, n. Worthless person, but originally a horse against which money could be laid without risk. Br slang.
SUGARALLY, n. Liquorice. Reduced form of *sugar alicreesh*. Scots. Also obsolescent *sugarallie hat*, a tall hat as originally worn by the police, hence 19th c *sugarallie*, police. Glasgow.
SWEDGER, n. Sweet (MacLaren). (Cf. Scots *swauger*, long drink of alcohol, from *swage*, v. settle down (of the stomach after a meal). Reduced form of *assuage*. Mainly North of Scotland).
SWEETIE, n. A sweet. St E *ex* Scots.
SWERRY-WORDS, n. pl. Swear words.
SYNE, conj. Then, next. Scots.
TAKE A BERKIE, v. phrase. Lose one's head. (Cf. Br slang *berk* n. fool).
TAKE A FLAKEY, v. phrase. Lose one's head. (Cf. Br slang *flak-happy*, reckless).
TAKE A HAIRY, v. phrase. Lose one's head. (Cf. Br slang *hairy*, excited, *ex* HibE).
TAKE A POWDER, v. phrase. Leave hurriedly. Br slang *ex* U. S. A.
TALLY MAN, n. phrase. Common law husband. Mainly North of England (Partridge, 1966); also a door-to-door salesman, selling goods on credit).
TART, n. Term for a girl. Originally complimentary, but now pejorative in Br slang.
TAWSE, n. Leather strap used in Scottish schools. Pl. of Scots *taw*, thong, reinterpreted as a sg. ScE.
TEABOY, n. Someone who cooperates with the authorities. (Cf. obsolescent Br slang *teaman*, a privileged prisoner, because entitled to tea).
TERR, n. Local form of *tear*, a spree. Scots.
THEEVIL, n. Porridge stick. Scots. Mainly East of Scotland, north of the Forth (LAS).
THRANG, adj. Busy. Scots form of *throng*.
TIM, n. Nickname for a Roman Catholic. (Unlikely to be the same as *tim*, term of personal abuse, 17th c St E (OED). Perhaps the proper name *Tim*, short for *Timothy*. Glasgow and more widely).
TIM, adj. and v. Empty. Also *tuim*, *toom*. Scots.
TOLY, n. Turd. Scots.
TOTTIE, n. Scots form of *potato*. Also *tattie*.
TUBE, n. Pejorative term for a man, literally 'penis'. Br slang *ex* HibE.

(Partridge, 1969).

TWA-THREE, adj. A few, literally 'two or three'. Scots.

WAARMUR, n. Scots form of *warmer*. Virago (Mitchell). Smart person; Br slang *ex* Glasgow (Partridge, 1949). Extreme example of its kind, either pejorative or ameliorative; Central and Southern Scotland.

WALLY, adj. Ornamental, hence made of china, perhaps via *wally dugs*, ornamental china dogs once favoured as mantelpiece decorations. Also *wally close*, a tiled lobby, and *wallies*, dentures. Scots.

WANCHANCY, adj. Unlucky, unreliable. Scots.

WARMER, n. See WAARMUR.

WEAN, n. Child. Reduced form of *wee ane*, little one. West of Scotland and Central Scotland.

WEARY, v. Become sad and dispirited, rather than tired. Scots.

WEE, adj. Little. Scots (and ScE).

WEEBER, n. or adj. (Nonce word, suggestive of *wee berr* little bare, *weaver*, *weeper*, and creature which makes a *weeb* noise).

WELLIES, n. pl. Reduced form of *wellington (boot)s*. Scots.

WHACK, n. A full share. Br slang.

WHEECH, v. Whizz. Scots; imitative in origin.

WINCH, v. Court, of either sex. West of Scotland and Scots.

WISE, adj. Same, clever. Rhymes with *advice*. Scots.

YELLOWBELLY, n. Coward. Br slang, cf. Am slang *yellow*, cowardly.

YETT, n. Gate. Scots form.

The accompanying cassette (one hour): contents and linking material

The following recordings illustrate the remarkably wide range of accents in the native English of Glasgow, Scotland's largest city. These range from an upper middle class accent approaching the so-called Received Pronunciation of British English to local accents as divergent from RP as any to be found in the British Isles.

SIDE ONE

Item 1 (T1 = 5.5 mins.) is part of a speech made by Jimmy Reid, a well-known figure on the left of British politics, who became a household name as the leader of a successful industrial campaign in the shipyards of the Upper Clyde in the winter of 1971-72. The speech comes at a crucial moment in the campaign, when Reid and other trade union leaders are mobilising the workforce to reject the findings of a government enquiry and to take industrial action in defence of their livelihood. It is clearly vital at this juncture for Reid to convince the men that the enquiry is biased, that the yards are viable, and that the workers have the intellectual authority to challenge the official view.

Item 2 (T3 = 2 mins.): The next speaker (W.H.) is another fairly young man, speaking in public to a large audience. The occasion this time is a university lecture, at a very basic level, and the speaker is careful to signpost his arguments and to give concrete examples of the abstract ideas he is discussing. The subject is the concept of culture, and the speaker is here explaining some of the ramifications of one definition of "culture".

Item 3 (T4 = 2.5 mins.): It is interesting to compare the last speaker with a younger speaker of the same class. In this extract we also have a more casual style of speech. The speaker (L.G.) is a student at Glasgow University. She's chatting about people that she knows, first of all one of her teachers at school, and then her friend Rosemary, who is transformed from a gauche teen-ager to a campus character in the course of the narrative.

Item 4 (T5 = 2 mins.): The next speaker (W.E.) is a young man from an inner city area. Although a very articulate and intelligent person, he had been almost continually unemployed since leaving school at the minimum age. The first ex-tract is from early in the conversation, where one of the speaker's favourite themes, the delinquency of children in his area, had led into a discussion of one young boy's glue sniffing. In the second extract, he is discussing the attitudes of the local community towards young people being in trouble with the police.

Item 5 (T6 = 2 mins.): This is a recording which was made with a concealed tape recorder, and the quality is therefore rather poor, but the extract does capture a very lively and natural piece of narrative. The speaker (Mrs. P.), a married woman from the inner city, is chatting to her tutor in an adult literacy scheme. She is telling how her son and his fiancée went to a dance in place of herself and her husband, and how the fiancée won a beauty contest.

Item 6 (T7 = 2 mins.): This recording was made in the home of the speaker (A.G.) a retired engineering worker and Labour Party activist. He is gamely keeping up his end of this rather one-sided conversation with a brief account of family life when he was a child.

Item 7 (T8 = 9 mins.) is a collage of street interviews recorded for BBC Radio Scotland. The speakers are making some very animated comments on unemployment, housing, and the inadequate response of the medical profession to problems such as alcoholism and depression.

SIDE TWO

Item 8 (T9 = 2 mins.): There now follows part of a discussion recorded in the classroom of a Glasgow secondary school. The speakers are four girls of average ability aged around 14 or 15. The girls are discussing a poem called "Work" by D.H.Lawrence, with the guidance of a worksheet, to which they refer from time to time. The situation is a rather artificial one. Up to this point, the girls had clearly been saying to each other the things which they would normally say to the teacher, and they had also been circulating the teacher's role amongst themselves. But the discussion now becomes lively, as one of the girls takes up a stance in defence of modern ways of life, and against the back-to-the-land approach advocated by the poem and explored further in the worksheet.

Item 9 (T10 = 1 min., T11 = 1.5 mins., T12 = 4 mins., T13 = 0.5 min., T14 = 4 mins.): We continue with some snippets from Tiger Tim's pop music programme on the local radio station, Radio Clyde. First of all Tiger Tim chats to another disc jockey, Billy Sloane. We then have part of a conversation with a listener who has phoned in to speak to Tiger Tim on the air and to take part in a competition. She has just given the right answer at the point where the extract begins. Then there is another phone-in conversation. This follows a regular format - Tiger Tim chats to the listener, then asks his opinion of the record just played. The listener has to sum up his own opinion and that of other listeners who have called by making funny noises. Next we have an exchange between Tiger tim and a female stooge called Maggie, whose voice is heard from time to time on the show. Finally, there is part of a third telephone conversation with a group of schoolgirls, who are participating in a spot where listeners sing aloud with a record. The listeners to this

Item 10 (T15a + b = 4 mins.): We now have two short extracts from a recording made for Transatlantic Records by Billy Connolly, a well-known Glasgow comedian. Connolly began as a musician, but is now admired as a raconteur. These extracts are from one of his most famous stories, the story of the crucifixion as prophesied by Christ in a Glasgow pub. The first part describes the scene at the Last Supper, with Judas as an insecure and unpopular little man, trying +o catch the eye of the charismatic Christ. In the second part, Christ reaches the end of his prophecy, and is mildly rebuked by his drinking companions for telling them such a tall story.

This brings us to the end of a selection of more or less natural Glasgow speech, within the limits of the Observer's Paradox. We conclude with a few stereotypes of various kinds of Glasgow accent, performed by mainly local actors and comedians.

Item 11 (T16/24- = 2.5 mins.) is from a recording made for EMI records in 1929 by the famous music hall artiste, Will Fyffe. Although his number "I belong to Glasgow" is one of his best known, Fyffe was in fact from Dundee. The song, and the monologue which interrupts it, ▉e a good-humoured defence of the hard-working labourer who likes to have a drink at the end of the week, and it is also a defence in general of the dignity and privacy of the workers as a class.

Item 12 (T17 = 3.5 mins.) features Stanley Baxter, a televison personality from Glasgow, as Professor Footer, one of his stock characters. Professor Footer is an outsider with a fruity English accent, who sets himself up as an authority on the quaint local customs and language of Glasgow, but who invariably misinterprets everything he hears. This is the sound track of a sketch recorded by Scottish Television.

Item 13 (T21-24 = 2.5 mins.): Finally, we have a series of advertisements from Radio Clyde for two local businesses. The first is constructed as an exchange between two men with "Kelvinside" accents, the second as a similar exchange between two men with working class Glasgow accents. The next two both feature a woman's voice, with a working class accent, who speaks with breathless excitement about the shop being advertised.

In the VARIETIES OF ENGLISH AROUND THE WORLD series the following volumes have been published thusfar:

Text Series

T1. TODD, Loreto: *Cameroon*. Heidelberg (Groos), 1982.
     Spoken examples on tape (ca. 56 min.)
T2. HOLM, John: *Central American English*. Heidelberh (Groos), 1982.
     Spoken examples on tape (ca. 90 min.)
T3. MACAFEE, Caroline: *Glasgow*. Amsterdam, 1983.
     Spoken examples on tape (60 min.)
T4. PLATT, John, Heidi WEBER & Mian Lian HO: *Singapore and Malaysia*. Amsterdam, 1983.

General Series

G1. LANHAM, L.W. & C.A. MACDONALD: *The Standard in South African English and its Social History*. Heidelberg (Groos), 1979.
G2. DAY, R.R. (ed.): *ISSUES IN ENGLISH CREOLES: Papers from the 1975 Hawaii Conference*. Heidelberg (Groos), 1980.

Scheduled for 1984:

G3. VIERECK, Wolfgang, Edgar SCHNEIDER & Manfred GÖRLACH (comps.): *A Bibliography of Writings on Varieties of English, 1965-1983*. Amsterdam, 1984.
G4. GÖRLACH, Manfred (ed.): *FOCUS ON: SCOTLAND*.
G5. VIERECK, Wolfgang (ed.): *FOCUS ON: ENGLAND AND WALES*.

- -

VARIETIES OF ENGLISH AROUND THE WORLD is a companion series of books to the journal

ENGLISH WORLD-WIDE
A journal of Varieties of English
ISSN 0172-8865

EDITORS
Manfred Görlach (*University of Heidelberg*)
Braj B. Kachru (*University of Illinois, Urbana*)
Loreto Todd (*University of Leeds*)

From vol. 4, onwards published by John Benjamins Publ. Co.
2 x p/y. ca. 320 pages.

Vol.4. 1983.	Subscr. price	Hfl.	110,--/$	44.00
	Postage	Hfl.	12,--/$	4.80

* Private subscriptions Hfl. 60,--/$ 24.00, postage included (Prepayment required).
Back vols. 1-3 available at current subscription price.